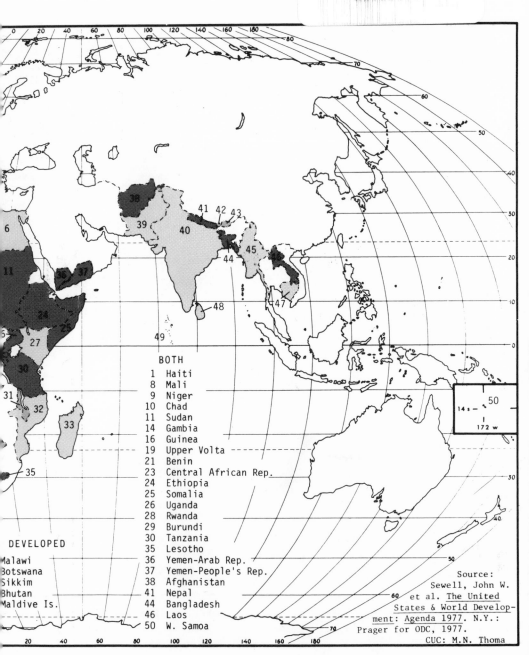

BOTH

1	Haiti
8	Mali
9	Niger
10	Chad
11	Sudan
14	Gambia
16	Guinea
19	Upper Volta
21	Benin
23	Central African Rep.
24	Ethiopia
25	Somalia
26	Uganda
28	Rwanda
29	Burundi
30	Tanzania
35	Lesotho
36	Yemen-Arab Rep.
37	Yemen-People's Rep.
38	Afghanistan
41	Nepal
44	Bangladesh
46	Laos
50	W. Samoa

DEVELOPED

Malawi
Botswana
Sikkim
Bhutan
Maldive Is.

Source:
Sewell, John W.
et al. The United
States & World Develop-
ment: Agenda 1977. N.Y.:
Prager for ODC, 1977.
CUC: M.N. Thoma

MAKING THE MOST OF THE LEAST

MAKING THE MOST OF THE LEAST

ALTERNATIVE WAYS TO DEVELOPMENT

EDITED BY
LEONARD BERRY AND ROBERT W. KATES

HM

HOLMES & MEIER PUBLISHERS, INC.

new york ● london

First published in the United States of America 1980 by
Holmes & Meier Publishers, Inc.
30 Irving Place
New York, N.Y. 10003

Great Britain:
Holmes & Meier Publishers, Ltd.
131 Trafalgar Road
Greenwich, London SE10 9TX

Library of Congress Cataloging in Publication Data
Main entry under title:
Making the most of the least : alternative ways to development.
   Bibliography: p.
   Includes index.
   1.   Underdeveloped areas—Economic policy—Addresses,
essays, lectures.   2.   International economic relations—
Addresses, essays, lectures.   I.   Berry, Leonard
II.   Kates, Robert William.
HC59.7.M254 1979   338.91'172'4   79-11619

ISBN 0-8419-0434-0

Manufactured in the United States of America

CONTENTS

ABBREVIATIONS

CUSO	Canadian University Service Overseas
DAC	Development Assistance Committee
EEC	European Economic Community
FAO	Food and Agriculture Organization
GATT	General Agreement on Trade and Tariffs
GDP	Gross Domestic Product
GNP	Gross National Product
GSP	Generalized System of [Tariff] Preferences
IBRD	International Bank for Reconstruction and Development
IDA	International Development Association
IDEP	Institut Africain du développement économique et planification
IDRC	International Development Research Center
IEO	International Economic Order
IMF	International Monetary Fund
ITCZ	Inter-Tropical Convergence Zone
LDC	Least Developed Country
LDN	Least Developed Nation
MSA	Most Seriously Affected
OECD	Organization for Economic Cooperation and Development
OPEC	Organization of Petroleum-Exporting Countries
ORSTOM	Office de la recherche scientifique et technique d'Outre-Mer
SDC	Special Drawing Currency
SIDA	Swedish International Development Agency
SITC	Standard International Trade Commodity
UNCOD	United Nations Conference on Desertification
UNCTAD	United Nations Conference on Trade and Development
UNDESA	United Nations Department of Economic and Social Affairs
UNDP	United Nations Development Program
UNDRO	United Nations Disaster Relief Office

UNEP	United Nations Environmental Program
UNESCO	United Nations Educational, Scientific, and Cultural Organization
UNICEF	United Nations Children's Fund
USAID	United States Agency for International Development
WHO	World Health Organization
WMO	World Meteorological Organization

FOREWORD

When we read, in John 12:8, that "the poor always ye shall have with you," we know who the poor must have been. They were those persons, families, and other social groups that, as parts of some given society, either existed at the margins of subsistence or could not survive without some aid, namely, charity, from others. Alas, the poor are still with us, although hopefully not indefinitely—at least within the more prosperous societies and/or those with systems permitting a more equitable distribution of wealth. In addition to these poor, a new phenomenon has appeared on the global landscape—the country or nation that is poor to the point where its very survival is at stake. How has this situation come about?

Two thousand years ago, indeed, until perhaps as recently as forty years ago, such a phenomenon was virtually unknown, at least for long periods. When a nominally independent country proved unable to "make it" economically or politically, its problems were solved, in one sense, as it passed out of existence and was absorbed by some larger entity, usually a neighboring country. But with the expansion of Europe over most of the globe, propinquity became less of a requirement for absorption. In fact, during the three centuries in which European expansion led to the development of a virtual worldwide network of imperialist powers and their colonial dependencies, most of the world's peoples passed from a state of independence to one of dependence.

It would be a mistake, however, to assume that the independence of states meant the independence of peoples; for the most part, the contrary was true. Most peoples of what came to be regarded as the colonial world, indeed, most peoples of the seemingly noncolonial world, were ruled by foreign dynasties long before European expansionism led to modern colonialism— witness Ch'ing China, Mogul India, and the Austro-Hungarian and Ottoman Empires.

The likelihood of success of such foreign-imposed political/military solutions to problems of national survival declined rapidly following World War I as notions of Wilsonian self-determination diffused rapidly, and it virtually disappeared following World War II. Some will dispute so sweeping a generalization, and there are, admittedly, some very recent exceptions to it, but by and large it represents a major truth. Mackinder was clearly premature when he described the world as a "going concern," in the sense of a closed system, after World War I, but Wendell Wilkie was only slightly so when he wrote *One World* in 1943. By the time the United Nations came into being and World War II had ended, a new political order was pretty well established. Historically, annexation of neighboring territories occupied by other ethnic groups—except where they were already faits accomplis, as in the Soviet Union and China—became outmoded and unlikely even by neighboring states.

During the ensuing thirty years and after, the world political map was further transformed as newer states made their appearance. Whereas at the close of World War II there had been some 69 commonly recognized, nominally independent states (whatever their degree of economic dependence upon other states might have been), by 1975 there were about 160 such entities—and the number has increased since then. In short, the nation-state has exhausted the land masses of the globe. There remains only the marine territory, and it too is beginning to shrink by at least two hundred miles as a result of new territorial-limits agreements.

Some of the newly defined states have voices in the United Nations and therefore exert some influence in the evolving global political order. Several had their origins in precolonial kingdoms and satrapies (e.g., Burma and Cambodia) and therefore were able to draw upon cultural history and political tradition to justify their new political autonomy. Most of them, however, were not so fortunate. To a considerable degree, they came into existence as a consequence of quite arbitrary divisions of territory that, often as a result of chance, ignorance, or administrative convenience, were imposed by the former imperialist power. Thus, peoples of the same culture frequently found themselves separated by new international boundaries that encompassed seemingly "closed national systems"—witness the numerous cases in Africa (i.e., Somalia). Inevitably, the states in which these peoples found themselves were multiethnic; the impact of multiethnicism on the evolution of viable new states is only now being properly appreciated. In the case of Malaysia, no political authority prior to the British had ever controlled and administered all of its territory as one unit. The same is true of Indonesia and the Dutch; the Philippines and Spain and the United States; and Laos and the French. In the case of the last named, there had, of course, been a kingdom of Laos for several centuries prior to the French occupation, but its territorial boundaries never encompassed all of its present territory and its relations with Thailand and Annam made its independence questionable in the first place. In short, many, perhaps even a majority, of the newer states, came into being as the products of colonialism. Their most important task, in the eyes of their elites, was the development of what Hartshorne called the "Idea of the State," with new nationalism as its underpinning.

These circumstances seem not to have been properly understood at a time when a spate of new nations appeared on the world scene and began to participate in the councils of the United Nations. A Wilsonian view of national autonomy echoed through the halls at Lake Success and in New York City. Numerous countries came into being (particularly after 1950), whose foundations were weak on political, ideological, and economic grounds, and of controversial value, but there were no acceptable international mechanisms for questioning their right to exist.

Throughout the 1950s the implications of this situation had yet to be made clear. In 1961 the *Atlas of Economic Development* (Ginsburg, 1961) recorded the fact that a few countries ranked well behind most others on the basis of a variety of indicators of economic development and national viability. In 1968, at the Second United Nations Conference on Trade and Development, some twenty-five countries (later expanded to twenty-nine) were identified as "least developed," and therefore presumably more problem-ridden and less viable than other less-developed countries. In 1971 the United Nations General Assembly came up with a similar list of twenty-five problem countries to which special attention would have to be paid during the Second Development Decade. To be sure, not all of these were new nations, but nineteen out of twenty-five were, and three more might have qualified if the definition of terms had been relaxed. The World Bank also defined its poorest countries at about this time. It was becoming clear at last that the developments of previous decades had created a new element in the world's political/economic landscape—the very poor country, unable to readily support itself—that would, under the newly established rules of the international game, always be with us.

Needless to say, something of a numbers game was being played out here. It was widely agreed that there was no simple cutoff at twenty-five, that the term *development,* however it was defined, represented a dimension along which countries were aligned without clear breaks in their statistical distribution, even apart from problems of definition and measurement. Thus, although concern was primarily focused on a small number of political entities, the issues also related to perhaps forty or even fifty countries of various sizes, problem sets, and ancestries.

By the early seventies, there was a growing awareness that the very poor countries and their seeming lack of long-term viability as political/economic units presented a serious challenge to the stability of the world order. Some of these countries had slipped into the status of client states of the former imperialist power, as was the case, for example, of Chad and other former territories of French West Africa. Sikkim was absorbed by India, its paternalistic neighbor, which had always maintained a protectorate over it. This, in turn, affected the client states' credibility as participants in the activities of world government and made them even more vulnerable to external forces beyond their control. Cold war politics also loomed larger as Africa in particular became a region of competition between, on the one hand, Russia and then China and, on the other, the Western powers. At the same time, a rising concern with management—or mismanagement—of the global resource endowment and with moral responsibilities of wealthier countries toward poorer nations led to often heated debate on the question of whether or not wealthier countries were indeed their brothers' keepers, to what extent that might be, and how they might best discharge their responsibilities.

One type of policy that emerged from this debate was that of *triage,* a term whose origin relates to the treatment of the most severely wounded in the carnage of World War I: those who could not be easily saved, given the fact of scarce medical resources, were simply allowed to die. An unholy alliance between hard-nosed "practical" politics at the international level and growing concern over environmental management became evident in the so-called "lifeboat ethic" of Hardin. Those who could not make it on their own, it was argued, without seemingly unlimited amounts of international aid, should be permitted to go their own way even if that way meant regional instability, war, and the death of innocent human beings. This prospect was abhorrent to those who believed, to paraphrase Mao Tse-tung, that people were "most precious" and that the right to life with security and dignity was part of the common heritage of mankind.

At the Center for the Study of Democratic Institutions in Santa Barbara, California, this issue came into focus relatively early in the debate. The need for systematic inquiry into the state of the most underprivileged, as well as the need for policies to deal with their problems, was brought to a head by Lord Ritchie-Calder of Balmashannar, a "Labour Lord" and great humanitarian, in a short, seminal paper entitled "Triage," which was presented at the center's "Dialogue" conference early in 1973. Meanwhile, at the opposite end of the continent, at Clark University's Program on International Development and Social Change, concern over the same issues was raised as a result of the suffering and environmental damage inflicted by the great Sahelian drought, the dimensions of which had only recently begun to be appreciated. The ethical perspective developed at the center merged, through informal conversation and correspondence between Robert Kates and myself, with the practical research and developmental perspectives at Clark University. The two institutions agreed to sponsor a major conference on the plight of and prospects for the "poorest of the poor," to be held in Santa Barbara in October 1974. It is a matter of some disciplinary pride that much of the impetus for such a meeting came from geographers such as Robert Kates and Leonard Berry at Clark University, myself at the University of California at Santa Barbara and the University of Chicago, and Gilbert White, acting as counselor, at the University of Colorado.

Unfortunately arrangements for the conference had to be suspended due to a basic reorganization of the center during the autumn and winter of 1974—75, by which time I had returned to the University of Chicago. In the summer of 1975 the center established a branch office in Chicago. Negotiations for holding the conference there were resumed, but the center's Chicago office did not have adequate facilities. At this point, the cooperation of two other institutions was sought and freely given. The Johnson Foundation, headed by Leslie Paffrath with Rita Goodman as program executive, offered the facilities of their beautiful conference center, Wingspread, near Racine, Wisconsin, as well as substantial financial support. In addition, the Norman Wait Harris Foundation in International Relations, at the University of Chicago—the executive secretary of which is Bert Hoselitz, editor of *Economic Development and Cultural Change*—also offered important conceptual and financial support. Thus, what had begun as a cooperative venture between two quite distinctive organizations at opposite ends of North America, became a quadrilateral enterprise involving like-minded interests in the Midwest as well.

It was generally agreed that no discussion of problems, solutions, and prospects should take place without representation from those countries whose futures were in the balance. As Berry and Kates mapped out the program and agenda for the conference, they sought participants from a significant sampling of very poor countries, participants whose perspectives were essential to any serious discussion of the what, where, why, and how of global poverty. Moreover, it was agreed that ideological orthodoxy, as reflected in the policies of the World Bank and even UNCTAD, must be balanced by views from a socialist perspective. The result was an exchange of views (held at Wingspread in 1975 from October 19 to 22) upon which most of the papers in this volume are based, providing a forum for dialogue cutting across national and ideological lines and involving both theoretical and practical dimensions.

To simply state that a major conclusion of the conference was that the condition and prospects of the "poorest of the poor" varied and were based upon complex factors of history, environment, and human organization would do the conference a great disservice. What is more important—and the reader of this volume may determine the validity of this assertion—the discussions clarified major issues basic to an understanding of national poverty and suggested possible remedies for its alleviation. They isolated important international forces that limit access of the disadvantaged to the resources of the rest of the world community. They determined the importance of idiosyncratic variables, ranging from the geographical and environmental to the social and political, which lend distinctiveness to the condition of some of the poorest countries. And they led to provocative and promising strategies that might be employed to diminish the vulnerability and enhance the welfare of these poor countries. Finally, they suggested the outlines of a research and action agenda that can serve as guidelines both to further inquiry and to the solution of specific problems in specific areas. Triage was rejected as inhumane and impractical. Judicious tempering of ardent nationalism with infusions of compassionate interest, more effective assistance in technological transfer, and the means for regional cooperation, which might involve surrender of a modicum of sovereignty, were presented and evaluated. Equally important, the responsibility of the wealthier toward the poorer and the more advantaged toward the disadvantaged was affirmed.

The results are a confirmation of the proposition that the improvement of the human condition is—or should be—the prime objective of international relations as well as a major objective of scientific enterprise. We are all in the global ark together, and on it humankind moves toward its destiny. Who can escape the responsibility for helping to determine the direction in which it sails and the ways in which life on board might be enriched?

Norton Ginsburg
University of Chicago
November 1978

PART I:

BEING LEAST DEVELOPED
IN AN AFFLUENT WORLD

The first section of this book establishes the rationale for least developed nations. R. B. Ford establishes the historical setting for G. K. Helleiner's current economic analysis of their status and T. Szentes's examination of the process of underdevelopment and its various solutions. The political status and stability of least developed nations is analyzed by C. H. Enloe through a case study of an Asian group of LDNs. The chapter by D. J. Campbell and C. Katz looks forward to the second section of this book in that it presents an analysis of similarities and differences among groups of countries within the least developed category.

1.
The starting point in this exploration of least development is history. Too often studies of development fail to recognize important insights gleaned from an understanding of sweeping changes in the status of areas and nations that have occurred over the centuries. The least developed include some of the most ancient (Ethiopia, Nepal) and most recent (Maldives) nation-states.

What seemed so firm has changed, is changing, and will continue to change. R. B. Ford uses a historical approach to pose questions, not provide answers. Why are the present West African Sahelian states, extremely powerful five hundred years ago, underdeveloped today? What happened to the era of productivity and advanced technology in Zimbabwe? Why is seemingly fertile Haiti the only least-developed country in the Caribbean?

Although Marxist theorists have relied heavily on the historical method, Ford argues that even this coherent approach leaves many questions unanswered. He concludes that no single factor provides an adequate evaluation of change and, like many other authors in this anthology, recommends a local/regional approach rather than a broader global perspective.

A number of historical studies are beginning to make clear the political and economic complexity of early African peoples and the devastating impact resulting from the incursion of Europeans and Arabs into Africa, particularly from the sixteenth century onward. For example, Philip Curtin's work on the agricultural history of West Africa (1975), I. N. Kimambo's study of the political history of the Pare (1969), and Walter Rodney's classic review of the slave trade (1974) utilize very different approaches. Increasingly, African historians are beginning to outline a national view of history (Ajayi, 1976; Kimambo and Temu, 1969).

As their work continues to provide a richer and a more complex picture of the African past, a somewhat more realistic background for a proper understanding of the present intricacies of development on the African continent will gradually emerge.

LEAST DEVELOPMENT: QUESTIONS IN SEARCH OF ANSWERS

R. B. Ford

History is rife with irony. What is it, for example, that determines which peoples shall be rich and which poor? Does the explanation lie primarily in the physical environment? Are not the variables essentially cultural? Why are wealth and poverty continually shifting? How ironic that among Arnold Toynbee's twenty-one great civilizations of the past, only a handful are still rich today.

The transitory nature of wealth and poverty is even more poignant when viewed in the context of twentieth-century development and underdevelopment. Many empires and kingdoms that once possessed great wealth, prestige, power, and stability are today numbered among the world's poorest nations. The West African Sudanic/Sahelian region supported large and powerful states five hundred years ago. Trade flourished northward across the Sahara, cities prospered, income grew, art and culture flourished, reliable tax revenues supported large armies and navies, and famine appeared to be a minor problem. According to historical sources describing the Sahel's preponderant sense of security in the fourteenth and fifteenth centuries, a traveler's life and property were safe thanks to a cohesive political organization and effective law enforcement. Erring or wayward villages and towns were kept in line either through the collection of tribute or by means of appropriate punitive expeditions. Yet today the Sahelian states are numbered among the world's poorest nations and are more vulnerable to natural disasters (e.g., the recent drought) than they were five hundred years ago.

In North Africa, ruins of ancient Rome stand as mute but dramatic evidence of the productivity that once prevailed. During the height of Roman power, ships laden with olive oil, grain, and other products regularly sailed for Rome and points north. Cities such as Leptis Magnus became powerful entities in their own right. Stability, resulting both from Rome's external dominance and local productivity, persisted for several centuries. Yet today these regions do not support high per-capita incomes (with the exception of recent oil infusions), nor is there a substantial export of food from, say, Tunisia or Libya.

In eastern Africa, particularly in the coastal area bordering the Indian Ocean, several city-states achieved comparable records. Trade goods moved regularly between Asia, the Near East, and Africa. Although the annual per-capita income in Somalia today is less than one hundred dollars, five hundred years ago the city of Mogadishu was a vital link in a commercial network that traded cloth, metalware, spices, gold, ivory, wax, meat, wheat, barley, horses, and several varieties of fruit. Off the Tanzanian coast, in the context of modern Tanzania's low GNP, Kilwa recalls the technological sophistication and worldwide influence that was common in eastern Africa five centuries ago. Farther inland, the massive ruins of Great Zimbabwe testify to the region's earlier productivity, trade, centralization, stability, and power.

Similar accomplishments are characteristic of many parts of Asia. In southern Asia, where Mogul princes reigned three hundred years ago, malnutrition today looms as an ever-present danger. The majestic Taj Mahal, built around 1650, contrasts with the struggle of modern Indian or Bangladeshi villagers to eke out a meager existence. Persia's Persepolis, although located in oil-rich Iran, is surrounded by arid land and marginally productive soil. In Southeast Asia, the grandeur of Angkor Wat seems curiously out of place in the midst of societies that today experience little of what Toynbee would call great civilizations.

In Latin America, the remains of Chichén Itzá in Yucatán or Machu Picchu in Peru represent vanished wealth and power. Yet the high Andes and the limestone shelf of Yucatán are no longer productive, nor is there any immediate prospect that the world's balance of power is about to shift back to its former state.

The irony is heightened when one examines the history of today's so-called rich nations. Using membership in OECD as an informal measure, one discovers that the bulk of monetary wealth is primarily found in northern Europe and North America. Yet at a time when northern Africa was feeding the Roman Empire, northern Europe was still considered barbaric. While Mayan rulers were constructing Chichén Itzá, the Vikings were pillaging the European coast. Similarly, while east and west African cities were trading with the rest of the world and Mogul craftsmen were constructing the Taj Mahal, North America had not yet entered the Iron Age.

The authors of a collection of essays concerned with the poorest among the LDNs can profitably pause to consider how shifts of wealth and power have occurred in the past and whether such shifts may recur in the future. What is it that determines whether and when a nation or region shall be rich or poor? And perhaps more important, are wealth and power the primary goals for nation-states to pursue?

Some historical explanations seek universal answers to account for these shifts. Toynbee argued that cyclical patterns pervade all of history. According to Toynbee's cyclical theory, every great civilization (a) originates with a physical challenge (e.g., a desiccated landscape for Egypt or a luxuriant tropical rain forest for the Mayans); (b) enters a formative period during which institutions emerge; (c) endures a time of crisis during which these institutions are challenged; (d) achieves a state of universal peace during which the society's religion, philosophy, and economic/political system dominate a large geographic region; and (e) eventually falls into a state of decline. Yet Toynbee's explanation falls short of analyzing why some regions with considerable physical challenges (e.g., the Amazon valley) produced no great civilizations. Toynbee is of little help in explaining why some groups overcame their time of crisis while others did not. Nor does he offer any analysis of the causes of decline.

A neo-Toynbee view could hypothesize that societies are similar to living organisms in that they experience inevitable stages of birth, infancy, adolescence, maturity, decline, and death. Strength and weakness, wealth and poverty, dominance and vulnerability are but opposite ends of the cyclical stages of growth and decline. In the light of this organic hypothesis, the rise and fall of ancient Egypt or Mogul India could be viewed as stages through which societal organisms pass, like all living things, eventually withering and dying. Although it is plausible that social institutions do undergo regular life cycles, this hypothesis does little to explain why particular groups rise or fall at particular times. Since it lacks such an explanation, the life-cycle hypothesis offers little guidance to account for the current imbalance in the allocation of world resources. Nor does it identify appropriate goals for nation-states.

Another universal explanation rooted in the concept of inevitability is the

Marxian view of history. Societies, Marx argued, pass through a series of stages, progressing from primitive communism to slavery to feudalism to capitalism to an eventual stage of socialism/communism. For Marx, the key variable is ownership and control of private property, which leads inevitably to a class struggle. This, in turn, ultimately brings about a socialist revolution. Wealth and poverty, Marx concluded, exist because different world regions are at different stages in the evolutionary process; power is consequently distributed unevenly. Thus, a slave society could easily dominate a primitive communist society and a capitalist society could readily rule a feudal society. However, Marx offered no inkling as to why such ancient civilizations as Egypt, Sumer, or Persia withered, or why, for that matter, ancient Rome did not endure for another thousand years. Moreover, Marx provided little or no explanation of how northern Europe became an industrial, political, and economic power *when* it did. To speak in terms of inevitability is to beg the questions of time and place. Although a Marxian analysis rooted in the concepts of private property and class struggle may have validity in the contemporary world, a historical application of the hypothesis leaves many questions unanswered.

In the absence of any universal explanations, analyses of individual situations may prove helpful. One view explains the presence or lack of wealth in terms of unique combinations of available natural resources. Egypt, China, and Babylonia grew strong because river basins provided abundant water and fertile soil, agriculture prospered, surpluses developed, specialization ensued, productivity increased—all of these factors contributing to wealth and power.

If wealth grows out of available resources, why does prosperity in these regions ever stop? At least three explanations exist. One explanation argues that decline is the result either of environmental depletion or actual resource destruction. Centuries of cropping wear out the soil. Years of irrigation silt up ditches and gradually increase soil salinization. Persistent land clearing reduces soil cover and therefore increases soil erosion. Expanding livestock populations exhaust grasslands. In all of these examples, poor management and improper land use combine to wear out what was once a productive resource. According to this view, the abandoned lands around Persepolis, Leptis Magnus, Chichén Itzá, and Timbuktu are depleted today because individuals or societies were careless in their use of resources. The depletion hypothesis can easily be projected into other settings: ancient Kush used up its iron ore reserves; nineteenth-century New England cut down all its timber; Europe and North America are today polluting their air and water resources.

Resource depletion, however, is a deceptive hypothesis. It implies that if Egyptians, Romans, New Englanders, and Kushites had been better managers of their physical environment, they would still be prosperous today. It suggests that the burden of responsibility largely rests with the leadership and decision-making system of the society in question. The hypothesis further assumes that an established system of resource use can and should be sustained, but in modes that make minimal demands on nonrenewable resources. This reasoning helps explain the adoption of policies that place a higher priority on environmental preservation than on increased productivity. Although environmental preservation is a worthwhile goal, it is questionable whether it should be sought at the expense of improved production. Rather, it may be more appropriate to pursue continually changing combinations of resource use instead of a fixed set of environmentally safe policies.

A second explanation accounts for a decline in productivity in terms of a shift in climate: a decrease in rainfall lowers the capacity of the land to produce food; surpluses slacken; more labor is required to produce food from the increasingly unproductive land; an increased emphasis on food production weakens specialization; comparative advantages slip away and stagnation sets in; with the onset of stagnation, poverty is soon to follow. Although this argument is especially compelling for Sahelian Africa, it fails to explain why Persia declined, Rome was toppled, and the Mayans fell victim to jungle encroachment.

Moreover, theories propounding a shift in climate are based on extremely sketchy data. For example, in the Sahel there is considerable evidence to support the view that lakebeds, rainfall, and vegetation patterns were quite different ten thousand or twenty thousand years ago, but there is no convincing documentation to prove that five centuries ago—the prime years of the Sudanic states—climate or rainfall differed substantially from today's conditions.

A third hypothesis seeking to explain why well-endowed regions may vacillate between extreme poverty and wealth relies upon questions of moral commitment and social discipline. This view claims that wealth results when people work hard and institutions enforce codes of moral dedication. When these codes are relaxed—Gibbon used this theory to explain the fall of the Roman Empire—social disintegration sets in. No matter how substantial the resource base, this hypothesis maintains that without discipline poverty will prevail.

The greatest problem with the "hard-work" hypothesis is that historically the people who have worked the hardest have been peasants involved in subsistence agriculture. Yet these are the very people who have found it difficult to free themselves from the burden of discipline and hard work in order to acquire new skills or perspectives and thereby increase their productivity and wealth.

These three perspectives on the natural-resource theory of wealth and poverty by no means answer all questions. Yet the foregoing discussion should suggest that availability of natural resources only partly determines whether or not different regions shall enjoy prosperity and, if so, when.

Yet another hypothesis suggests that technology is the key variable in the attainment of wealth. With adequate technology, other problems (e.g., natural resources) can be managed. The two best historical examples of this view are eighteenth- and nineteenth-century Great Britain and twentieth-century Japan. Although both nations are largely deficient in natural resources, they have managed to achieve unprecedented levels of influence and wealth despite major external dependencies for such basic needs as energy, food, and industrial raw materials. Some proponents of the technology hypo-thesis, furthermore, argue that the unique appearance of Europe's military/industrial power several centuries ago can be traced back to specific accom-plishments in the field of naval navigation and the use of gunpowder and the steam engine. Others argue that the U.S. conquest of the Great Plains could not have occurred without the development of barbed wire (to control cattle), the windmill (to provide water in a region where energy derived from wood and coal was scarce), and the repeating six-shooter (to overcome the skill of native American plains dwellers who could shoot three or four arrows in the time it would take a muzzle-loaded rifle to fire a single shot).

But technology does not tell the whole story of rich and poor nations. Recent experiences in development and technology transfer suggest that tech-nology is culture-bound. Western agricultural equipment, for example, pre-assumes particular land-ownership patterns, wage relationships, and mar-keting techniques. In the absence of a set of supporting institutions, new technology will make little improvement in productivity and may even lead to a decline. Therefore, if technology seemingly results in wealth in one setting (Kansas) but fails to do so in another (Niger), one can safely conclude that the key variable in determining wealth or poverty must lie elsewhere.

In short, how can one respond to the basic question: Why have wealth and power continually and dramatically shifted from one civilization to another throughout history? First, it is clear that no universal or general explanation exists. Second, it seems equally clear that the simple answers based on theories of resource availability and technological capability (examined in a limited number of individual situations) do not provide adequate explanations.

One must therefore conclude that not only is there no single answer but there is no single approach that will correct the current imbalance in resource allocation. Instead, it seems apparent that the causes of underdevelopment vary from case to case. In some instances variables are rooted in local social, political, or economic practices; in others poverty exists because the local resource base is not coordinated with planning and policy activities; in still other cases underdevelopment prevails because unequal power relationships create dependencies, making it difficult, if not impossible, for poor societies to free themselves from an umbilical relationship with the industrial world.

In contemplating strategies to reduce poverty, particularly among LDNs, it is necessary to move away from general or universal solutions. Instead, policy must grow out of a conviction that local situations vary considerably. A broad range of alternative approaches and choices should be explored. Unique circumstances require individual responses. Insofar as the other essays in the present anthology extend the range of possible developmental approaches, they shall have made a useful contribution to the field.

FOR FURTHER READING

Ajayi, J. F. A. and M. Crowder. 1976. *History of West Africa.* London: Longmans.

Curtin, Philip et al. 1978. *African History.* Boston: Little, Brown.

Davidson, B. 1959. *The Lost Cities of Africa.* Boston: Little, Brown.

Dudley, G. 1973, *A History of Eastern Civilizations.* New York: John Wiley.

Farmer, E. et al. 1977. *Comparative History of Civilization in Asia.* Reading, Mass.: Addison Wesley.

Ford, John. 1971. *The Role of Trypanosomiasis in African Ecology.* Oxford: Oxford University Press, Clarendon Press.

Hargreaves, John D. 1974. *West Africa Partitioned.* Madison: University of Wisconsin Press.

Hopkins, A. G. 1973. *An Economic History of West Africa.* New York: Columbia University Press.

Julien, C. A. 1970. *History of North Africa from the Arab Conquest to 1830.* London: Routledge and Kegan Paul.

Kimambo, Isaria N. and A. Temu. 1969. *A History of Tanzania.* Nairobi: East Africa Publishing House.

Meillassoux, Claude. 1972. *The Development of African Markets and Trade in West Africa.* London: Oxford University Press.

Munro, J. Forbes. 1976. *Africa and the International Economy, 1800–1960.* London: J. M. Dent.

Rodney, Walter. 1974. *How Europe Underdeveloped Africa.* Washington, D.C.: Howard University Press.

Toynbee, A. 1972. *A Study of History.* 2 Vols. New York: Weathervane Books.

Vansina, J. 1968. *Kingdoms of the Savanna.* Madison: University of Wisconsin Press.

2.

By definition, the least developed are least influential in the current economic order, but what about a new economic order? G. K. Helleiner reviews the relative position of the least developed in terms of existing and possible new economic orders. In neither are prospects particularly pleasing. He notes that up until the worldwide rise in prices in the early 1970s, the export purchasing power of the least developed had remained at fairly steady levels, only to plummet to 63 percent of 1963–65 levels by 1974.

In addition, the least developed appear to have achieved little or no effective growth in per capita GNP over a considerable period. While some developing countries have begun to join together in order to negotiate from a position of greater strength, the least developed, for the most part, do not have the resources or political strength to make this a very effective bargaining position.

In fact, the one growth area among the least developed during the last few years has been development assistance. Helleiner suggests that there are two alternatives that many of the least developed will utilize to some degree. First, they will make a more concerted effort to work out commodity agreements. Second, they will attempt to reduce their degree of individual dependency on the outside world. (These themes are expanded upon in chaps. 12 and 13.) A judicious combination of a self-reliant and hard-headed approach to the outside world may be the best possible route. But the fact remains that the gap between the rich and poor is increasing at a more rapid rate for the least developed.

THE LEAST DEVELOPED IN THE INTERNATIONAL ECONOMIC ORDER

G. K. Helleiner

There have been two major new thrusts in the development literature and experience of the last few years. The first concerns a greatly increased emphasis upon employment and, more broadly, the distributional effects of different development strategies and projects. Growth, as conventionally defined, is no longer considered an adequate proximate target if poverty alleviation is the ultimate objective; there can be no assurance that its gains will trickle down to those at the lower end of the distribution spectrum. Some individuals have set about trying to construct new measures of aggregative national development performance that better reflect these new perceptions— either by developing social indicators or by revising the weighting system employed in more conventional growth accounting. Others have tried to incorporate them into the methodology of benefit/cost analysis for use in assessing microlevel projects. At the international level, there has been a corresponding increase in concern, at least as officially expressed, over the effects of total trade, aid, and other resource flows upon the least developed countries. A "trickling down" from world growth is no more assured (probably less so) than that from growth within nations.

A second major new thrust is of more recent vintage and can be summarized under the heading "new international economic order" concerns. Growing disillusion with developed countries' performance with respect to aid, trade, and financial policies vis-à-vis less-developed countries as a whole was galvanized by OPEC's success into a much more aggressive and determined Third World international stance. The less-developed countries, both singly and as a group, appear far readier now to employ whatever bargaining strength they possess to extract maximum concessions from developed countries and even to employ unilateral initiatives where the bargaining process proves unproductive. Their new objectives are not solely related to possible income gains; they also include increased "distance," decreased "packaging" (whereby a variety of separable inputs must be purchased together), increased reversibility in their foreign economic relations, and increased power in international institutions. Not surprisingly, this new mood is accompanied by a resurgence of interest in Third World cooperation—or what has become known as "collective self-reliance." All of this potential disruption emanating from the Third World burst upon the scene at a time when the international economic order of the post-World War II period was experiencing unprecedented stress from inflationary pressures, severe recession among industrialized countries, and international financial crises.

This chapter will explore the area of concern where these two new thrusts converge. Unfortunately, the world economic order that might be consciously planned by people of goodwill is unlikely to resemble the economic order that actually emerges from the complex process of accommodation among competing governments in the rough-and-tumble world of international politics. What is the position of the poorest of the poor in the present international economic (dis)order? What must they inevitably do for themselves? (Chapter 13 examines what eventually might be gleaned from ongoing efforts to build a new economic order at the international level that would be of assistance to the poorest nations.)

Let it be said immediately that the poorest of the poor are found within relatively well-off countries, including the United States and Europe, and not merely among the least developed. Focusing on the poorest *nation-states,* as one tends to do in discussions of international affairs, is politically and statistically expedient, but it is not necessarily more correct than analyzing the problems of the poorest *people.*

It is also important to be aware of the fact that the term *least developed,* as employed in UN documents, is not synonymous with *poorest.* As part of a complex political process intended to improve the distribution of overall gains resulting from international-bargaining activities in the second UNCTAD (1968), some twenty-five countries (later expanded to twenty-nine) were designated least developed. The objective criteria employed for this designation included per capita income, literacy, and the share of manufacturing in total national output. Unfortunately, this least developed grouping excludes some very large and extremely poor countries, notably India and Pakistan. (Indonesia and Nigeria are other large and poor countries excluded from the definition, but both have petroleum and other resources and are not generally considered problem countries, i.e., members of what has come to be termed the Fourth World.) One must therefore be careful to distinguish between the two definitions of the term *least developed,* which can either refer to a specific UN-defined category consisting of twenty-nine countries or simply to the poorest nation-states.

The fact that this chapter focuses upon the international dimensions of problems associated with the world's poorest nation-states should not be taken as an indication that purely local problems—environmental, social, political—should be regarded as unimportant. On the contrary, they are of crucial importance. Structural changes and reforms at the international level may be necessary, but they are certainly not sufficient to guarantee significant improvements in the plight of the poor. Indeed, if one is prepared to assign substantially greater significance to nonmaterial measures of welfare having to do with the quality of life and human relationships, one might also argue that international change is frequently not necessary. At all events, since major international change is unlikely, it follows that domestic policy must be the key element in feasible and independent antipoverty activities in poor areas. Relatively marginal external changes that are politically feasible can expand opportunities and assist these efforts to succeed, but they can do no more. This chapter, therefore, shall be primarily concerned with international dimensions as they relate to the problems of the poorest nation-states since they are important for an understanding of the constraints that efforts to help them must overcome.

The Least Developed in the International Economy

Development assistance is no longer seen as the base upon which relations between rich nations and the Third World rest. Always overemphasized and misunderstood in the developed countries, the role of development assistance has at last been recognized as secondary, relative to trade and financial issues that poor countries have long tried to bring to the fore. Table 2.1 shows the principal components of the balance of payments of the Third World as a whole and of the least developed countries (as defined by the United Nations). Even for the latter, where development assistance is of greater importance, it usually amounts to less than one-third of imports. For much of the Third World, the mid-1970s signaled the end of the "aid era"—if, in fact, there had ever been as much aid as talk about its purported existence. The Third World now has fewer illusions about the willingness of developed countries to offer significant assistance. It has formulated new objectives (e.g., greater self-reliance and increased arms-length relations with more powerful nations) and, consequently, new instruments and approaches for their attainment. Much more determined and sophisticated bargaining can now be expected from Third World representatives in their dealings with foreign firms and governments, including an increasingly greater reliance upon unilateral initiatives.

For some poor countries, however, the new mood apparent in the less-developed world is small comfort in view of the enormous losses they recently incurred in relation to trade account terms or the extraordinarily bleak trade

TABLE 2.1
KEY ELEMENTS IN BALANCE OF PAYMENTS
OF LEAST DEVELOPED COUNTRIES
(In Constant 1974 Per Capita Dollars)

	Least Developed Countries		All Other Developing Countries[a]	
	1965–1968 Average	1974	1965–1968 Average	1974
1. Export-purchasing power	20.2	12.8	49.4	62.2
2. Total financial flows[b], including:	8.2	11.4	18.3	20.8
Official development assistance[c]	6.8	6.9	9.9	6.7
Loans and grants from OPEC countries[d]	-	2.7	-	2.5
3. Total foreign exchange available (= 1 + 2)	28.4	24.2	67.7	83.0
4. Import volume	26.2	22.1	61.9	80.7
5. Gross National Product[e]	101.0	102.0	248.0	316.0

SOURCE: UNCTAD, *Least Developed among Developing Countries, Developing Island Countries, and Developing Land-locked Countries* (Item 13—main policy issues), TD/191, Nairobi, May 1976, p. 4.

a Excluding major petroleum exporters.
b Includes: (1) net disbursements of loans and grants from DAC member countries and multilateral institutions; (2) net disbursements on loans from socialist countries of Eastern Europe; (3) net disbursements on loans from China; (4) net disbursements on loans and grants from OPEC countries; (5) net private investment flows from DAC countries; and (6) estimated net disbursements on Euro-currency borrowings for 1974.
c From DAC member countries and multilateral institutions.
dIncluding OPEC-financed flows from the IMF Oil Facilty.
eAt 1973 constant prices.

prospects they now face. For these countries, bargaining can achieve little additional progress, and there is no option but to plead with whomever will listen for increased voluntary assistance. While trade is still more important to them in the aggregate than aid, present prospects are so somber that their only hope lies in the dawning of a new aid era. They are already extremely aid-dependent by Third World standards.

Instability and recession at the core of the world's economy have historically generated even greater problems in peripheral areas. Demand for the periphery's products and capital flow have traditionally been the principal channels through which the impact of the center has been felt in the periphery. In the most recent recession, although the usual forces operated in a traditional manner, they were aggravated by coincidental sharp increases in relative prices for fuel, food, fertilizer and, in some areas, by abnormal weather conditions. The effect was not merely to stop development efforts in these countries but also to inflict additional human suffering upon those least able to bear it.

For the non-oil-exporting developing countries, the commodity terms of trade deteriorated at a rate of over 2 percent annually from the early 1950s until 1973. This deterioration was more pronounced among the least developed countries, as a consequence of which the per capita purchasing power of their exports scarcely changed from the mid-1960s until the recession and oil crisis of 1973. (The foregoing is documented in a confidential World Bank report cited in the 1975 issue of *The Economist*.) The precipitous collapse of their terms of trade at that time reduced the per capita purchasing power of their exports to 63 percent of its 1965–68 average (table 2.1). Per capita import volume of the least developed countries, which had risen slightly from the mid-1960s to 1973, plummeted to only 84 percent of its 1965–68 level despite some growth in development assistance. Total import volume was lower in 1974 than it had been in 1970—not only for the twenty-nine least developed countries but also for India and Pakistan. While total import volume recovered somewhat in 1975, per capita import volume in the least developed countries was nearly 10 percent lower than it had been in 1970 (OECD, 1977).

Largely as a consequence of this experience, real per capita income hardly grew at all for the least developed countries collectively considered as a group, while over half of the group's total population actually suffered a decline. This dismal experience followed a decade in which the annual growth rate in the group's per capita income was only 0.7 percent (UNCTAD, 1976a). The World Bank does not anticipate that per capita income of the poorest countries (under $200 per capita) will grow by as much as 1 percent annually for the balance of the decade (World Bank, 1975).

This unfortunate scenario is the result, in large part, of the unfortunate assortment of products the poorest countries export. (This is itself a reflection of other factors, most notably each country's resource base.) With very few exceptions, the exports of the poorest countries consist of food, beverages,

TABLE 2.2
COMMODITY STRUCTURE OF EXPORTS OF HARD-CORE
LEAST DEVELOPED COUNTRIES, 1972

		Share of Major Commodity Groups in Total Exports				
Hard-core Least Developed Countries	Value of Exports ($ millions)	Food and Beverages	Crude Materials	Fuels	Nonferrous Metals, etc.	Manu-factured Goods
Afghanistan	90	25.0	46.7	10.9	—	17.4
Bangladesh	253	36.8	37.5	—	—	49.4
Benin	47	36.8	57.9	—	—	2.6
Bhutan	—	—	—	—	—	—
Botswana	46	40.9	26.9	—	32.0	—
Burundi	25	80.0	16.0	—	—	4.0
Central African Republic	39	31.0	34.9	0.2	32.1	1.3
Chad	39	11.1	83.3	—	—	5.6
Ethiopia	167	68.5	29.1	0.6	—	1.5
Gambia	19	16.2	83.8	—	—	—
Guinea	68	18.6	12.9	—	67.1	2.9
Haiti	42	44.2	9.3	—	—	41.9
Laos	3	—	100.0	—	—	—
Lesotho	8	26.0	52.7	—	—	3.2
Malawi	81	72.8	16.0	2.5	—	6.2
Maldives	4	100.0	—	—	—	—
Mali	34	38.9	55.6	—	—	5.6
Nepal	30	42.3	38.5	—	—	19.2
Niger	54	22.2	75.9	—	—	1.9
Rwanda	19	55.0	45.0	—	—	4.5
Sikkim	—	—	—	—	—	—
Somalia	42	92.5	7.5	—	—	0.7
Sudan	360	9.5	89.4	0.8	—	—
Uganda	283	66.3	22.9	0.6	6.1	0.3
United Republic of Tanzania	319	48.6	29.4	9.4	4.3	2.4
Upper Volta	20	60.0	35.0	—	—	—
Western Samoa	12	60.0	40.0	—	—	—
Yemen, Arab Republic	4	25.0	75.0	—	—	—
Yemen, Democratic Republic	108	5.2	7.6	68.5	—	5.4
TOTAL	2,220	37.1	40.9	5.5	4.7	9.1
All Developing Countries	75,040	21.0	15.6	39.9	3.6	19.5

SOURCE: UNCTAD, *Least Developed among Developing Countries, Developing Island Countries, and Developing Land-locked Countries* (Item 13—supporting paper) TD/191/Suppl. 1, Nairobi, May 1976, table 6, p. 24.

and crude materials (table 2.2.) Fuels, nonferrous metals, and manufactured products—areas in which market prospects are brightest—are conspicuously absent. Only one least developed country (viz., Democratic Republic of Yemen) has significant fuel exports; those of Tanzania are simply re-exports. Nonferrous metals are important only in Botswana, Guinea, and Central African Empire—all of which have developed significant exports of this material relatively recently. The few manufactured products consist primarily of such items as jute fabrics, carpets, and so forth. In twenty of the twenty-nine countries listed in table 2.2, food, beverages, and crude materials comprise over 90 percent of total exports.

Table 2.3 shows the leading exports of the twenty-nine least developed countries. Three items (cotton, coffee, and oilseeds) account for 40 percent of total exports from these countries; despite recent price gains, none of them can be described as having strong, long-range market prospects.

The very weakness of their economic prospects, of course, makes these countries less creditable. They therefore do not have the same access to private capital (either with respect to quantity or terms) as do the better-endowed Third World countries. While others hail the opening up of Euro-dollar markets to less-developed borrowers, the poorest countries derive no direct benefits from this phenomenon. (They may benefit indirectly if their more fortunate Third World allies thereby reduce their claims on total development assistance.) Nor are they attractive candidates for direct investments. Per capita receipts of private capital in the least developed countries totaled less than a quarter of those received by the less-developed countries as a whole in 1973 (UNCTAD, 1975a).

The least developed countries are thus peculiarly dependent upon resource flows and foreign-exchange receipts, which are not commercially motivated. Indeed, official development assistance is the only balance-of-payments item that has recently been showing any sort of favorable change. As can be seen in table 2.1, while per capita (constant-dollar) aid receipts in the developing countries have elsewhere been falling, those in the least developed countries have risen very slightly between the late 1960s and 1974. However, real aid to India, the population of which alone is two and one-half times that of the entire least developed group, fell not only in per capita terms but absolutely (Edelman and Chenery, 1977). Thus, not even in this area can it really be said that the poorest countries have fared better than they previously did.

Prospects for a New International Economic Order

What is immediately apparent in the clamor surrounding the proposal to create a new international economic order is the fact that the seriousness with which it is being discussed in Washington, London, and Paris does not stem from a sudden burst of conscience on the part of governments of developed countries or from their disenchantment with their own positions in the order. Rather, it stems from the power of the protesters to do positive harm to the

TABLE 2.3
LEADING EXPORTS OF HARD-CORE
LEAST DEVELOPED COUNTRIES[a]
(Ranked According to 1972 Value in $ Million)

SITC	Item	Value in 1972	As % of Total Least Developed Exports	As % of All Developing-Country Exports of Products Shown
263	Cotton	396	17.9	19.7
071	Coffee	353	16.0	11.2
221	Oil seeds	144	6.5	23.7
657	Floor covering, tapestries, etc.	141	6.4	61.5
332	Petroleum products	104	4.7	2.5
264	Jute	94	4.3	53.9
051	Fruit (fresh), nuts, etc.	69	3.1	7.6
001	Live animals	62	2.8	21.9
121	Tobacco, unmanufactured	58	2.6	11.5
211	Hides and skins	57	2.4	21.2
074	Tea and maté	51	2.3	9.0
513	Alumina	45	2.0	41.5
667	Diamonds	44	2.0	7.7
075	Spices	42	1.9	15.9
292	Crude vegetable materials	39	1.8	12.4
011	Meat: fresh, chilled, or frozen	32	1.4	2.8
081	Feeding stuff for animals	30	1.4	5.2
054	Vegetables (fresh), etc.	21	1.0	3.8
265	Vegetable fibers (excluding jute & cotton)	21	1.0	22.9
682	Copper	19	0.9	1.0
042	Rice	19	0.9	4.4
341	Gas, natural	18	0.8	5.7
052	Dried fruit	18	0.8	16.4
212	Fur skins, undressed	16	0.7	76.2
283	Nonferrous base metal ore & concentrates	16	0.7	0.9
421	Fixed vegetable oils, soft	14	0.6	4.2
013	Meat and preparations	13	0.6	4.9
262	Wool and other animal hair	11	0.5	7.1
422	Other fixed vegetable oils	9	0.4	1.6
286	Uranium concentrates	9	0.4	—
072	Cocoa	8	0.4	0.9
TOTAL[b]	(26 least developed countries)	2,210	100.0	8.4

SOURCE: UNCTAD, *Least Developed among Developing Countries, Developing Island Countries, and Developing Land-locked Countries* (Item 13— supporting paper) TD/191/Suppl. 1, Nairobi, May 1976, table 8, p. 27.

NOTE: Data for twenty-six least developed countries, accounting for about 99 percent of the total exports of the twenty-nine hard-core least developed countries.

a Against data for twenty-six least developed countries.

b Including products not shown above.

defenders of the present order. It is the exercise of power over commodity supplies and the threat of more to come that has forced governments of developed countries to consider new commodity arrangements. Similarly, increased revenues accruing to host countries from the operations of transnational enterprises in less-developed countries and improvements in the enterprises' "behavior" (where they have occurred) are the product not of reduced interest in private profit but rather that of the use of host governments' power. The gains being realized by some Third World countries stem from their possession of previously underutilized power; new cards are being played—and there may also be some bluffing as to what cards are still being held.

In the new order it would seem that it is realpolitik—the sophisticated and cold-blooded use of power—that is to determine the outcome. As one commentator has put it, we are developing a system for "winners." What, however, is to become of the "losers"? Some countries have no cards to play, or have such weak ones that they are of little account. If the new aggressiveness of the Third World destroys the limited consensus by which the developed countries accepted some of the claims on their resources for the alleviation of world poverty, what will become of the "Fourth World"?

There are two possible outcomes, each buying at opposite ends of the economic spectrum: (1) either the new order will be one in which "the devil takes the hindmost," international responsibility for poverty (or, indeed, for much else) will evaporate, and the world will enter a period of disorder and anarchy in which the weakest are bound to fare worst; or (2) the exercise of power by some of the countries formerly categorized as poor will enable them to reduce their claims for international assistance and even to share the responsibility for its provision to those countries remaining at the lowest absolute levels, thus raising the overall scale of efforts to assist them.

It would be foolhardy to select the more realistic scenario. In any case, the real outcome is likely to contain elements of both. It is important, however, to be aware of the risks inherent in the first alternative and the opportunities for the realization of the second.

It is obvious that the poorest countries are technically least equipped to deal with the new risks and uncertainties in the world economy: fluctuating exchange rates; volatile commodity markets; and rapidly changing institutions. If one projects a slower growth rate for the world economy as a whole (as many now do), including increased instability and uncertainty in its functioning, the implications for the poorest countries are very serious.

Even the most optimistic attitude cannot remain very sanguine when confronted with the medium-term outlook for the world's poorest countries or peoples. Their market prospects are bleak and their hopes for increased noncommercial assistance are highly uncertain. Nor can one forget that the levels of income from which they begin are so low that even the attainment of rates of growth as great as those of other countries—an unlikely prospect—would generate absolute improvements of slight overall consequence. A 4 percent average per capita income growth rate for India or Tanzania, for example, would still leave each country with barely two hundred dollars per capita by 1990.

Self-Reliance and the Least Developed Countries

What can be the response of the poorest countries to the prospect of an unstable world economy in which more powerful players possess all the cards? They must, of course, continue to press for international arrangements that will protect them against the worst blows from external sources. They should seek emergency relief systems for such crises as droughts, natural disasters, or pronounced deterioration in the terms of trade—all of which have been experienced by many poor nations in the past few years. Commodity arrangements that both stabilize prices and offer some guarantee of earnings are both highly desirable and politically feasible; and there are prospects of at least some redirection of total official development assistance toward poorer countries.

Faced with the prospect of weak markets for exports, limited access to foreign capital, and a highly uncertain international economy, the poorest countries might reasonably be expected to turn somewhat "inward" in their preoccupations. There is little enough that the weakest countries can do about the international environment.

What can they do about their own economies—in terms of production structures, distribution, and buffers against further adversity? There is, at the outset, the issue of the size and nature of their international links. If one perceives the world primarily as a source of severe external shocks rather than as a source of increased income—it is actually both—it would not be unreasonable to proceed cautiously and lessen the degree of risk by limiting the extent of one's outward orientation. Unfortunately, savings rates and government revenues are likely to be positively related to a nation's degree of openness.

Some poor countries are as yet so little involved with the world economy that major international disruptions do not greatly affect the overall level of domestic economic activitity or welfare. In most poor countries, the vicissitudes of weather and pests are of greater importance to the majority of the population than are international economic factors, however crucial the latter undoubtedly are to the formalized exchange economy. In these relatively unaffected countries, however, even the exchange economy is either small or relatively uninvolved in international exchange. (It may nevertheless be true that marginal changes in the external account may be critical to the success of particular development programs; many have argued that this has typically been the case in India.)

Table 2.4 shows the shares accounted for by external trade in the GNPs of selected least developed countries. In some countries, imports make up a far greater proportion of the GNP than exports, the difference being financed from abroad (e.g., Chad, Laos, Mali, Upper Volta, and the Yemen Arab

Republic; in 1974 disasters led to the addition of several more countries to this list, including Bangladesh). Such countries are extremely vulnerable to shifts in their patrons' willingness to finance their purchases despite their relative insulation from the direct impact of the world market. Other countries (e.g., Burma, Nepal, and India) are unambiguously less involved in the international economy. If one had data showing the extent of external involvement of particular districts or regions within countries, they would undoubtedly reveal many more that "remain so isolated from the world economy that they have been spared some of its shocks" (Low and Howe, 1975).

There are, of course, other dimensions to the degree of openness of a country besides that shown by trade statistics. The share of domestic capital formation accounted for by external sources and the share of total skilled-manpower positions occupied by foreign personnel are other relevant measures. None of these measures, however, reflects the extent to which the country in question exercises selectivity and control over world influences that have an impact upon its society and economy—and this may be most important.

TABLE 2.4
OPENNESS OF SELECTED LEAST DEVELOPED COUNTRIES,
1974

	Exports as % of GNP	Imports as % of GNP
Afghanistan	12	13
Bangladesh	6	19
Burma	8	5
Burundi	10	14
Chad	11	29
Ethiopia	11	11
Haiti	12	18
India	5	7
Laos	2	17
Mali	9	25
Nepal (1973)	4	6
Pakistan	13	20
Upper Volta	9	34
Yemen Arab Republic	2	28

SOURCE: Data for all countries except Nepal were calculated from data in: Overseas Development Council, *The U.S. and World Development Agenda for Action, 1976* (Washington, D.C., 1976), pp. 132–135. Nepal data are from UNCTAD, *Review of Progress in the Implementation of Special Measures in Favour of the Least Developed among the Developing Countries, Statistical Annex,* TD/B/AC. 17/3/Add.1, June 1975, Tables 4 and 5.

There is bound to be disagreement as to the degree of risk or income involved in external orientation, and consequently in policies relating to it. Wherever possible, however, it is generally agreed that such external links that do exist should be managed in such a way that their unexpected severing or disruption does a minimum degree of damage: exports that can also be consumed at home are preferable to those that cannot; aid attached to "marginal" projects is preferable to aid assigned to "core" sectors; dependence upon foreign sources for food and mass consumer goods should, in many countries, be reduced, and so forth.

The nature of the links with external "players" is also a matter for policy, not merely to be accepted passively as a given. A greater degree of control over relations with the rest of the world is now being assumed by poorer countries. Foreign enterprises and aid donors can no longer expect to have a free rein in the development of projects. Nor are domestic exporters or importers still free to do as they please with receipts and expenditures. External relations are increasingly being viewed in terms of their functionality with respect to national objectives. Unfortunately, in the least developed countries there is frequently limited planning capacity and/or doubtful political purpose, with the result that attempts to manage the overall external impact do not always achieve a development purpose. Therefore, one cannot in good faith offer a generalized recommendation to all poor countries' governments to increase their controls over external relations. One can, however, promote the view that these relations with the rest of the world should be assessed in terms of their developmental function; and one can recommend that their management be improved to this end.

As far as the direction of external links themselves is concerned (regardless of their size and nature), there is again room for disagreement concerning strategy. Should a poor nation align itself closely with one powerful "protector" government or firm? Should it seek maximum diversification of contacts? Above all, should it seek to develop a maximum number of links with other Third World nations to present a common front vis-à-vis the world's rich? What about developing close links with the newer oil-rich states? The majority of observers would agree that the most prudent course is diversification. A weak state must be especially careful when making such calculations. The disadvantages inherent in being a client state of some major power are obvious. But the danger involved in forming Third World alliances with more powerful (but not major) states may be almost as serious.

In any case, economists are increasingly abandoning the search for international or externally oriented answers to the problems of the poorest countries. Domestic policies can and should be geared to the creation of relatively self-reliant economies in which incomes, though low, are reasonably and equitably spread. Unfortunately, there is no universal agreement as to what, precisely, can be achieved on a self-reliant basis in the poorest parts of the world. To cite a recent report (UNCTAD, 1975b) on the problem:

Despite growing interest, there has not yet emerged any particularly different development approach or strategy calculated to respond more effectively to the special needs of the least developed world. Neither the least developed countries themselves nor the multilateral or bilateral donors involved have come forth with a conceptual framework delineating strategies differing from those being applied to other developing countries.

This is, of course, a much larger issue. And one may well ask whether this is any more feasible in domestic political terms than major international action is in world political terms.

FOR FURTHER READING

Amin, Samir. 1977. "Self-reliance and the New International Economic Order." *Monthly Review* 29, no. 3: 1–21.

Caldwell, Malcolm. 1978. *The Wealth of Some Nations*. London: Zed Press.

Edelman, J. A. and H. B. Chenery. 1977. "Aid and Income Distribution." *The New International Economic Order: The North-South Debate*. Edited by Jagdish N. Bhagwati. Cambridge, Mass.: MIT Press.

Fishlow, Albert et al. 1978. *Rich and Poor Nations in the World Economy*. New York: McGraw-Hill.

Helleiner, G. K., ed. 1976. *A World Divided: The Less Developed Countries in the International Economy*. Cambridge: Cambridge University Press.

Jolly, Richard. 1974. "International Dimensions." *Redistribution with Growth*. Edited by Hollis Chenery. London: Oxford University Press, pp. 158–180.

International Labor Office. 1977. *Employment, Growth and Basic Needs: A One-World Problem*. New York: Praeger.

Low, Helen C. and J. W. Howe. 1975. "Focus on the Fourth World." *The U.S. and World Development: Agenda for Action, 1975*. Washington, D.C.: Overseas Development Council, p. 36.

Organization for Economic Cooperation and Development. 1972. *Development Cooperation: Efforts and Policies of the Members of the Development Assistance Committee, 1972 Review*. Paris: OECD.

Sampson, Anthony. 1975. *The Seven Sisters: The Great Oil Companies and the World They Made*. New York: Viking.

Singer, H. W. 1958. "The Mechanics of Economic Development." *The*

Economics of Underdevelopment. Edited by A. N. Agarwala and S. P. Singh. London: Oxford University Press, pp. 381–399.

Streeten, Paul. 1977. "The Distinctive Features of a Basic Needs Approach to Development." *International Development Review* 19, no. 3: 8–16.

Tanzania Delegation to the Nonaligned Nations Summit Conference. 1973. "Cooperation against Poverty." *The Political Economy of Development and Underdevelopment*. Edited by C. K. Wilber. New York: Random House, pp. 373–389.

UNCTAD. 1976(a). *Least Developed among Developing Countries, Developing Island Countries, and Developing Land-locked Countries*. Item 13—Main Policy Issues. TD/191. Nairobi: United Nations.

3. Tamas Szentes, a former member of the UN Commission on Trade and Development (which first proposed that a select group of countries be designated "least developed"), provides a sharp look at the theory of underdevelopment* and its relevance for the least developed. Writing from this vantage point, he emphasizes the pragmatic issues involved in the designation of the least developed, namely, the need for special monies to provide assistance to the poorest countries. The main theme Szentes stresses concerns the international economic and political links, operating throughout recent history, that have caused the least developed to become either relatively or totally underdeveloped. There is, he argues, no special theory for the least developed, only the theory of global development and underdevelopment.

Important for subsequent chapters is Szentes's emphasis on regional differentiation as especially affecting the least developed (chap. 12). In a region comprised of developing countries, the peripheral countries may become the least developed. Furthermore, at least one set of alternatives suggests that an international division of labor will replace the traditional colonial arrangements.

Solutions are presented in terms of major socioeconomic and structural changes, though the details echo, in part, points made elsewhere in this book (chaps. 10 and 11): increased self-reliance; national control of the national economy; regional and national economic integration; and complex rural development, followed by appropriate types of industrialization.

LEAST DEVELOPMENT IN THE CONTEXT AND THEORY OF UNDERDEVELOPMENT

T. Szentes

The modest aim of this paper is to outline briefly the historical and socioeconomic background of what is called least development, why it is so called, and to provoke debate by raising questions and issues of political or ideological relevance.

*Underdevelopment theory (Frank, 1970) is increasingly being used to provide a more coherent and credible explanation for the widening gap separating the global rich and poor. Scholars, including many non-Marxists, have found that the assumptions of neutrality or Pareto optimality for global economic processes simply do not fit the observed conditions. Economic development and growth affect an individual, group, class, region, nation, or tier faction in such a way as to leave some counterpart worse off, both in absolute as well as relative terms. The successful development process, in effect, "underdevelops" the more vulnerable group.

Why Use *Least Developed* Now?

As is well known, the international category of least developed countries is of rather recent origin, though throughout history it was always possible to isolate certain countries, regions, or areas that, in a given historical period, lagged behind others in terms of developent.

The first question, therefore, is: Why had such a distinction not been made before? Was it due to a lack of adequate information on the level of development or "performance" of individual countries of the world, or was it the result of imperfections in the methods used to measure it? Was it the result of ambiguities in the definition and interpretation of the term *develop-ment* or simply a lack of interest that retarded social science in making such a classification?

The answers to each of these questions contain a part of the truth, but no single answer provides a full explanation. As to the reliability of the statistical information or the appropriateness of measurement, we are still faced with problems, uncertainties, and shortcomings that are just as serious today as they were a decade ago. Statistical information is scanty and sets of national-income calculations and census figures are unreliable. It is difficult to assess the output of subsistence economies because of the arbitrary choice of indicators and borderlines. Often the sterile character of the per capita indicators conceals the dispersion behind the average, the income-distribution system, and the appropriation and utilization of the surplus. The interpreta-tion of the content and characteristics of development of a country has remained just as debatable and ideologically conditioned as it was in the past, though the narrow, vulgarized variants on both sides have no doubt lost some space. Emphasis on the improvement of the position of the masses vis-à-vis the quantitative growth of output or national income has definitely been strengthened even in the nonsocialist approach.

However recent the widely applied category of the least developed coun-tries with measurable characteristics is, the differences between the develop-ment level of the national economies and the causes of the latter have attracted the attention of social scientists for a long time. Various theories of the stages of economic development, each containing different approaches, methods, and conclusions, have all been used to explain why certain countries are economically more advanced while others still lag behind—from the German "historical" school (Roscher, 1861) up to the theories of W. W. Rostow (1960) and Raymond Aron (1962). Insofar as the least development category was only an outgrowth of these theories, it would be sufficient to investigate their applicability to countries today considered least developed among the developing countries (Szentes, 1971).

The selection of these countries, however, is much more the result of certain practical requirements rather than theoretical approaches. The fact that a number of countries could hardly benefit from the international actions, measures, and assistance framed in the First Development Decade (e.g., the general system of preference, commodity agreements) and are increasingly lagging behind other developing countries—they are relatively disadvantaged or less developed—has made it necessary to create and implement special measures in their favor. This real and practical need has accentuated the problems of measurement and identification as well as those relating to development strategy.

Since the practical implications of this classification have, to a considerable degree, intertwined with theoretical and, by extension, ideological implications, the term *least development* has gained a rather ambiguous double meaning—just as *underdevelopment* had before it. From a practical standpoint, the term implies a group of countries that, at a given moment and from certain concrete considerations, find themselves in a relatively disadvantageous position vis-à-vis other countries. From a theoretical standpoint, the term suggests a particular stage of development, thereby explaining the country's disadvantages in the area of international relations. Which of these meanings is accepted, either implicitly or explicitly, is an ideological decision having far-reaching conclusions in the area of development strategy.

What Is *Least Development*?

The false theoretical interpretation of the term *least development* (similar to that of *land locked*) is based upon the same unhistorical assumptions as those in the axis of conventional underdevelopment theories. Developing countries in general, and least developed countries in particular, are implicitly conceived as primarily independent national economic units in the sense that their development, i.e., its direction and tempo, has been negatively determined by their own internal conditions and factor endowments; the potential benefits accruing from international economic relations (e.g., capital assistance and trade) are likewise diminished by the same local conditions. If these countries are primarily independent units that only secondarily engage in dependent or interdependent international relationships, then least development, like underdevelopment, can simply be explained by such unfavorable internal conditions as geographical location, small size of the country, poor natural resources, low per capita income, underdeveloped industry, high illiteracy, low productivity, shortage of skills, traditional production systems, and weak administration. The concomitant conditions, consequences, and measures of least development seem to account for this explanation, one in which external factors do not bear any primary responsibility.

The countries of least development are assumed to be on the same road of economic development, trailing behind the relatively more advanced developing countries, which, in turn, follow upon the heels of the developed industrial countries. Least development is considered a natural yet lower stage of the same development process that more advanced developing countries have experienced.

The interpretation of least development (and underdevelopment) as simply a "falling behind" might be more or less acceptable for (and applicable to) the historical period preceding the rise and expansion of the world capitalist economy, with its center-periphery relations first embodied in the colonial division of labor.

The assumptions concerning the basically independent advance of national units, developing more or less rapidly, collectively considered as a theory of least development are not only unacceptable from a scientific point of view but are extremely dangerous with respect to implicit or explicit recommendations concerning the direction of development strategy. Apart from the possibility of one or more countries discovering rich natural resources and achieving rapid growth by intensifying the specialization of primary production, for the majority of countries the example of the relatively more advanced developing countries, with their lopsided structure and open-door policy for foreign investment capital, is not a way out of least development—and even less so with respect to underdevelopment.

Least development as a theoretical category delimiting a defined quality to explain the disadvantages of a number of countries is a false concept, one that can easily be manipulated to deny historical responsibility to support the misleading "diffusionist" approach (Frank, 1967a) in international assistance, and even to stimulate conflicts of interest within the Third World.

The Practical Value of the *Least Developed* Designation

The foregoing critique of least development as a *theoretical* category, however, does not necessarily dispel the *practical* need to isolate a group of countries for concrete, specific purposes by means of related indicators within a given period. If international assistance and trade measures affect—and they do—the countries of the Third World in a different manner, it is fairly evident that special or additional measures are necessary for those countries that do not significantly benefit from the general situation. An important methodological requisite is to make certain that the criteria used for classification suit the purpose of distinction and, in addition, to apply the identification exclusively for the same purpose.

Those countries identified by various UN bodies as least developed represent a similar case—only from a specific and by no means homogenous point of view. The countries have been identified by the United Nations on the basis of per capita GDP share of manufacturing in the total GDP and the literacy rate (UNCTAD, 1976). They differ widely with respect to actual pattern of national economies, income distribution, size and character of the traditional sector, export commodity, land problem, population density, and chosen policy and direction of postindependence development. From a qualitative and dynamic point of view, such differences may prove to be much more important than the partial and static similarities revealed by quantitative indicators. United Nations criteria may accurately describe their actual position in comparison to other countries, but such criteria cannot explain their manner, direction, and tempo of development, which might be very different in the longer view. To explain the latter, a complex socioeconomic analysis is required in the context of the functions of the periphery in the world capitalist economy.

Over and above some specific, narrow purposes, the classification, from a dynamic point of view, of the least developed countries (not necessarily the same as those countries identified as such according to static, quantitative indicators) may correctly serve the purpose of expressing the differentiation process of the Third World. In other words, the term *least development* may acquire a more meaningful (i.e., more general) significance if it is based upon an analysis of the reasons underlying regional differences and historical modifications of the periphery's functions in relation to the center's development. (Here least development is interpreted as the subsystem of the international capitalist economy, i.e., in the context of center-periphery relations.)

Least Development in the Context of Certain Periphery Relationships

The differentiation process among Third World countries is by no means a new phenomenon, though it has gathered impetus only recently. These countries or territories differed greatly in terms of level of economic, social, and cultural development; rate of growth; mode of production; and social organization—this even before they fell victim to the colonial system. Their geographical positions and natural and human resources varied enough to ensure that there would be advantages for some countries and less so for others in a given period and mode of development.

Ever since that historic moment, however, when colonialism incorporated them into the world system of capitalist economy, the differences among them have been shaped by metropolitan capital according to the advantages they had with respect to development needs of the metropolitan economies.

Colonialism has embodied and realized the peculiar and original system of international division of labor, namely, the link between the industrialized center and its primary-producing periphery, which corresponded to a given level of technical and economic development of metropolitan capitalism (Szentes, 1972a). The catalyst and vehicle of this colonial pattern of international division of labor was the export of metropolitan capital, which, first of all, shaped the socioeconomic structure of the dependent periphery by means of direct investments and spontaneous market forces.

It is primarily the motivations of the exporters of capital and the "choice pattern" of the exported investment capital (i.e., the choice of economic sector, technique, and product orientation) that explain not only the basically similar features of the colonial or semicolonial economies but also their differences and changes according to the preferences of the metropolitan capital.

In tropical Africa, for example, the case seems to be particularly clear, given the fact that early colonialism and the slave trade virtually destroyed all previous internal development. On the basis of the same qualitative features of the periphery (viz. structural deformations, socioeconomic "dualism," economic dependence, and exploitation), different types of peripheral economies came into being here, reflecting the advantages or disadvantages individual territories could provide to colonial capital and personnel. Accordingly, five types of economies can be distinguished in tropical Africa:

  1.   Subsistence economies remained predominant in production, while foreign capital penetrated the limited spheres of foreign trade and finance.

  2.   Peasant farming became dominant in the export-oriented ore-crop production, under the rule and influence of foreign commercial and finance capital.

  3.   European settlers' estates and foreign-owned plantations made up the dominant sector of agrarian production, supplemented in the modern sector by certain industrial, trading, and financial positions shared by settlers and foreign companies; the traditional sector became a labor reserve.

  4.   Extractive industries, including the foreign-owned mining sector, became the dominant one, supplemented by the traditional sector as a labor reserve and the settlers' economies (though not necessarily).

  5.   The dominant traditional sector, comprising practically the whole economy, became the source of labor supply for other countries (Szentes 1967, 1973b).

One of these types of peripheral economy reflects less attractive conditions for the growth of the colonial economy (in terms of geographical position, climate, and natural resources for developing plantation economies or mineral production, European settlements, or even for the controlled expansion of peasant export-crop production). It seemed to have left its mark on many of those economies not called least developed in Africa. Though sharing the decisive disadvantages with the others, they missed even the relative and debatable advantages of the growth of periphery economy.

Least Developed and Landlocked Countries

Since many of the least developed countries are also landlocked, it may be worthwhile to stress the special meaning of the term *landlocked* in the context of underdevelopment (Szentes, 1972b). The present problem of landlocked developing countries arose in a very specific historical and political/economic context, one that differs considerably from that of the European landlocked countries not only of today but of the past. The difference between the two cases is much greater than the mere question of distance or navigable waterways, though in most cases the problems of developing landlocked countries are aggravated by their great distances from the sea and/or the limitation of inland river transport facilities.

  The roots of the problem are structural in nature, being related to the international division of labor and its impact on the local economy and environment. The very fact that not only landlocked developing countries but also their littoral neighbors have been playing the role of the "periphery" in the system of international division of labor—oriented toward the overseas center and subordinated to it (at least economically)—explains the specificity and gravity of the problem.

When external economic relations develop in consonance with, and are induced by, the inner development of a national economy, the growing needs of the former tend to be in harmony with the material conditions and capacity of the latter to satisfy those needs. The expansion of the circle of market relations is accompanied by a further development of the inner division of labor and its completion from outside. This process creates for itself the necessary infrastructure. The countries that enter into regular market relations and division of labor with one another are mutually interested in building up the transport network. Transport facilities expand in proportion to the demand for expansion of economic and market development. Though natural transport routes are, no doubt, enormous promotive forces for economic development, normally the demand for them stems from the latter.

However, what characterizes developing countries is the excessive size (in relation to the size and development of local market relations) and abnormal orientation and structure of their foreign trade. Consequently, their economy demands long-range (overseas) transport facilities before short- and medium-range facilities have been adequately developed. Market relations with overseas partners, which involve great distances and different (and more expensive) means of transport, are extremely premature in contrast to the actual level of internal market relations. The known—though sometimes forgotten—reason for this distortion is the colonial heritage of specialization for primary production, that is, the adjustment of both economic structure and infrastructure to foreign interests.

These same interests have obviously dictated an investment policy that has led over and beyond structural deformations, which are similar in all developing countries, to considerable differences in the infrastructure development between littoral and landlocked countries; the latter, apart from those subregions rich in some natural resource, could, as a result of transport costs, offer far less attractive investment opportunities for foreign capital in primary production.

In other words, the colonial type of international division of labor, though it has incorporated landlocked territories into the same pattern, has basically discriminated against such territories. At the same time, by diverting the production and market orientation, as well as the infrastructure, of their coastal neighbors, it deprived them of the opportunities to develop intraregional trade and division of labor. Consequently, in landlocked countries the same relative enforced adjustment to the colonial type of division of labor evolved under even less favorable conditions, with smaller benefits accruing in infrastructural development than is true of other countries.

Differentiation within the Third World

The differentiation process of the Third World has considerably accelerated since the collapse of the colonial system. This has led to greater divergencies of development according to chosen patterns and internal policies. Besides political changes, however, the concomitant crisis in the machinery of the colonial pattern of international division of labor and the rise of more elements of a neocolonial system (motivated by shifts in the center economies as well) have contributed to the widening of differences among countries of the Third World.

The colonial pattern of international division of labor—with the dependent periphery serving as raw-material supplier, sheltered market for manufactured commodities, and monopolized sphere for profitable investments—has been operating with increasing difficulty since World War II, particularly since the late fifties. Its crisis became obvious in the international economic and political events of the last few years, particularly during the energy crisis. As with all economic phenomena and processes, the crisis and shift in the capitalist international division of labor are related to both material/technical and sociopolitical factors.

Undoubtedly, the scientific/technical revolution is one of the factors fundamentally influencing the reallocation process of the world capitalist economy and market, the orientation of capital export, and investment patterns—as well as, directly and indirectly, the positions of developing countries. The development of productive forces with revolutions in science and technology, leading to the increasing internationalization of the reproduction process, is an objective tendency independent of, though influenced by and affecting, the actual socioeconomic formations. Under the capitalist system, this tendency has been interrelated with further concentration and centralization of capital, including the rise and strengthening of multinational or supranational corporations.

The scientific/technical revolution has changed the pattern of leading industries, has given rise to new ones, and has created new centers of technological research and development. It has demonstrated where the decisive links are located in the vertical chain of production. The scientific/technical revolution has resulted in far-reaching shifts in the production structure of the "centrum" countries, thereby modifying their input and output patterns, the commodity pattern of foreign trade, as well as the demand for products, services, marketing facilities, and investment opportunities provided by the periphery. Capital export to developing countries is also changing accordingly, not only in terms of the composition of the exporters (shifting in favor of the multinational corporations) but also in the choice of investment sphere, technique, and product orientation. For vertically integrated corporations expanding their capital-goods production at home, market interests specifically suggest the development of consumer goods-producing industries with capital-intensive techniques abroad. Similarly, these interests also suggest the maintenance of a blockade against the development of the capital goods-producing sector in the periphery and particularly of industries that are the centers of technical progress.

In addition to, and connected with, market interests (i.e., the orientation of the capital export-serving commodity export), profit considerations (i.e., the orientation of capital export as direct profit source) have also changed. Instead of the absolute cheapness of local unskilled labor and natural resources, both of which were guaranteed in the past by the colonial administrative and economic machinery, it is the relative wage differences (i.e., as they relate to productivity differences and the indirect economizing on wage costs) or other costs (e.g., environmental) which are increasingly important in the choice of investments.

But there have been changes even in the function of raw-material supply since the scientific/technical revolution made an impact, particularly through the synthetic substitutes on the demand pattern of traditional raw materials imported from the periphery.

Since the actual role of various primary products in the technical and scientific progress is widely different (and changing), differentiation among the primary producing countries is a natural process inasmuch as their one-sided specialization is natural.

The consequences of these shifts on world market prices and terms of trade have been amply discussed in the international literature, as have the problems of demand elasticities. In this context, one should stress, however, that the price and/or income elasticities of demand of the typical primary products exported by the developing countries do differ considerably according to whether the prices or incomes are changing in an upward or downward direction. Here again, one may point to the favorable position of, say, oil or the unfavorable position of such luxury-food products as cocoa, coffee, and tea, which, unlike the durables, do not face an exploding demand in developed countries; nor can they meet the expanding need of Third World masses for basic necessities. This is one reason for the difficulty in organizing OPEC-like strong cartels in the case of the latter.

Though the policy of readjustment to a neocolonial investment pattern resulted in spectacular growth and specific advantages in trade and finance in a few countries, most of the developing countries suffered additional losses due to the disturbances of the colonial division of labor. In some cases, the accumulation of additional economic burdens and negative effects resulting from both the colonial mechanism and its disruption were so severe that they led to indebtedness, population and food-supply problems, mass unemployment—virtually producing a chronic crisis.

Countries Grouped by Differentiation

In the light of the above processes and the resulting differentiation of the Third World, one can isolate four groups of developing countries (Szentes, 1975):

1.   A group in which, for various reasons (e.g., landlocked position, with a lack of attractive natural resources) neither the colonial-investment pattern with a primary-producing export sector nor the new one have developed to a considerable extent. Therefore, the production spheres have remained subservient to the traditional sector, alongside and subordinated to the activity of foreign capital in commerce and finance.

However, the fact that most of the so-called least developed countries and a few landlocked countries belong to this group proves not so much the relative disadvantage resulting from short or absent colonial investments per se as it does the consequence of the turning away by their natural, neighbor-partners from intraregional trade and cooperation. Therefore, solutions to the trade problems of this group can hardly be found by encouraging similar structures and their overseas orientation, even if this may make benefits from preference systems more accessible. Instead, the promotion of regional trade and cooperation, the avoidance of structural distortions arising from the often impressive and attractive growth of enclave sectors, and an increase in adequate financial as well as technical assistance for a more balanced and internally planned development seem to promise a way out.

2.   A group of countries with a predominantly colonial production structure that has borne the burdens of the colonial heritage as well as those generated by the crisis of colonial division of labor and the reallocation process. Most of these countries are negatively affected by world-market changes on both sides: as exporters of widely substituted marginal products (such as mineral or agricultural raw materials)—or faced with an almost stationary consumption demand (such as relatively luxurious food products)—and also as importers of a great many expensive manufactured commodities as well as some primary products at increased prices.

3.   A group of countries whose inherited, colonial-type production structure or its still dominant remnant in a primary-producing export sector has been favorably affected by changes in international production and consumption patterns. The most obvious case is that of the exporters of crude oil.

4.   Finally, there is an expanding group of countries that has developed urban industrial enclaves connected with, and dependent upon, metropolitan industrial powers, thereby displaying the characteristic neocolonial pattern. Wide differences exist within this group, depending upon whether these countries have export-oriented or import-substitutive industries and to what extent false industrialization follows from the policy established by local forces or foreign multinationals. Common features, however, in their pattern of industrial investments (viz. the bias in favor of capital-intensive techniques to produce products appealing to an elite consumer and the bias against the centers producing basic means of production and developing techniques for the local economy) as well as resulting external ties (i.e., intensive technological dependence) lead to similar problems in international trade and economic relations.

This group, however, represents the kind of alternative that develops in the wake of the reallocation process and modifications of the center-periphery relations under the influence of multinational corporations or their local agencies and allies. If this remains the only alternative followed by more and more developing countries, the colonial pattern of international division of labor will be replaced by a division of labor between the centers of scientific and technological progress and the periphery of all those countries relying on regular imports of technical innovations and scientific results. Although this alternative may add new features to the economy of developing countries through a certain type and level of industrialization, it will create an even wider gap between center and periphery than presently exists.

These groups, products of the differentiation of the Third World, do not represent clear-cut categories; there are a substantial number of mixed, overlapping, or marginal cases (not to mention the effects of counteracting factors and efforts). If an attempt is made to diagnose the differential problems of various developing countries or country groups, and to develop practical measures of amelioration adapted to their different positions, this activity may prove beneficial.

Insofar as the differentiation process and its main products, stemming from the same background tendencies, show up both the crisis of the former colonial type of international division of labor and the warning signs of the negative consequences and dangers of the emerging new (i.e., neocolonial) pattern—both of which are inadequate to bring about international equality and serve the common welfare—there is need for a new international economic order with a truly alternative pattern of international division of labor.

Overcoming Least Development

Following the model implicitly suggested by the conventional theory implies for both least and underdeveloped countries:

- Increasing reliance and dependence on foreign capital
- Inappropriate transfers from metropolitan countries, with subsequent losses for least and underdeveloped countries
- Further growth of old or new enclaves (whether primary-producing or industrial) in the economy of the latter
- A widening gap not only internationally but internally (i.e., between the elite and the masses, the modern and the traditional, the urban and the rural sectors)

Overcoming least and underdevelopment requires a long-term development strategy of far-reaching structural changes and socioeconomic transformation. Though the concrete details and time dimensions can be outlined only in relation to and inside each individual country, such a strategy necessarily involves:

- The principle of increasing self-reliance (without autocracy and isolation)
- National control of the national economy
- Internal socioeconomic integration and, where possible, regional integration
- Complex rural development in a collective manner and for collective interests
- A real form of industrialization that serves the whole economy, furthers its technical progress, particularly the development of agriculture and the needs of the masses

● Expansion and democratization of appropriate cultural, training, and research facilities

That such a strategy can only be implemented by a democratic, people-oriented political regime that deliberately strives for a more equal and related distribution of the burdens and benefits of development among society's members is quite obvious. A few examples drawn from least developed countries (e.g., Tanzania, Mozambique) of efforts and results in this direction seem to show a promising, though by no means easy start, which, if supported by the required changes in the international economy, can lead these countries out of least development.

FOR FURTHER READING

Barnet, R. J. and R. Muller. 1974. *Global Reach*. New York: Simon & Schuster.

Frank, A. G. 1970. "The Development of Underdevelopment." *Imperialism and Underdevelopment*. Edited by R. Rhodes. New York: Monthly Review Press.

Green, R. H. and A. Seidman. 1968. *Unity or Poverty? The Economics of Pan-Africanism*. Harmondsworth: Penguin.

Hymer, S. 1972. "The Multinational Corporation and the Law of Uneven Development." *Economic and World Order from the 1970s to the 1990s*. Edited by J. Bhagwati. Riverside, N.J.: Collier Macmillan, pp. 113–140.

Leys, Colin. 1975. *Underdevelopment in Kenya: The Political Economy of Neo-Colonialism*. Berkeley: University of California Press.

Mandel, E. 1975. *Late Capitalism*. London: New Left Books.

Palloix, C. 1977. "The Self-Expansion of Capital on a World Scale." *Review of Radical Political Economy* 9, no. 2:1–17.

Radice, H., ed. 1975. *International Firms and Modern Imperialism*. London: Penguin.

Rodney, Walter. 1974. *How Europe Underdeveloped Africa*. Washington, D.C.: Howard University Press.

Rostow, Walter. 1960. *The Stages of Economic Growth: A Non-Communist Manifesto*. New York: Cambridge University Press.

Szentes, Tamas. 1971/1973. *The Political Economy of Underdevelopment*. Budapest: Akademiai Kiado.

Trajtenberg, R. 1977. "Transnationals and Cheap Labor in the Periphery." *Research in Political Economy*. Edited by P. Zarembka. Greenwich, Conn.: JAI Press, pp. 175–206.

UNCTAD. 1976. *Least Developed among Developing Countries, Developing Island Countries and Developing Land-locked Countries*. Item 13: Main Policy Issues, TD/191. Nairobi: United Nations.

4.
Least development has already been defined in economic terms. Does it apply equally to political life? Cynthia Enloe was asked to examine the political situation of the least developed, to study the proposition that there are common political circumstances either for the least developed as a whole or for groups of countries within the least developed. Her conclusions are not unexpected: there is as much diversity in terms of political systems among the least developed as there is among most other groups. One-party civilian rule and military regimes of varying complexions are most common. A certain vulnerability on the part of some systems to external political pressure is exemplified by the disappearance of Sikkim from the list of world countries as well as lists of the least developed.

In her examination of the Asian least developed, Enloe highlights the internal resource constraints within which the least developed must work. Political development may have to be increased in terms of subtlety of mobilization and cohesiveness of ideology.

The least developed are hard pressed on all fronts. Recently Chad and Ethiopia were desperately in need of external support to maintain internal cohesion. The least developed also encounter difficulties in pursuing independent lives in the face of strong external economic pressures. There are, moreover, the continuing difficulties of administering large countries with meager financial resources and qualified personnel. Considering all these factors, the relative stability of such least development governments as Kenya, Tanzania, and Nepal is remarkable.

LEAST DEVELOPMENT AND POLITICAL DEVELOPMENT: SOME ASIAN EXPERIENCES

C. H. Enloe

The political experiences and current structures of the countries officially designated as least developed are disparate. One cannot argue that a single pattern of politics is either the cause or the consequence of socioeconomic developmental lag. Among the several dozen countries designated in the UN list are those that have experienced long-term and short-term colonization. The category includes countries that won independence through armed struggle and those that were granted independence without experiencing the mass mobilization of an anticolonial war. Within the least developed group are countries that have historically exercised imperialist control over neighboring societies and those that have constantly been at the bottom of the international hierarchy.

The current forms of political structure within the category are varied as well. One can find systems of one-party civilian rule, states with military regimes, and states with elitist rule plus a minimal mass-party organizational infrastructure. Some experienced multiparty parliamentary politics and subsequently rejected it, while others have never governed through such structures.

Moreover, in the political attributes that these poor countries do share, they are not dramatically set apart from many contemporary political entities. It is true that a sizable percentage of the designated LDNs have experienced violent changes in regime due to the intrusion of foreign powers and internal conflicts for central power. Similarly, a great number of the LDNs have experienced civil wars in the postindependence period, wars that have been precipitated, in large part, by disparities and distrust among ethnic groups. While these political characteristics certainly have undermined efforts to alleviate poverty, they have not prevented other countries that have experienced similar political events from achieving some progress. Finally, although many, though not all, LDNs have had difficulty in creating lines of access to a multitude of states, all of them, be they landlocked or not, have always been vulnerable to external manipulations and hegemony. Thus, like all Third World states, these countries have had a vital stake in finding the necessary leverage to control foreign intervention.

From the perspective of "nation theory," it is a misnomer to refer to these countries by their designated label. They are not least developed nations at all; most of these countries are not nations in any but a narrow legal sense. That is, they are not polities whose central governmental authority is derived from shared values and a mutual sense of belonging among persons subject to that central authority. In this they are not unique. With the evolution of political science, we are learning, albeit rather belatedly, that surprisingly few entities conventionally referred to as nation-states are, in fact, national in terms of the bases of their governmental authority.

For countries whose political authorities are faced with compensating for and overcoming extreme poverty, the absence of nationhood to underpin legalistic statehood is especially dysfunctional. Spain's problems concerning alienated Basques and Catalonians and Canada's difficulties in reformulating the state to allow for the continued allegiance of disaffected French-Canadians share many characteristics typical of Ethiopia's problems in resolving Eritrea's alienation and Burma's problems in winning the trust of insurgent Shans and Karens. What sets Ethiopia and Burma apart, nevertheless, is the extent to which their nation-aborting cleavages sustain and exacerbate socioeconomic underdevelopment.

What distinguishes the politics of the LDNs, therefore, is neither their peculiar political experience nor their current forms of governmental structure, nor even their lack of a national base. Rather, what marks them off analytically is the demands imposed on their political systems. Coping with the demands imposed by poverty coupled with international vulnerability are the distinguishing characteristics of political development processes in LDNs.

The conventional model of mobilization for catch-up development in the sixties—a centralized, single-party, all-embracing mobilization—often prescribed for ex-colonial states, may be inappropriate for many of today's

LDNs. This inappropriateness is the very reason why many of them are so culturally fragmented and short on the sort of administrative and communications infrastructure that makes a centrally organized mobilization feasible. Rather, the type of mobilization most appropriate for the LDNs is more subtle, capable of utilizing village structures, in closer contact with local interests and not simply involved with larger national concerns.

The fact that this alternative mode of mobilization is less centrally controlled and less organizationally coherent does not make it less difficult to achieve. In fact, it may well call for superdevelopment. It requires a meshing of established and new structures and a linkage of localized needs and nationwide goals. Multiple levels of interest and cooperation will generate confusion and spark old antagonisms unless there is a clearly delineated set of objectives and a guarantee of just distribution, that is, an accepted ideology. (The term *ideology*, as used in this context, refers to a basis for consensus and intergroup trust; it is not a rigid doctrine.) Only in this fashion can governments both cope with scarcity and achieve growth without completely sacrificing what minimal autonomy their states have in the existing international system.

The Asian Experience in Mobilization

Several states in Asia that fall under an expanded rubric of LDNs have approached the politics of scarcity with disparate modes of human and material mobilization resulting in different political consequences. Burma tried to isolate itself internationally and to centralize its political system, only to find that such premature consolidation set off a protracted and multisided civil war that has drained scarce resources for two decades. Nepal retrained its monarchy and attempted little genuine mobilization while becoming increasingly dependent upon the political/economic needs of neighboring India. Vietnam, subsequent to its own civil war, pursued a multilayered mobilization effort much like that outlined earlier, conducted a growing assortment of international negotiations, and deviated significantly from the Chinese model.

What is striking about these three cases of Asian LDNs is the relationship between, on the one hand, types and degree of success of mobilization and, on the other, the capacity for controlling relationships with the international political-economic system. Those countries that have been most ideologically coherent and subtle in designing mobilization appropriate for fragmentation and scarcity have also been most able to create a sufficient degree of autonomy to relate to, and yet not be wholly at the mercy of, stronger international actors (Semin-Panzer, 1975, and correspondence dated Jan. 1977). The three states are not similar enough in their available and potential resources to formulate specific conclusions about the relationship of types of mobilization and real growth (table 4.1). Nonetheless, growth in and of itself matters little if a society is so internally skewed that growth is consistently

TABLE 4.1
COMPARATIVE INDICATORS FOR
SELECTED ASIAN COUNTRIES

	Population (millions)	GNP Per capita, 1975 (U.S. dollars)	Annual Average GNP Growth Per Capita	Life Expectancy at Birth (years)
Bangladesh	80	100	−2	36
Burma	30	100	2	
Cambodia	7	100	−6	45
Indonesia	135	200	4	51
Laos	3	100	2	40
Malaysia	12	700	4	59
Nepal	13	100	0	44
North Korea	16	450	3.5	61
Vietnam (N & S)	45	150	−1	48

SOURCE: "A Survey of Asia." *The Economist*, May 7, 1977, pp. 62–65.

unevenly distributed, or if a society is so internationally vulnerable and short on political integrity that whatever growth does occur is siphoned off or ghettoized into those sectors of the economy that suit its external markets rather than its own long-range needs.

Burma.   The Burmese were subject to direct rule by British colonial authorities as a result of their defeat in the Anglo-Burmese wars, which destroyed Burma's monarchal system. Until the 1930s, Burma was administered as an adjunct of India. (For an insightful description of change in lower Burma peasant society, see Nash, 1965.) During the British hegemony, lower Burma became a major rice-exporting region. The various ethnic groups in the country were treated differently by the British, with smaller groups increasingly relying on the British to protect them against possible future domination by the lowland ethnic Burmese. World War II was fought in such a way as to disrupt Burma's rice production and to further separate the various ethnic groups from one another. Independence was based, in part, on a fragile reconciliation of interethnic differences vis-à-vis the degree of Rangoon's central authority, as well as on an alliance of disparate Burman political factions under a single-party umbrella. Both bases for national consolidation proved too thin to withstand postindependence pressures for rapid development and international participation. Dissident ethnic groups—Karens, Shans, Chins—as well as the two communist factions in the ruling alliance, declared separate wars on the central government in 1948 (Tinker, 1976). The army intervened in the early 1960s and sought to solve the problems of political disintegration and economic decay by means of centrally administered mobilization and a severing of most international ties. Today it is clear that this formula was too artificial to succeed.

There is a tendency among certain foreign observers to express smug satisfaction at the fact that the regime of General Ne Win greeted the World Bank's delegation in 1976 and apparently agreed to the international banking consortium's stipulations as the groundwork for any large-scale foreign loan. The World Bank required antiinflationary controls, whereas the Burmese consultation group (six Western nations plus Japan and UNDP) required access for foreign investment (Harriman, 1976a and b). Such smugness is the result of a too facile assumption that the root of Burma's inability to reverse its postwar decay, which pushed it into the LDN category, lies in its isolationist stance and its socialist program. It may be far more useful and accurate to look for the source of Burma's acute problems in the artificiality of the military regime's concept of mobilization. The Ne Win regime assumed that mobilization could be achieved by a party structure designed by the central elite, with little natural mass base, plus a militarily imposed administrative consolidation in the regions of ethnic alienation. Lower Burma had the potential for making Burma food-sufficient and a major rice exporter, while the hill regions, the home of most non-Burman groups, contained valuable untapped mineral resources. World Bank loans and foreign investments from such industrialized countries as West Germany (which is most interested in Burmese development) may make Burma more accessible to international actors, both governmental and extragovernmental, but may not enhance the country's domestic bonds of cooperation and trust, which will insure that growth is widely distributed and that the sense of commitment to Burma as a whole is great enough to permit the central government to negotiate with outside actors from a base of strength. In fact, acceptance of World Bank loans and West German investments may only mislead central government officials into thinking that funds for road building can act as a surrogate for effective linkages between local needs/identities and national needs/identities.

Nepal. The government of Nepal has never experienced such a far-reaching internal conflict, though it is a fragmented society both ethnically and regionally, nor has it ever attempted such a thoroughgoing international withdrawal. What little mobilization has been attempted has either been designed to serve foreign, delineated objectives or has been organizationally nebulous, dependent on the authority and charisma of the ruling monarch. In 1960 King Mahendra dismantled the country's parliamentary institutions, abolished scores of political parties, and concentrated all decision-making power in his own hands. While Mahendra was popular with the Nepalese, his twenty-nine-year-old son, Birenda, who has since succeeded to the throne, has increasingly cut himself off from the general citizenry (Bloomfield, 1976). This atrophying of mobilizing linkages, minor though they were at their peak, has come at precisely that period in Nepal's political/economic evolution— one can hardly call it development—when domestic cleavages have deepened and international interventions have escalated.

Inequalities between Nepal's plains and hill peoples have been growing (Gange, 1976). A "Go to the Village National Campaign," first instituted in

1967, was still failing to elicit genuine popular mobilization by 1973 because of its top-down operation (Baral, 1976). The military is considered by some current observers to be the only institution capable of replacing the monarch. By the mid–1970s, Nepal depended on India for 75 percent of its food (Jayaramen and Shrestha, 1976). International aid agencies have scores of projects under way in Nepal, some of which are said to have had disastrous effects on Nepal's slender resources, particularly its timber supply. In Katmandu it is common to hear the boast that the capital of Nepal probably has more foreign advisers per square foot than any other less or least developed country. Among the foreign-assistance agencies currently operating in Nepal are USAID, the Indian Cooperation Mission, the Japanese Overseas Cooperation Volunteers, the German Volunteer Service, Cornell University, the World Bank, UNESCO, and FAO. Foreign-aid funding entering Nepal has run to over $500 million, or about $40 per capita for the Nepalese, which is more than the average resident's annual income (Sterling, 1976). However, conflicting aid objectives, overemphasis on production for export, and the apparent inability of agencies to reverse priorities—even when damage from existing programs has been documented—have all served to keep Nepal within the LDN category.

The creation of horizontal and vertical linkages among the Nepalese, which the subtle mode of mobilization requires, will not in and of itself prevent deforestation, landslides, regional inequalities, or the confusion resulting from a variety of international programs, but it might provide a basis for Nepalese planning to encourage the sort of growth, however modest, that would reduce international vulnerability resulting from an absence of effective indigenous authority and goals.

Vietnam.   The most interesting country to watch among the Asian LDNs may be Vietnam. It is coping with scarcity and international-market participation by employing political formulas that do not duplicate any of the well-known models now featured in scholarly or technocratic literature. Vietnam's international pressures and internal fragmentations are no less severe than in Burma or Nepal. China, the Soviet Union, the World Bank, and French and American petroleum companies must all be dealt with. Domestically, the Hanoi government continues to express concern over the possible disaffection of the small but commercially significant Chinese minority, as well as the diverse hill peoples who played so strategic a role in the 1945–72 war. Furthermore, in its 1976 and 1977 policy announcements Hanoi demonstrated a keen awareness of the cultural and political discontinuities still persisting between North and South Vietnam (Loche, 1976).*

What is perhaps most interesting about the Vietnamese strategy for coping with, and eventually overcoming, poverty is the multilayered character of

---

*Since this was written the question of the "boat people" has made the ethnic Chinese of Vietnam an issue of international concern. Ed.

political mobilization made possible by virtue of a clear ideological statement of common, long-term objectives and distribution values. This type of mobilization allows for considerable decentralization. It is also occurring at a time when Hanoi is cautiously accepting joint ventures with foreign capitalist firms (Brown, 1976; Chanda, 1976). Decentralization was necessitated by bombing raids during the war. More fundamentally, it grew out of a conclusion by Hanoi decision makers that individual peasant communities would have to be reorganized around their own perceived needs as well as the larger national needs (Elliott, 1976). Moreover, while the dominant political party has maintained its primacy in the political system, mobilization has not been confined to party structures. Extraparty associations have been formed both in order to incorporate those sectors of the population that remain shy of the party and to prevent an all-embracing party from becoming stagnant and rigid. Third, various subgroups in Vietnamese society have been treated differently. Various montagnard ethnic groups (a misleading umbrella term encompassing what is in reality a host of distinct cultural groups) have been given special representation. The Chinese have at times been exempted from certain official requirements as long as they continue to demonstrate basic loyalty. The South Vietnamese have been told that their progress toward socialism will be more gradual than that of the North Vietnamese in recognition of the consumerist and entrepreneurial tendencies entrenched during the 1945–72 era.

Decentralization, multiple mobilization vehicles, and differentiated treatments of subgroups make for a very risky development package. It is a necessary risk when scarcity puts a premium on equitable distribution and when fragmentation and inadequate infrastructure disperse available resources. What makes such a risky package a viable formula for development in a LDN is a coherent ideology that spells out shared goals among the disparate subgroups and a governing group that has sufficient popular legitimacy to make decisions on behalf of the entire citizenry. Without these prior conditions—each of which should be enhanced, and not merely confirmed, by the subtle mobilization process—dealing with international firms, agencies, and governments is likely to exacerbate underdevelopment. Thus, how successful Vietnam is in negotiating with the World Bank, Japanese electronics firms, and French petroleum corporations will ultimately depend on how successful the government is in refining a mode of mobilization suited to poverty and fragmentation.

LDNs are not politically unique. They are internally diverse and share past experiences and present strains with many other political systems, one of the most profound being their common lack of nationhood. What does distinguish the LDNs is the severity of strains that their various decision-making and decision-implementing vehicles must cope with. In particular, politics in the LDN must maximize scarce resources and ensure wide distributions of whatever inadequate resources and rewards do exist. Given such conditions, political development may have to be measured not in terms of the conventional Western criterion of structural complexity but rather in terms of subtlety of mobilization and cohesiveness of ideology. Political mobilization that sustains state integrity in the midst of international penetrations and permits public planning to lessen scarcity will most likely be such that ideological coherence will be coupled with decentralization and multiple vehicles of popular participation. Development strategies that merely attempt to overcome poverty through administrative innovation and international intervention, without concomitant intrasocietal mobilization, will only further skew the distribution of minimal rewards, isolate the central elite, and accelerate dependency on external markets and authorities.

FOR FURTHER READING

Blaut, J. 1977. "Are Puerto Ricans a National Minority?" *Monthly Review* 29, no. 1 (May):35–55.

Deutsch, Karl. 1953. *Nationalism and Social Communication: An Inquiry into the Foundations of Nationality*. Cambridge, Mass.: MIT Press.

Emerson, Rupert. 1960. *From Empire to Nation: The Rise to Self-Assertion of Asian and African Peoples*. Boston: Beacon Press.

Enloe, Cynthia H. 1973. *Ethnic Conflict and Political Development*. Boston: Little, Brown.

Fitzgerald, Frances. 1973. *Fire in the Lake: The Vietnamese and the Americans in Vietnam*. New York: Random House.

Gaige, Frederick H. 1976. *Regionalism and National Unity in Nepal*. Berkeley: University of California Press.

Kearney, R., ed. 1975. *Politics and Modernization in South and Southeast Asia*. Cambridge, Mass.: Schenkman.

Nash, M. 1965. *The Golden Road to Modernity*. Chicago: University of Chicago Press.

Socialist Republic of Vietnam: Structure and Basis. 1976. San Francisco: China Books.

Tinker, H. 1976. "Burma: Separations as a Way of Life." *Politics of Separation*. Edited by W. H. Morris-Jones. London: Institute of Commonwealth Studies, pp. 57–68.

Trager, F. N. 1976. *Burma: From Kingdom to Republic*. Westport, Conn.: Greenwood Press.

Weiner, Myron. 1965. "Political Integration and Political Development." *Annals of the American Academy of Political and Social Science* 358 (March):52–64.

5.   In 1968 UNCTAD prepared a list of twenty-five LDNs representing the poorest countries of the world. The United Nations recommended special assistance to these countries in order to alleviate their poverty. In this chapter the distinctiveness of the LDNs as opposed to other poor countries is examined on the basis of a wide variety of social, economic, political, and environmental characteristics.

Based on these additional criteria, it is shown that thirty-eight countries may be considered to form a distinct set of LDNs. Coherent groups of nations with similar characteristics exist within this set. An examination of the geographical location of the countries within these groups demonstrates regional association.

The emergence of regional groups of LDNs sharing common social, economic, political, and environmental characteristics suggestsd that it may be appropriate to go beyond the familiar approach to development problems, namely, that of examining social and economic constraints to the development of particular countries, and examine the relevance of environmental constraints and the possibility of proposing regional rather than national development strategies. A discussion of the interaction between environmental and socioeconomic factors in the Sahel serves to illustrate the importance of environmental constraints to the development of this particular group of LDNs; it also demonstrates the need to follow a more holistic approach to development planning both in this area and in other LDNs.

THE LEAST DEVELOPED AND THE REST

D. J. Campbell and C. Katz

Criteria for Definition, Data Analyses, and Country Groupings

In 1968 UNCTAD resolved to initiate special measures designed to promote greater international assistance and increase existing assistance for the least developed nations (LDNs). This resolution was a recognition of the fact that among the underdeveloped countries there were some that were relatively more underdeveloped and could thus be regarded as the hard core of underdevelopment.

According to the UNCTAD "group of experts" (UNCTAD, 1971, pp. 6–7):

> . . . countries having all three of the following characteristics should be classified as least developed: per capita gross domestic product of $100 or less; share of manufacturing in total gross domestic product of 10 percent or less; and literacy rate—proportion of the literate persons in the age group of fifteen years and more—of 20 percent or less. In addition, certain borderline cases were considered eligible for inclusion in this classification. Countries with per capita gross domestic product of $100 or less but with a manufacturing ratio or literacy rate somewhat exceeding the limit just mentioned were included, especially if their average real rate of growth during recent years had been exceptionally low.

Similarly, countries where per capita gross domestic product is over $100 but is not more than around $120, and which satisfy the other criteria, were also included. However, in considering the borderline cases, the Committee exercised judgment in order to take account of special circumstances which might have distorted the recent picture. Finally, some countries (Maldives, Bhutan, Sikkim, and Western Samoa) were included although relevant data are not available. The absence of data for these countries was taken as an indication of the low level of their development.

Table 5.1 includes those countries named as LDNs on the basis of the above criteria.

TABLE 5.1
CLASSIFICATION OF TWENTY-FIVE LEAST DEVELOPED NATIONS

Africa		*Asia and Oceania*	*Latin America*
Botswana	Mali	Afghanistan	Haiti
Burundi	Niger	Bhutan	
Chad	Rwanda	Laos	
Dahomey (Benin)	Somalia	Maldives	
Ethiopia	Sudan	Nepal	
Guinea	Uganda	Sikkim	
Lesotho	U.R. Tanzania	W. Samoa	
Malawi	Upper Volta	Yemen	

SOURCE: Committee for Development Planning, UN (UNCTAD, 1971, p. 4).

Though the committee used three socioeconomic indicators to designate the twenty-five countries, it was recognized that there were additional characteristics of these countries that pointed to problems for which special measures might have to be formulated. These indicators included low levels of labor productivity, scarcity of skilled labor, inadequate knowledge about existing natural resources, low levels of physical and institutional infrastructure, high levels of subsistence production, dependence on primary goods for export, and a lack of integrated industrialization. These characteristics also refer to the social and economic effects of the undevelopment process. In reviewing such characteristics, the committee concluded that other factors might be important as well. For example, of the twenty-five LDNs, fifteen are land-locked or otherwise isolated from the world's markets (UNCTAD, 1971, p. 8), fifteen arid or semiarid, eight are tropical or subtropical montane lands, and most have one dominant ecosystem (Clark University Program in International Development and Social Change, 1974). Many of these countries are contiguous; the special measures may thus require both regional and national programs. It is important to note that the above-mentioned problems are simply descriptive characteristics indicating appropriate areas for development assistance. The roots of these characteristics *as problems* may be traced historically as forming part of the process of underdevelopment. Hence, solutions may be sought, at least in part, in the restructuring of existing international relations. Such a historical analysis, however, is not the focus of this introductory chapter (for a detailed discussion, consult O'Keefe, 1975, and Campbell, 1977).

In 1974 a group in the Clark University Program in International Development and Social Change conducted a study of LDNs that included environmental and locational characteristics in addition to social, economic, and political indicators. The study demonstrated that thirty-eight countries (see Table 5.2) might be considered least developed and that they might be grouped

TABLE 5.2
THIRTY-EIGHT LEAST DEVELOPED NATIONS

Africa

1. BENIN*
2. BOTSWANA*
3. BURUNDI*
4. CAMEROON
5. CENTRAL AFRICAN EMPIRE
6. CHAD*
7. ETHIOPIA*
8. GAMBIA
9. GUINEA*
10. KENYA
11. LESOTHO*
12. MALAGASY REPUBLIC
13. MALAWI*
14. MALI*
15. MAURITANIA
16. NIGER*
17. RWANDA*
18. SIERRA LEONE
19. SOMALIA*
20. SUDAN*
21. SWAZILAND
22. TOGO
23. UGANDA*

24. UNITED REPUBLIC OF TANZANIA*
25. UPPER VOLTA*
26. ZAIRE

Asia

27. AFGHANISTAN*
28. BHUTAN*
29. BURMA
30. KHMER REPUBLIC (Cambodia)
31. LAOS*
32. MALDIVES*
33. NEPAL*
34. SIKKIM*
35. YEMEN, Arab Republic of (North)*
36. YEMEN, Peoples Democratic Republic (South)

South America: Central America

37. HAITI*

Oceania

38. WESTERN SAMOA*

SOURCE: Clark University Program in International Development and Social Change, 1974.

*Designated by the UN as being among the twenty-five LDNs.

MAP 5.1 **LEAST DEVELOPED COUNTRIES**

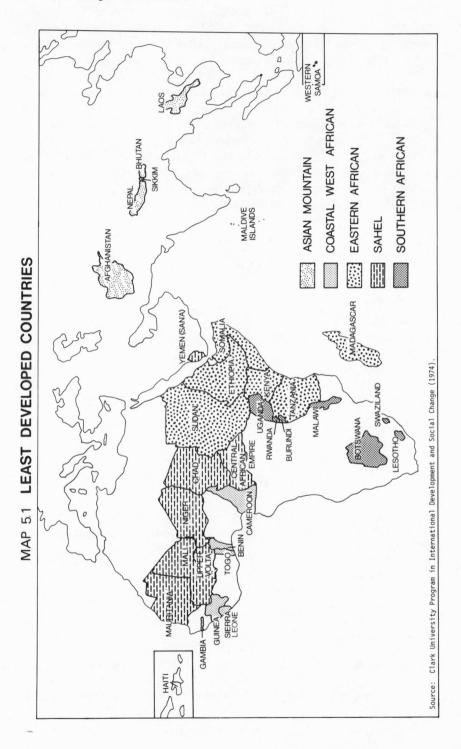

ASIAN MOUNTAIN

COASTAL WEST AFRICAN

EASTERN AFRICAN

SAHEL

SOUTHERN AFRICAN

Source: Clark University Program in International Development and Social Change (1974).

according to similarities in a variety of characteristics. These countries and their groupings are shown in map 5.1.

It should be noted that the UNCTAD committee recognized that it might be necessary to add to the list of twenty-five countries those countries which are similar to hard-core LDNs and which, in the context of a particular problem, may be indistinguishable in their characteristics from those countries specifically listed as hard-core (UNCTAD, 1971 p. 8).

This chapter does not seek to explain either the conditions or the process of underdevelopment. Lesser developed nations share many characteristics with other Third World countries. These are often the result of their interaction with capitalist imperialist states, a historical process that disrupted indigenous patterns of economic and social evolution. This process is referred to as the "development of underdevelopment." The conditions resulting from this process have been analyzed and described elsewhere (Frank, 1967b; Baran, 1957; Amin, 1974; and Szentes, 1971). The present chapter aims to:

- Describe some characteristics of groups of LDNs
- Identify some fundamental problems of groups of LDNs
- Lead readers to examine the importance of environmental factors in the development of LDNs through an in-depth analysis of the dynamics of the Sahelian drought of 1968–74

Groups of Least Developed Nations

The principal components analysis conducted on thirty-eight LDNs at Clark University utilized thirty-seven indices representing a broad range of social, political, economic, and environmental factors (see Table 5.3). These data were derived from secondary sources and were often constrained by the types of indicators available for the dynamic processes of economic, political, social, and environmental interaction. Hence both technique and data have limitations that must be recognized. Given these limitations, the analysis did indicate the existence of five strong groups among the LDNs (see Table 5.4). (For a detailed description of the principal components analysis, consult Clark University Program, 1974.)

The most cohesive group considered in the analysis is comprised of nations of the Sahelian region of West Africa (Group A). These countries possess arid and extensive land, are primarily landlocked, generally lack those characteristics associated with modernization, are all dependent on traditional forms of agricultural production and pastoral subsistence, and were all severely affected by the Sahelian drought.

This situation may be viewed as the result of the historical process of European penetration into the area. In the past, a symbiotic relationship existed between the inland and coastal areas of West Africa. The Sahelian countries were then the center of trade between North Africa and the western coastal areas. Traditional reciprocal relationships were severed during the period of penetration; the coast became the focus of trade and the Sahel was relegated to a more peripheral status. Colonialism broke down the existing

Table 5.3
DATA USED IN THE FINAL ANALYSIS

1. Population—mid-year 1972
2. Percent urban
3. Crude birth rate
4. Crude death rate
5. Percent of population less than fourteen years of age
6. Rate of growth GNP in thousand U.S. $
7. Exports per capita in thousand U.S. $
8. Imports per capita in thousand U.S. $
9. Percent of GDP from agriculture
10. Percent of GDP from mining
11. Percent of GDP from manufacturing
12. Percent of students in secondary education
13. Literacy—percent of adult population
14. Population per hospital bed
15. Population per physician
16. Caloric intake per capita
17. Number of commercial vehicles (thousands)
18. Radio, TV—broadcasting receivers per thousand people
19. Percent of GDP from construction
20. Energy consumption per capita
21. Percent of population in largest town
22. Area, km^2
23. Crop or mineral as major export
24. Significant nomadism
25. Rapid onset of natural hazards
26. At least 40 percent of land area arid
27. Percent of population living in mountains
28. Landlocked
29. Aridity index
30. Density of population in nonarid areas
31. Urban water supply
32. Riots, 1948–67
33. Armed attacks, 1948–67
34. Percent of land under arable cultivation
35. Ethnic fractionalization
36. Total executive adjustments
37. Defense expenditure as percent of total

SOURCE: Clark University Program International Development and Social Change, 1974.

Table 5.4
MAJOR COUNTRY GROUPINGS
DERIVED FROM THE CLARK UNIVERSITY ANALYSIS

A	E
Chad/Mali/Niger/Upper Volta/ Central African Empire	Benin/Togo [Afghanistan/Nepal [Haiti Gambia

A

Chad/Mali/Niger/Upper Volta/
Central African Empire

B

Rwanda/Burundi/Lesotho/
Botswana

C

Bhutan/Sikkim
Maldives/Western Samoa
Cameroon
Laos

D

[Kenya/Sudan
Tanzania
Ethiopia
Malagasy Republic
[Khmer Republic
Burma
Zaire
Somalia

E

Benin/Togo
[Afghanistan/Nepal
[Haiti
Gambia

F

[Guinea
[Sierra Leone
Swaziland

G

Mauritania/North Yemen
(Arab Republic of Yemen)

H

South Yemen
(People's Democratic Republic of
Yemen)

Legend: /= firm pair
[= weaker grouping

trade and communication networks, replacing them with routes facilitating the extraction of economic surplus from the interior. The Sahel continued to provide goods for export but had lost its integrative role.

The 1968–74 drought brought to light several basic and all-pervasive consequences stemming from colonial policies in the area. An example of this is crop marketing structures, designed to improve agricultural production and movement of cash crops on a national and international level with little regard for the impact of such structures on local food production and nutrition. The usual means by which people cope with crises are destroyed by the colonial process; vulnerability to an environmental crisis such as drought is consequently increased. This problem will be examined in greater detail in the second part of this chapter.

A second group of nations identified in the principal components analysis consists of relatively small landlocked states of central and southern Africa (Group B plus Swaziland [Group F]). These nations depend upon traditional agricultural systems for their subsistence. Their economic trade relationships are dominated by the export of one or two primary products—either minerals or cash crops.

Being landlocked, these nations are in a vulnerable situation with respect to their ability to maintain a flow of imports and exports. For example, Uganda has in the past been forced to airlift some of its coffee crop out of the country due to the closing of export routes via Kenya. In addition, they are vulnerable because they have strong trade relationships with a single industrial country, the Republic of South Africa in the case of the three southernmost nations. For many of the countries in this group, the dependent relationship, particularly vis-à-vis South Africa, is aggravated by the migration of a significant proportion of the labor force to other countries. This migration creates an obvious drain of productive labor power from these countries. Clearly, new patterns of regional and economic integration would be beneficial, particularly for those countries whose trade is tightly bound up with South Africa.

Group C includes countries for which statistical information was largely absent. Lack of information is a clear indication of underdevelopment. However, any discussion of causes and conclusions about unifying factors would be inappropriate given the absence of such information.

Group D includes nations with characteristics similar to those of Group B, except that the former are larger and have a greater amount of industrial and infrastructural development. Several of the nations in Group D are beset by environmental problems associated with aridity. These nations—Ethiopia, Somalia, Sudan, Kenya, Tanzania, and Malagasy—comprise an East African coastal group. Large areas of these nations are arid or semiarid. In some lands of potentially greater yields there is evidence of land fragmentation, a decline in fertility, soil erosion, and migration to towns and areas of marginal agricultural productivity.

In addition to environmental problems, these nations are constrained by patterns of development and infrastructural investment, both of which are the legacy of past colonial policies. The concentration of investment in a primary and secondary city and the lack of attention to rural development during the colonial period presented the independent nations with a pattern of development that ran counter to the aspirations of African socialism. While Kenya's postindependence policies have reinforced the colonial pattern of development, other countries—notably Tanzania, Somalia, and Malagasy—have made strenuous efforts to break through the constraints imposed by the colonial pattern of development.

The three northern nations (Sudan, Ethiopia, and Somalia) share a number of common problems, including poor communications, difficult terrain, lack of linkages with other African nations, and considerable ethnic diversity and conflict. All are dependent upon one or two crops for foreign exchange, a fact that increases their economic vulnerability. Much of their trade was and, to some extent, remains tied to one industrial nation, again increasing their economic vulnerability.

If a group-oriented problems approach implies, as we have indicated, some group-oriented solutions, then the current political and military divisiveness among the three nations is even more tragic. Several sources of divisiveness can be traced back to the European partitioning of these areas into nation-states, as a result of which homogeneous regions and peoples were split apart. Moreover, their strategic geographical position has made them vulnerable to exploitation—particularly their ethnic aspirations—by the modern forces of imperialism which have waged a continual struggle to divide and control Africa.

Within groups E and F, the West African coastal nations (Benin, Togo, Gambia, Guinea, Sierra Leone) and Haiti form a coherent group. The grouping procedures used in conjunction with the principal components analysis demonstrated that although the nations in this group did not have very similar characteristics, their regional and ecological coherence might suggest strategies for development. All of these countries are small, their frontiers being a result of colonial demarcation. Many of them face the challenge of developing a diversified economy with a small ecological and population base. Climatic constraints limit agricultural production to the southern portions of these West African countries. The heavy concentration of European activity in the coastal towns has further accentuated the dominance of the south over the north.

The principal components analysts identified coherent groups of LDNs sharing environmental as well as more familiar social and economic constraints to development. A similarity of characteristics among nations within the same group suggests that factors operating at a regional, rather than a national, level may be impeding the development of countries within a particular group. Some of these constraints may have had their origin in colonial development policy, particularly in Africa, where colonial power tended to govern a much wider area than the nation-states created at the time of independence. These nations were hindered by an infrastructural pattern that may have been appropriate under the objectives of colonialism but was often an impediment to the implementation of policies to which they aspired. Group-oriented development programs may therefore be appropriate where the objective is to overcome constraints at the regional level. If solutions are only proposed at the national level, imbalances may persist. For practical purposes, namely, to study and take action with respect to cohesive groups of countries rather than individual nation-states, the Clark study clustered the countries under investigation into seven groups (see Table 5.5).

The geographical pattern of grouping LDNs suggests that environment factors should be considered together with social, political, and economic constraints to development. In a number of groups, semiarid and arid regions are widespread, amount and duration of rainfall is unpredictable, and drought is a recurrent problem. Technological advances (e.g., boreholes, medical assistance, and the development of crops able to flourish despite low rainfall) have enabled a larger number of people to live in semiarid areas under

Table 5.5
COUNTRY GROUPINGS DETERMINED BY A COMBINATION OF COMMON CHARACTERISTICS AND REGIONAL LOCATION

A. *Largely West African Sahelian (plus North Yemen)*
Chad, Mali, Niger, Upper Volta, Mauritania, Central African Empire, and Arab Republic of Yemen
(North Yemen is included in this group because of similar enivronmental characteristics and a population with a cultural background similar to those of the West African states.)

B. *Semiarid East African Coastal Countries*
Kenya, Sudan, Tanzania, Ethiopia, Somalia, and Malagasy Republic
(This grouping is significant because it breaks with traditional Anglophone definition of East Africa and suggests dissimilarities among these states.)

C. *West African Coastal Group (plus Haiti)*
Benin, Togo, Gambia, Guinea, Cameroon, Sierra Leone, and Haiti
(Haiti is included in this group because its environmental and cultural characteristics are similar to those of the West African group.)

D. *Asian Mountain States*
Afghanistan, Nepal, Bhutan, Sikkim, and Laos
(Although these states have different patterns of development, their similar environmental problems justify their being considered as a group.)

E. *Landlocked States in Eastern and Southern Africa*
Rwanda, Burundi, Lesotho, Botswana, Uganda, Malawi, and Swaziland
(The climates of most of these states are basically semiarid. Their economies are largely cattle-oriented.)

F. *Islands*
Maldive Islands and Western Samoa
(Their status as islands, plus a meager share of natural resources, provide common characteristics for these two nations.)

G. *Miscellaneous*
Burma, Khmer Republic, the Peoples Democratic Republic of Yemen (South Yemen), and Zaire.
(These four countries do not fall into any of the above groups for a variety of statistical, regional, and ecological reasons. However, as with the other groups, they demand special attention and research in terms of approaches to development and pattern and objectives of development aid.)

average rainfall conditions. The emigration of people from more crowded, higher-potential areas to marginal lands has been facilitated and encouraged by such technological change. The problem of recurrent drought, however, still remains; when it occurs, it affects a larger population often unable to adapt to drought conditions. Under such circumstances, major famine relief efforts, which impose a severe burden on national resources, become necessary. If resources are diverted from development programs to critical relief operations, the vitality of national development efforts may be reduced. The postindependence development programs of a number of LDNs have been disrupted by the effects of environmental hazards.

Environmental problems such as drought can result in the disruption of national and regional economies, as will be illustrated in the second part of this chapter. Studies of societies subjected to recurrent environmental hazards suggest that in most cases the local people have developed mechanisms for coping with such problems. These coping mechanisms, however, are inadequate in dealing with a prolonged period of environmental stress, which can occur when environmental conditions are too severe or the adaptive mechanisms have in some way broken down. When a major hazard occurs at a time when a particular society's coping mechanisms are not functioning at optimum levels, a major calamity such as the recent Sahelian drought may result.

R. W. Kates (chap. 9) has demonstrated that national hazards inflict considerably greater costs on LDNs than on more developed countries—a fact that underscores the relationship between socioeconomic conditions and the effects of environmental conditions. In order to gain an understanding of the extent to which national hazards may affect development, it is necessary to analyze the social and economic context of the area since development among LDNs may be hindered if the social and economic processes serving as mediators between hazards and their effects are not operational.

The present writers have repeatedly argued, as have others, that the very process of development can mitigate or exacerbate the impact of environmental hazards. As LDNs become more closely integrated into the modern global economic system, their traditional social and economic systems alter in response to new opportunities and constraints. The changes occurring during the process of modernization may either strengthen the mechanisms designed to cope with such environmental problems as droughts, cyclones, or floods or weaken them to the point where the effects of these hazards may be increased (Lofchie, 1975).

Recent studies investigating the effects of the drought that spread over wide areas of Africa in the early 1970s have demonstrated the importance of social, economic, and political conditions in explaining the severity of these effects. A number of writers have argued that the people of the Sahelian countries were more vulnerable to the impact of drought in the late 1960s because of the modifications they made in their lifestyles in order to accommodate the colonial policies of the French (Bugnicourt, 1974; Raynaut, 1975; Campbell, 1977a). Davidson (1976) notes that the impact of the 1974—75 drought in Somalia, though severe, was lessened as a result of the initiatives taken by the Somali government to mobilize people in an effort to aid those affected.

The Origins of Least Development: A Case Study of the Sahel

In the following pages an assessment is made of the severity of environmental problems as a constraint to the development of LDNs in the interior of West

MAP 5.2

The West African Sahelian – Sudanic Group

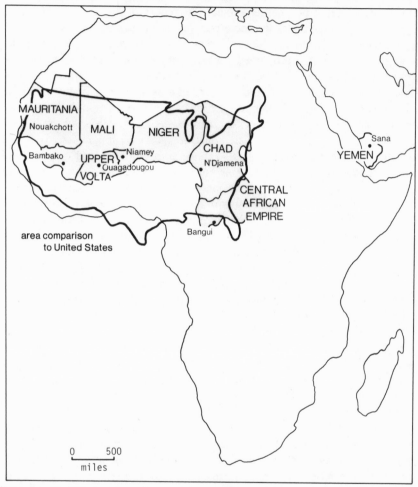

MAURITANIA
Nouakchott MALI   NIGER
Bambako   UPPER   Niamey   CHAD
         VOLTA   Ouagadougou   N'Djamena   YEMEN   Sana
                                 CENTRAL
                                 AFRICAN
                                 EMPIRE
area comparison
to United States   Bangui

0   500
miles

Africa, with Niger serving as the principal example. The historical approach
utilized traces changes in the ability of some of these societies to cope with
the environmental hazards to which they are prone. The principal hazard
facing the peoples of the West African interior and East and North Africa is
that of recurrent drought, with those inhabiting the drier areas of such regions
being most vulnerable. Emphasis is placed on the ability of inhabitants of the
semiarid regions to cope with drought.

The West African Sahel-Sudan Zone

The Sahelian countries of West Africa (map 5.2) occupy a zone extending
from Senegal in the west to Chad in the east, between twenty-seven and seven

degrees north latitude. They comprise two ecological zones, the Sudan (200mm–600mm rainfall per annum) and the Sahel (600mm–1,200mm rainfall per annum), respectively. Inhabitants have developed a predominantly agricultural economy in the wetter southern areas and a pastoral economy in the north, where drier conditions prevail. These economies have not been isolated from each other; trade and conflict between them have been common. Some peoples (e.g., the Fulani) include farmers, herders and mixed agro-pastorialists. The major agricultural groups include the Toukouleur, the Mossi, the Zarmas, and the Hausa; the Fulani and the Tuareg are the principal pastoral groups.

In the previous analysis of characteristics of LDNs, it was demonstrated that the Sahelian LDNs grouped together with the West African Sahelian group share a number of socioeconomic developmental factors that can generally be explained within the context of French colonial policies (Amin, 1973), while the environmental constraints are a consequence of prevailing climatic conditions, drought being a recurrent hazard. Major droughts affected the entire area from 1910 to 1917 and from 1968 to 1974, while less widespread droughts occurred in the 1930s (Salifou, 1975) and the early 1940s (Boudet, 1972).

The rainfall pattern of the region is controlled by seasonal fluctuations in the position of the intertropical convergence zone (ITCZ), a frontal system moving seasonally as the sun shifts relative to the equator and marking the limits of rain-bearing winds from the Gulf of Biafra. In the summer months, the ITCZ penetrates northwards across West Africa, reaching the farthest point, which varies between eighteen and twenty three degrees north latitude (Kelly, 1975), and then retreats southwards. The movement of this front results in a maximum period of rainfall in the region, usually occurring in August, though some rain may fall between April and October.

Most of the precipitation falls as thundershowers; its distribution is thus highly variable. The utility of the rain that does fall is also variable, as it is a function of local conditions such as infiltration, runoff, and evaporation. However, latitude acts as the principal determinant of the amount of rainfall (Boudet, 1972) and its potential utility (Cochemé and Franquin, 1967, p. 68; see fig. 5.1).

The intensity and distribution of rainfall is a primary determinant of the distribution of vegetation, though even dry zones, valleys, and areas where the water table is high may support a denser vegetation than their surroundings. The Sahel zone has sparse vegetation covering less than 30 percent of the ground surface in the wet season and even less during the dry season. The Sudan zone has a continuous cover in the wet season plus a greater number of bushes and trees. Valleys and areas with a high water table support vegetation throughout the year.

It is within this environmental context of seasonal shortages of water and vegetation, and under the recurrent threat of drought, that the people of the region have developed their pastoral and agricultural economies. Each economy

FIGURE 5.1

Diagrammatic Summary Of "Availability Of Water" Periods In The Sahelian Zone

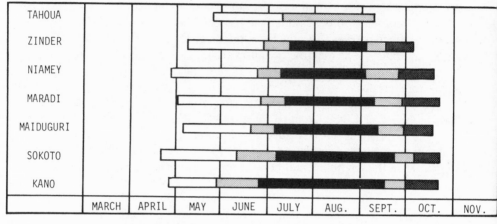

KEY:

☐ PREPARATORY

▨ INTERMEDIATE

■ HUMID

▦ INTERMEDIATE WITH STORAGE

Source: Cocheme and Franquin, 1967, p.68.

has incorporated mechanisms to facilitate its survival by mitigating the impact of regular seasonal water deficits and occasional drought. However, during the most recent drought in 1968–1974 new patterns of adjustment were observed, including intense migrations to more favorable areas or to food distribution centers (Bugnicourt, 1974; Sawadogo, 1974; Campbell, 1977a). This suggested that traditional mechanisms had become less effective, forcing people to resort to mechanisms that increased their dependency on forces beyond their control.

Traditional Mechanisms for Coping with Drought

In this section, emphasis will be placed upon the Tuareg peoples of Niger and the Hausa of southern Niger and northern Nigeria. Though these are admittedly specific examples, it is not unlikely that the pattern of adjustment to the hazards of drought is similar in its general characteristics, for peoples in other areas.

It has already been stated that the mechanisms for coping with drought are integral characteristics of a particular socioeconomic system. Some are continuously operative (e.g., the maximizing of animal numbers among pastoralists and grain storage among farmers), while others are resorted to only in the event of a drought. (The Tuareg have traditionally migrated to live with and requisitioned food from vassal agricultural tribes in times of scarcity.) The effectiveness of these mechanisms in reducing the social and economic impact of drought during the precolonial period was not always sufficient to prevent widespread losses, but such losses took place within coherent social systems that could absorb them without fundamental disruptions.

The Hausa.   Prior to the colonial period, the Hausa, who practiced agriculture in the Sudan zone, had developed a variety of mechanisms for reducing the impact of drought. These involved arrangements for land use and social and religious structures. The settlement pattern was nucleated, providing protection against hostile neighbors, but the location of the villages and fields reflected the need to have easy access to water and rich soil. Agricultural activities took place in valleys where fertile soil was plentiful and groundwater was sufficiently close to the surface to permit the digging of wells to provide water during periods of low rainfall. The fertility of such areas was maintained by the washing-in of new soil during floods (Raynaut, 1971).

Whereas valleys could be cultivated throughout the year, agriculture on the plateau was possible only during the wet season, namely, from June to December (Nicolas, 1963). The fertility of plateau soil was maintained by means of mixed cropping, through the application of animal manure, and through regular fallowing. Animal manure became available during the dry season, when the herds of the Fulani moved southwards in search of better grazing pastures. A symbiotic relationship existed between the Fulani and Hausa whereby the Hausa exchanged grazing rights for manure; trade in grains for animal products also took place.

The land-use system was closely bound up with Hausa religious beliefs (Nicolas, 1966; Nicolas et al., 1968). The allocation of labor and fields for various crops was organized on an extended-family basis and was controlled by the head of the family, the *mai gida*. This leader was responsible not only for the land-use system but also for the allocation of the harvest for immediate consumption, for short-term storage in connection with trading activities and during the dry season, and for long-term storage in the event of a drought.

The major drought-resisting strategy was the storage of food in family granaries, but a surplus could only be stored if the whole land-use system functioned efficiently. Land clearing, planting, weeding, and harvesting were all organized within the extended family, as were the distribution and consumption of the harvest. Regular fallowing and manure obtained from pastoralists ensured the fertility of the land.

The Hausa also maintained links with neighboring villages from which assistance might be obtained in times of scarcity. During a period of food shortage, villages with more food would help their associate villages and thus mitigate the effects of drought. The donor village could expect this assistance to be reciprocated in the event that it experienced a similar scarcity of food at a later time (Faulkingham, 1975).

Thus, the Hausa socioeconomic system incorporated mechanisms for mitigating the effects of drought through grain storage, which was facilitated by careful land management and the controlled use of labor and food supplies through the extended family. Contact with herding groups permitted a diverse diet to be maintained. The use of animal manure increased soil fertility. Lastly, association with neighboring villages offered the potential of assistance in time of need.

The Tuareg. The Tuareg are a pastoral people who occupy the northern areas of the Sahel/Sudan zone. Their economy, based upon animal husbandry, is constrained primarily by the availability of water and pasturelands for their herds. Their main strategy for mitigating the impact of drought has been to keep as many animals as possible, allowing numbers to build up during years of adequate rainfall in anticipation of losses during periods of drought. According to Johnson (1975, p. 79), the emphasis on sheer number of animals has its roots in the desire to enhance the individual's economic security. It is the survival of a residual flock that is of crucial importance to the nomad, since it is upon this fraction of his predrought herd that he hopes to rebuild.

In order to keep large numbers of animals, the Tuareg had to gain control over the resources required by their herds, namely, water and pasturelands. Military control of dry-season sources of water and grazing lands was organized through clans made up of groups of families. Within the clans, a complex social hierarchy existed in which particular classes were charged with military, trading, religious, herding, and agricultural responsibilities (Bernus, 1966 and 1975; Nicholaisser, 1963). Slaves and vassals performed the manual labor, while nobles organized trade activities and ensured the protection of the clan, its herds, and its grazing lands. The Tuareg also dominated farmers in the dry-season grazing areas, extracting tribute from them and expropriating grain in times of need.

Their herding practices and seasonal movements were designed to minimize risk by reducing the possibility of overgrazing and by diversifying their stock. The Tuareg kept animals for a variety of reasons—food, transport, currency and savings, and for various social purposes. The goats and sheep provided food and skins, while cattle and camels were the principal symbols of wealth and the mainstay of the subsistence economy. By keeping a variety of animals, the herders reduced the possibility of total loss through disease or drought. The various pasture and water requirements of the different animals, however, necessitated a complex herding system. The animals were herded separately and their seasonal movements were coordinated with those of other pastoral groups (e.g., the Fulani), so that the herders whose animals required the least water would leave for the north first and return last (Dupire, 1972).

The Tuareg also controlled lucrative trade routes in the region. These included the trans-Sahara route, along which gold, ivory, and ostrich feathers were traded for Arab and European goods (Nicholaisser, 1963; Boahen,

1962), and local trade routes involving the export of salt from Bilma and Fachi in exchange for grain and animal products from the Sudan zone (Nicholaisser, 1963; Baier, 1974). The profits from these activities were considerable, enabling the Tuareg to amass savings that could be used to purchase grain and animals during periods of scarcity.

A rigid social system, control of basic resources, extensive land use, and a diversified economy were among the elements of the Tuareg way of life that enabled them to reduce the impact of drought.

The Colonial Period

Colonial administrative and economic policies required great changes in the functioning of indigenous societies of the Sahel/Sudan region. The objectives of colonial rule were outlined in 1908 by Ivory Coast Governor Angoulvant (Hargreaves, 1969, p. 203):

> To subdue all hostile elements; to win over the waverers; to encourage the masses, who can always be drawn to our side by self-interest until one day they are drawn there by sympathy; in short, to establish our authority beyond dispute; and, finally, to express these results in such tangible ways as the full collection of taxes, the rendering of assistance by the natives in the creation of public fixed capital and economic and social progress.

In Niger, these objectives were fulfilled through the military conquest of the area, which culminated in the defeat of the Tuareg at Agadès in 1916, and by the subsequent activities of the civilian regime, including taxation, forced labor, and the stimulation of cash-crop production for export.

The implementation of these policies disrupted the social system of the Tuareg and the Hausa, altered their economies, and set in motion a variety of processes which, over the next fifty years, combined to reduce the efficacy of many of the traditional mechanisms for coping with the environmental constraints of the region.

The Hausa. The Hausa were more quickly drawn into the new economy imposed by the French than were the Tuareg, for they were sedentary and could most easily be taxed, provide labor for public works, and grow cash crops. The colonial peace enabled the Hausa to break away from the restrictions imposed upon them by their Tuareg and Fulani overlords, and to take advantage of their freedom within the colonial system.

In a number of areas, the lifestyle of the Hausa was relatively unaffected by economic changes, permitting the continuation of traditional practices (Faulkingham, 1975). In other areas, however, the effect of taxation and the availability of imported goods stimulated the need for money and cash cropping (Collins, 1974). Labor migration developed as means of earning cash (Rouch, 1956 and 1957). The principal cash crops were groundnuts and cotton. Coastal nations were the primary destinations of migrant laborers.

The increasing demand for cash crops was just one of a number of factors that stimulated the expansion of the area under cultivation during the colonial period. The defeat of the Tuareg at Agadès and the Fulani at the hands of the British enabled the Hausa to disband their nucleated villages and to evolve a more dispersed settlement pattern, with each village clearing sufficient land to meet its own needs. An increase in population in Niger (Dankoussou et al., 1975) and northern Nigeria, together with greater cash-crop production, particularly after World War II, resulted in a further increase in the area under cultivation.

A second factor affecting the land-use system of the Hausa was the disruption of their social system, resulting in a weakening of communal values and a strengthening of values associated with individual gain. The communal system lost much of its influence when the French replaced traditional chiefs with others of their own choosing and demanded that the new chief collect taxes, recruit labor, and check on anti-French movements in their area (Crowder, 1968). By performing these tasks for the colonialists, the appointed chiefs lost the sanction of their community. The respect and authority formerly held by the *mai gida* also declined since the expanding economy increased opportunities for individual gain outside the traditional extended-family system. Migrants returning from towns brought with them ideas of individual independence plus a variety of merchandise which soon became associated with wealth and esteem. These returning migrants challenged the authority of the *mai gida* through their acquisition of independent values and access to symbols of wealth associated with the new socioeconomic system. Young men who felt constrained within the extended-family system of production and consumption departed in search of more lucrative monetary opportunities by means of which their individual needs and aspirations could be better satisfied (Nicolas, 1960).

In a number of areas, changes in values and social relationships resulted in major alterations in the system of land tenure and production. The extended family lost much of its cohesiveness, splitting up into its component families, each farming its own parcel of land and responsible for the production of sufficient crops to meet its food and cash needs.

This division of land among individual families meant that land use was now determined by individuals rather than the group as a whole. Control over the choice of crops to be grown and the practice of fallowing passed to the individual farmer; there has been a tendency toward specialization in terms of food or cash crops, leading to a reduction in size of the area under fallow (Nicolas, 1960). The individualization of production and consumption also undermined the traditional practice of communal grain storage, particularly once grain acquired a commercial value at the market. With the development of individual farms, land acquired a commercial value (Raulin, 1969; Raynaut, 1975), causing some farmers to sell their land. Problems arose over the availability of sufficient labor during peak periods (e.g., clearing and weeding); hired labor consequently became an increasingly important part of the work force (Nicolas et al., 1968; Raynaut, 1971).

Individual landholding, population growth, and the expansion of both food and cash-crop production led to an increased demand for agricultural land. This demand was met in Niger by reducing the amount of land left under fallow, decreasing the length of the fallow period, and cultivating the better-watered areas to the north of the traditionally cultivated zone. This northward expansion, facilitated by favorable rainfall conditions prevailing in the 1950s, posed such a threat to some of the better pastoral areas that the government of Niger tried, first in 1954 and again in 1961, to set a northern limit for such cultivation (Bernus, 1966; Rep. de Niger, 1961).

These developments involved a risk to crop production. The shortening of the fallow period threatened to reduce fertility, while the northward expansion occurred in areas more susceptible to water shortages. While the production system lost some of its resilience, the demand for food and cash crops increased. Some farmers specialized in the cash-crop production of ground-nuts and cotton. Both they and the growing urban population came to depend on commercialized food crops for their subsistence. Thus, while the amount of food crops available for storage declined, the amount required for consumption by the growing rural and urban population increased; moreover, the possibility of increasing output was limited by the availability of suitable land and the need to produce cash crops.

The major traditional strategies for coping with the effects of drought involved food storage, the latter facilitated by a well-organized extended-family production system. As these strategies declined others replaced them. Savings in the form of cash and labor migration to earn extra money were important safeguards whose efficacy depended upon the modern system. The holding of savings in the form of cash rather than grain (the traditional form), was less effective, however, for during a period of shortage cash was devalued relative to grain (Campbell, 1977a, p. 98). For example, during the recent drought grain prices increased by over 200 percent in some areas (Lallemand, 1975).

Seasonal labor migration had been a major source of income for many people from the Sahelian countries for decades. As the colonial economy expanded, additional labor was needed for the development of infrastructure and to service the coastal cities. However, a limitation on the emigration of laborers from the Sahelian states to the coastal nations was imposed in the 1960s as a consequence of labor surpluses in these countries (Peil, 1971). This fact served to limit the possibility of securing an alternative source of income through labor migration in times of drought.

Thus, during the colonial period traditional strategies for mitigating the impact of drought became less effective. Though new strategies were developed, their usefulness was limited by the functioning of the very system that had necessitated their development. Whereas in the past indigenous agricultural societies, such as the Hausa, tried to deal with the effects of drought within their own social, economic, and religious structures, their recent dependence upon sources of work away from their home areas, food markets and, in many cases, upon famine relief greatly reduced their self-sufficiency.

The Tuareg.   As was previously described, the precolonial pattern of Tuareg life included strategies for coping with drought that sought to control access to dry-season water supplies and pasturelands and to build up the size of herds as an insurance against losses anticipated during a drought. The Tuareg did not expect these mechanisms to protect them completely against the effects of drought; rather, they were ultimately designed to ensure the survival of the nobles and a sufficient number of animals to permit the rebuilding of herds in the postdrought period. The Tuareg economy had developed under conditions reflecting the availability of extensive pasturelands, great freedom of movement and action, and little population pressure (Swift, 1975). These fundamental parameters of their socioeconomic system were radically disrupted after the French conquered the area and initiated the administrative and economic policies previously discussed.

The traditional social hierarchy so important to the organization of the Tuareg economy collapsed soon after their final defeat at Agadès in 1916. The nobles lost control over their dependents, the French increased the political power of priests by installing them as chiefs, and slavery was nominally abolished. Though the French granted freedom to the Bouzou, the Tuareg slaves, they were loath to enforce this policy. It was only after Niger's independence in 1960 that most slaves left their masters. Some became herders or took up trading, while others settled as farmers alongside the Hause (Nicolas, 1962). As the society lost the coherence which was provided by the nobles, and each family became responsible for its own subsistence, animal husbandry became less specialized, and the size of herds increased (Bernus, 1975, p. 243).

The military and political defeat of the Tuareg was also reflected in a lessening of control over the Hausa, their vassals, who had paid them tribute, traded grain in exchange for animal products and salt, and provided hospitality during periods of drought (Lovejoy and Baier, 1976). The colonial peace enabled the Hausa to escape the constraints imposed upon them by the Tuareg and to expand their agricultural and trading activities.

A combination of events occurring around World War I led to a reduction in the diversity of the Tuareg economy by totally disrupting their trading patterns. The requisition of camels by the French for military purposes, the 1910–17 drought, and the abortive rebellion at Agadès resulted in a major loss of animals and curtailed the trans-Saharan and regional trading activities of the Tuareg. At the same time, traffic on competitive routes—by sea to the West African coast and then inland via the rivers, and later the railways and the motorized trans-Sahara route via Tamanrasset—was in the process of expanding. The Tuareg's trans-Sahara trading activities never fully recovered; even though trade in salt recommenced in the 1920s (Rodd, 1929), it was not until the 1960s that salt from the oases of Bilma and Fachi again supplied a significant proportion of Niger's needs (Baier, 1974, p. 117).

The social, political, and economic bases of Tuareg society were rapidly disrupted by the forces of colonization. As the Nigerian economy adapted to

French policies, that freedom of movement so fundamental to an ecologically sound pastoral economy was curtailed.

The process of agricultural expansion occurred in the most favorable areas already under cultivation (with a consequent reduction in fallow land) and in new areas where water was most readily available. As has already been mentioned, many new areas were important dry-season grazing lands for the Tuareg herds. As a result, their whole seasonal migratory cycle was necessarily shifted northward. The reduction in size of the pastoral domain took place during a period when the demand for pasturelands was increasing as a result of the growth of the animal population. This rise in the number of animals was the result, first, of vaccination and well-drilling programs designed to improve conditions in the pastoral zone and, second, of a breakdown in the clan system of animal management, which allowed each family to develop its own herd. The danger of overgrazing the more meager pastures in these northern areas was increased; in some cases, the heavy concentration of animals around permanent wells so depleted the surrounding vegetation that treks of up to twenty kilometers were necessary to find adequate pasturelands (Bernus, 1966, p. 30).

Though the higher amount of rainfall in the 1950s concealed some of the dangers inherent in this situation, it is clear that in the period preceding the 1968 drought the traditional mechanisms developed by the Tuareg to cope with drought had been disrupted. The cohesiveness of their social system had disintegrated, traditionally varied economic activity was reduced, and mobility was restricted to more northerly areas where the risk of drought was greater.

The changes that colonialism and modernization occasioned in Tuareg and Hausa societies not only affected the capacity of these societies to deal with the climatic phenomenon of drought but also altered their land-use practices to such an extent that, even in the absence of drought, degradation of the environment was taking place. Traditional land-use practices acknowledged the importance of the land as a resource requiring careful management if the productivity of the agricultural and pastoral economies was to be maintained. For example, the Hausa left land fallow in order to increase its fertility; likewise, the nomads moved their herds frequently to prevent overgrazing of available vegetation and denudation of the soil in any one place. Such management techniques were developed during a period when sufficient land of suitable quality made extensive pastoral and agricultural activities viable.

After World War II, in particular, land became scarce as the region's animal and human populations increased rapidly (Conde, 1971; Diakite, 1971; Dankoussou et al., 1975; Ganon, 1975). In Niger, the demand for agricultural land grew as the number of farmers increased, the latter a result of natural population growth, emigration from northern Nigeria, and sedentarization of nomadic groups. These farmers required land to grow not only subsistence crops but also cash crops. They met this need by clearing bush land and unused fallow areas in the cultivation zone, incorporating land north of the traditional area of cultivation, and intensifying the use of land already being farmed. Among the nomads, an increase in population led to a greater demand for animals to meet subsistence needs; larger pasturelands were consequently required to feed them.

Thus, two competing demands were made upon the land resources of the region: while agriculturalists were extending the area under cultivation, nomads were demanding more pasturelands. As a consequence, wider areas were utilized and more fertile land was used more intensively—nomads tended to concentrate their herds around permanent water wells during the dry season, while farmers cultivated their plots more intensively.

The productivity of the Sahelian environment is related to rainfall and the fertility of the soil. The presence of vegetation is important for the preservation of soil fertility; it protects the soil against weathering caused by high temperatures, the impact of raindrops, and trampling by animals, and reduces erosion by holding the soil together with its roots and preventing topsoil from being windblown, thus decreasing rainwater runoff (Ahn, 1970, p. 246).

In the years prior to the 1968 drought, a reduction in Sahelian vegetation occurred as a consequence of a variety of processes, including overgrazing, clearing of bush land for agriculture, reduction in size of the fallow area, and tree cutting for firewood and building materials. Such processes set in motion the following cumulative cycle: the removal of vegetation encouraged erosion; this, in turn, reduced soil fertility both on the plateau, where topsoil was removed, and in the valleys, where sandy, eroded materials were deposited over more fertile clays; reduced fertility inhibited the growth of crops and vegetation, thus necessitating the clearing of larger areas in order to produce sufficient foodstuffs and cash crops. This process of environmental degradation resulting from human activity has been recognized for many years in the Sahelian region (Stebbing, 1935; Pelissier, 1951; Tricart, 1956; Pouquet, 1956; Dubourg, 1957).

Implications for Development

The adaptations effected by the pastoral and agricultural societies to accommodate the demands and opportunities of the colonial system resulted not only in the reduced effectiveness of traditional mechanisms for coping with drought but also in degradation, both actual and potential, of the environment, thereby reducing the ability of the area to meet the food and grazing needs of its growing human and animal populations. Figure 5.2 illustrates how a complex interaction of various processes over a period of time created a situation very different from that originally anticipated.

In general, one can safely conclude that the traditional ability of the people of this region to cope with drought by utilizing the resources available within their own communities was reduced as a result of their adaptation to modern conditions. Whereas many of the Hausa were able to take advantage of the opportunities presented by a commercial economy and found viable alternatives to some of their traditional adaptive strategies (e.g., labor migration and cash savings), the majority of the Tuareg remained outside the mainstream of new economic forces, isolated geographically, politically, and socially; they were simply unable to replace their traditional coping mechanisms with others linked to the modern sector.

Any attempt to understand the impact of the recent Sahelian drought must therefore proceed beyond an analysis of the severity of the climatic phenomenon and explanations centering on processes such as land degradation and overgrazing. A broader perspective is required to explain the historical context of contemporary problems. Environmental constraints hindering the development of Sahelian LDNs are indeed formidable, but the extent to which they hinder development depends upon the ability of the people of the area to mitigate the environment's detrimental effects. The ability to cope with environmental constraints is conditioned by social and economic factors. Development planning must therefore recognize that social and environmental processes constantly interact and are not independent of one another.

The foregoing discussion of the relationship between socioeconomic change and environmental conditions in the Sahel illustrates the need to consider environmental factors in any discussion of development planning for LDNs. The fact that environmental factors operate at a regional rather than a national level presents a challenge to planners to consider some of the problems of individual LDNs in a regional context.

Population pressure as a prime factor resulting in the movement of people into more marginal lands is not limited to the Sahelian LDNs; it has been recognized as a serious problem in the East African LDNs, particularly in Kenya (Mbithi and Wisner, 1972; Mbithi and Barnes, 1975; Campbell, 1977b) and Tanzania (Kates and Hankins in G. F. White, 1974b).

The designation by UNCTAD of the twenty-five LDNs served to highlight the plight of the poorest nations. The present analysis has suggested that in order to develop strategies for the development of the poorest nations it may be necessary to consider more than the twenty-five LDNs, examine regional as well as national constraints to development, institute a group-oriented approach where appropriate and, finally, emphasize the importance of the interaction between environmental and social change among LDNs.

According to Berry (1975, p. 43), a new context for the preparation of development plans may be required: "Development efforts, at present, tend to be based on specific projects, but there is a great need to work with total systems rather than just with parts. Each investment must be seen in context, both environmentally and socially. It may be that an important prerequisite is the definition of a set of development zones which add a human component to the environmental activities."

Social and environmental contexts cannot be clearly explained if they are

FIGURE 5.2
THE IMPACT OF SOCIOECONOMIC CHANGE
ON AGRICULTURAL AND NOMADIC RESOURCES

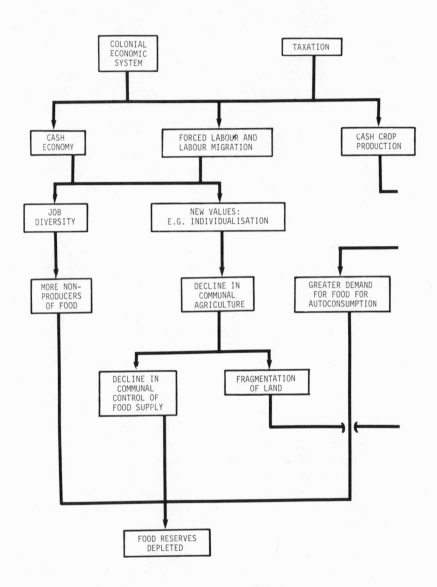

SOURCE: Campbell, 1977, p. 147.

Note: For the sake of clarity, feedback mechanisms resulting in complex effects have been
omitted; these processes, however, did not always occur in a linear fashion, as shown.

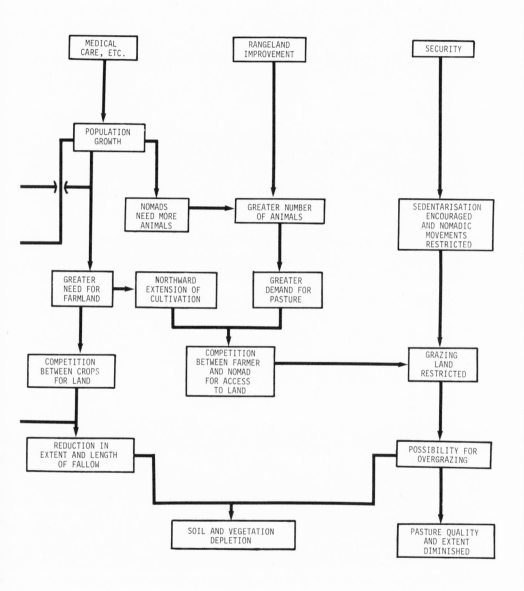

regarded as a static concept. The present is the product of a historical process. Development plans are unlikely to succeed unless they are based upon a clear understanding of the origins and directions of contemporary processes. This chapter has attempted to demonstrate that LDNs are subject to a variety of social, economic, political, and environmental constraints to their development. These constraints interact in a complex system, thus providing the context within which development plans should be conceived and implemented.

FOR FURTHER READING

Amin, Samir. 1973. *Neo-Colonialism in West Africa*. Harmondsworth: Penguin.

————. 1974. *Accumulation on a World Scale*. New York: Monthly Review Press.

Baran, Paul. 1957. *The Political Economy of Growth*. New York: Monthly Review Press.

Bradley, P. et al. 1977. *The Guidimaka Region of Mauritania: A Critical Analysis Leading to a Development Project*. London: War on Want.

Caldwell, J. C. 1975. *Population Growth and Socio-Economic Change in West Africa*. New York: Columbia University Press.

Clark University Program in International Development and Social Change. 1974. *Delimitation of Groups of Least Developed Nations on the Basis of Socio-Economic Data*. Worcester, Mass.; Clark University.

Crowder, M. 1968. *West Africa under Colonial Rule*. Evanston, Ill.: Northwestern University Press.

Frank, A. G. 1967b. *Latin America: Underdevelopment or Revolution; Essays on the Development of Underdevelopment and the Immediate Enemy*. New York: Monthly Review Press.

Green, R. M. and A. Seidman. 1968. *Unity or Poverty? The Economics of Pan Africanism*. Harmondsworth: Penguin.

Johnson, D. L. 1969. *The Nature of Nomadism: A Comparative Study of Pastoral Migrations in Southwestern Asia and Northern Africa*. Chicago: University of Chicago, Department of Geography, Research Paper 118.

Joyce, Stephen J. and Françoise Bendot. *Elements for a Bibliography of the Sahel Drought*. Paris: OECD, 1977.

Lofchie, M. F. 1975. "Political and Economic Origins of African Hunger." *Journal of Modern African Studies* 13, no. 4:551–567.

Meillessoux, C. 1974. "Is the Sahel Famine Good for Business?" *Review of African Political Economy* 1:27–33.

Monod, I. 1972. *Pastoralism in Tropical Africa*. Oxford: Oxford University Press.

O'Keefe, P. 1975. "The Process of Soil Erosion." *African Environment: Special Report I—Problems and Perspectives*. Edited by P. Richards. London: I.A.I., pp. 63–65.

—— and B. Wisner. 1975. "African Drought the State of the Game." *African Environment: Special Report I—Problems and Perspectives*. Edited by P. Richards. London: I.A.I., pp. 31–39.

Salifou, A. 1975. "When History Repeats Itself: The Famine of 1931 in Niger." *African Environment* 1, no. 2: 22–48.

Seers, D. 1972. "What Are We Trying to Measure?" *Journal of Development Studies* 8, no. 3.

Szentes, T. 1971 and 1973a. *The Political Economy of Underdevelopment*. Budapest: Akademiai Kiado.

UNCTAD. 1971. *Special Measures in Favour of the Least Developed among the Developed Countries. Report of the Ad. Hoc Group of Experts on Special Measures in Favour of the Least Developed among the Developing Countries*. New York: United Nations.

UNISD. 1970. *Contents and Measurement of Socio-Economic Development*. Report 70.10. Geneva: United Nations Institute for Social Development.

PART II:

ALTERNATIVE APPROACHES TO BASIC NEEDS

Many of the standard approaches to development problems attempted in the 1960s and early 1970s have not succeeded in dealing effectively with the problems set forth in the preceding section. The hope for a "trickle down" has faded, the possibilities of industrial engines of growth appear quickly only for the few and not for the least developed. Goals established for increased aid and trade have either not been met or have increased dependency. These shortcomings suggest that alternative strategies may be appropriate in confronting the problems of underdevelopment.

The alternatives outlined in Parts II and III are illustrative of themes rather than definitive. Ultimate choices have been dictated, in part, by the interests of the various participants in the editors' network; they have also been governed by the practicality of an alternative viewpoint. The various topics discussed in the second part, including pastoralism, nutrition, water supply, and disaster reduction, are all of major importance to LDNs; their inclusion in this volume needs no defense. Given the scope of problems faced by LDNs and the recent crop of alternative strategies attempting to deal with such problems, these topics are necessarily subjective selections drawn from a broad field of equally important alternative approaches to varying constraints to development within these areas. The editors trust that their choices are both meaningful and practicable in dealing with the problems of LDNs.

6. Although there is an incomplete correlation between pastoralism and least development, many LDNs have high percentages of their population engaged in pastoral nomadic activities (table 6.1). An important component of the development problem of the least developed is thus related to the future of pastoral nomads. They occupy large areas of land and represent significant strong minorities in the national resource base.

The recent UN Conference on Desertification (UNCOD, 1977) debated the issue of modernization of pastoral nomads at some length. D. L. Johnson was a coauthor of one of the conference papers on this topic.* The ensuing discussion of alternative futures provides four hypotheses: the preservation of current lifestyles; the addition of new futures to an essentially unchanged lifestyle; sedentarization; and, lastly, slower adaptive changes. Government processes in many countries have favored sedentarization; this tendency was reinforced by the drought that occurred in the early 1970s. The process of slower adaptive change is theoretically preferable, but it is difficult to achieve in practice. Alternatives to sedentarization tend to involve the welding of "modern" activities to more traditional lifestyles. No one has thus far discovered the answer to the problem of making effective use of dry lands in developing countries—except perhaps the pastoral nomads themselves!

PASTORALISM: SOME ALTERNATIVE FUTURES

D. L. Johnson and F. Vogel-Roboff

Predicting the future is analogous to weather forecasting: the shorter the time span involved, the more accurate the prediction is likely to be. Trying to foresee the condition of the pastoral nomadic lifestyle during the next decade or so is fraught with difficulties. Nonetheless, the broad outline of contemporary trends and an examination of recent history suggest the likely parameters of future events. No consideration of the future, however, can be on firm ground without an understanding of the past role of the nomadic lifestyle and its present status as a socio-economic form. This chapter briefly advances a model of the nomadic economy as an exploiter of marginal resources, discusses some of the salient pressures impacting pastoral life in a modernizing era, and devotes most of its attention to outlining the major potential futures awaiting the nomadic way of life.

Specific concern for the future of pastoral nomadism is appropriate when discussing the development opportunities and problems of LDCs. There are at least five reasons for singling out the practitioners of pastoral livelihoods

---

*R. W. Kates, D. L. Johnson, and K. Johnson Haring. "Population, Society, and Desertification." *Desertification: Its Causes and Consequences*. Oxford: Pergamon Press, pp. 261–317.

TABLE 6.1
PASTORAL POPULATION OF SELECTED
LEAST DEVELOPED AND DEVELOPING COUNTRIES

Country	Total GNP (millions $US)	GNP Per Capita ($US)	Total Population (millions)	Nomadic Population	% Nomadic of Total Population
Least Developed					
Afghanistan	1,620	100	018.80	400,000	2
Botswana	180	270	.66	14,000	2
Chad	360	90	3.95	1,800,000	46
Ethiopia	2,550	90	27.24	1,600,000	6
Mali	410	70	5.56	1,500,000	27
Niger	470	100	4.48	800,000	18
Somalia	260	80	3.09	1,700,000	55
Sudan	2,560	150	17.32	3,900,000	23
Developing					
Algeria	9,840	650	16.28	500,000	3
Angola	3,370	580	5.79	500,000	8
Egypt	10,090	280	36.42	100,000	<1
Iran	35,120	1,060	32.14	400,000	1
Iraq	10,400	970	10.77	75,000	1
Kenya	2,580	200	12.91	1,500,000	12
Libya	7,530	3,360	2.35	300,000	13
Mauritania	290	230	1.29	900,000	70
Mongolia	860	620	1.40	900,000	64
Saudi Arabia	16,690	2,080	8.71	700,000	8
Senegal	1,310	320	3.96	350,000	8
Syria	3,480	490	7.12	340,000	5

SOURCES: Demographic Yearbook, 1975; S. Sandford, "Size and Importance of Pastoral Populations." London: Overseas Development Institute, 1976. Pastoral Network Paper 1C; J. I. Clarke and W. B. Fisher, *Populations of the Middle East and North Africa* (New York: Africana Publishing Company, 1972); *World Bank Atlas* (Washington, D. C: World Bank, 1975).

for special consideration. First, as table 6.1 indicates, pastoral communities make up a significant percentage of the population of LDCs. In those LDCs with substantial dry-land areas, the proportion of nomads to the sedentary population may exceed 50 percent. In contrast, even where nomadic pastoralists exist in substantial absolute numbers in developing countries, they rarely comprise more than 15 percent of the total population. Exceptions to this generalization, such as Mauritania and Libya, reflect the importance of massive royalties from a limited array of mineral resources. At least in the case of Mauritania, there is no indication that national average per capita income figures represent reality for most of the country's inhabitants. Mongolia represents a socioeconomic anomaly in which the absence of alternative income-generating possibilities has encouraged the devotion of resources to pastoral development. Simply as a result of their numerical importance, pastoral communities merit sensitive and sustained attention.

Second, much remains to be learned about the numerical and income characteristics of pastoralists. Difficult to enumerate and to study, pastoralists are likely to share neither the demographic characteristics nor the socioeconomic attributes of settled populations. If both population-growth pattern and income characteristics differ from those of sedentarists, alternative development policies for pastoralists may be necessary.

Third, whatever may have been their political situation in the past, with few exceptions pastoralists today are far removed from positions of political power and economic influence. Agricultural objectives dominate the planning horizons of most central bureaucracies; pastoral communities have become marginalized denizens of peripheral districts in the LDCs.

Fourth, pastoralists make good use of marginal resources that cannot be used for alternative primary-production systems. With much of the best grazing land consumed by agricultural expansion, pastoral nomads are worthy of special attention by virtue of their ability to make the most of the least. In the constrained context of the economies and ecosystems of most LDCs, this ability to utilize marginal resources is of particular importance.

Finally, as the following discussion will suggest, pastoralists are not rigid traditionalists, hidebound and resistant to change. Indeed, when presented with viable opportunities that remove constraints in the traditional system or offer alternatives supportive of group objectives, pastoralists are often quick to shift to new activities. This gambler's instinct, perhaps the product of the flexibility required to cope with a fluctuating environment, predisposes pastoral communities to adaptive change. This flexibility merits the creative attention of planners concerned with the future productivity and survival of indigenous pastoral systems.

The Contemporary Setting of Pastoral Peoples

Arriving at a suitable definition of pastoral peoples is no easy task. Much debate has been generated concerning the "purity" of one form of nomadism over another. Traditionally, camel-herding Bedouin have been regarded as the prototype of the pure nomad because their involvement in agricultural activity has often been minimal and their presumed disdain for any activity associated with tilling the soil is a conspicuous feature of nomadic literature. Yet numerous instances of nomadic involvement in agriculture can be cited (Salzman, 1971; Dyson-Hudson, 1972). For many nomadic communities, direct participation in crop production is required to ensure their livelihood. Thus, it seems more reasonable to regard any group as nomadic that places paramount value upon herd animals as their primary economic and cultural activity, engages in a regular pattern of ecologically based migration to bring animals into contact with seasonal pastures, and lives in an impermanent dwelling for all or part of the year (Johnson, 1969). The fundamental distinction between pastoral nomads and agricultural peoples is that nomads exploit resources that are marginal in an agricultural sense. Given the existence of high-risk areas in which recurrent drought makes farming hazardous on an annual basis, investment in mobile animal capital (and in the peripatetic lifestyle that supports its most efficient development) is a rational resource-use system. Whereas the farmer's crops would wither if subjected to drought, the nomad can anticipate moving his animals to better areas, thereby escaping the worst effects of drought. Where this pattern fails to operate, it is generally due to the interference of values and technologies that are alien to nomadic culture (Bernus, 1974a). Mobility permits the nomad to graze more animals on the range than would be possible under a ranching system, since seasonal movement away from agricultural zones during rainy periods enables use to be made of grass and water resources beyond the reach of the sedentary farmer or stockbreeder. It is this specialized adaptation on the margins of the more secure irrigation or rainfall agricultural zones that underlies a nomadic livelihood (Lees and Bates, 1974).

Because the nomadic way of life is not self-sufficient and requires large agricultural and material inputs from sedentary society to achieve viability, a symbiotic exchange of animals and animal products for desirable and necessary commodities is an essential feature of most nomadic adaptations (Bernus and Bernus, 1972; Bisson, 1964; Dupire, 1962). The wealthy and the poor in the nomadic community tend to flow into the sedentary community, while upwardly mobile investors among the settled population frequently move into the nomadic group. These movements of the population along a sedentary-nomadic continuum take place within an ethnic and kinship setting, with some members of a clan or family being sedentary at any given time. The result is a moderate-income population in the nomadic sphere characterized by values that support capital accumulation. Large herds are thus both a symbol of wealth and a form of mobile capital generated on otherwise unproductive semiarid grasslands. The nomad and the farmer, despite their separate, specialized ways of life, are linked by population flows between each community and by symbiotic exchanges of products. Their activities are generally complementary rather than antagonistic with the nomad playing a vital role in the larger community as an exploiter of an otherwise unusable ecological niche.

This simplified and generalized picture ignores most of the features that characterize the contemporary setting of pastoral nomads (Johnson, 1944a and b). A series of changes in political and economic relationships have reduced the nomad's former central role in economic activity to a peripheral and often nonviable position (Asad, 1973). Changing transportation technology and trade routes have eliminated the nomad's role in caravan trade activities both as suppliers of beasts of burden and as guides and guards (Bulliet, 1975). Shifts in the balance of military power have obviated the nomad's superior mobility and conferred a decisive advantage upon sedentary society. Alien technological devices, such as deep-bore wells and novel philosophies concerning their use and control, have removed many of the traditional constraints in nomadic society on the use of pasture and water. Indigenous responses to modernization have either placed nomads at a distinct disadvantage or have encouraged their movement into new, often urban-based, activities. Frequently, nomadic pastoralists are seen as recalcitrant and unprogressive types who must be settled and reformed as soon as possible. In the course of the domestication process, much knowledge about the use of local resources has been lost (Bailey, 1974); prospects for long-term productive use of marginal resources have also been compromised.

Responses to Change: Scenarios for the Future

Culture exists to ensure the survival of man. It is a mediator between man and his environment. Its laws, passed down through generations, enable man to materially and spiritually survive in his chosen milieu. We use the biological analogy of ecological niches to demonstrate how particular nomadic cultures attempt to ensure their viability. As in nature, the more flexible a culture, the more niches it can fill and the less vulnerable it is to threats against its people. Living cultures continuously undergo change. Always interacting with changes in the environment, cultures adopt new forms, adapt older ones, and discard those no longer considered useful. But when a crisis occurs, either through natural causes (e.g., climatic change) or human-induced pressures, this gradual evolutionary pace accelerates. A culture in crisis must either adjust, thereby rapidly absorbing change, or be destroyed. The outcome depends on both the level of internal strength and adaptability of a culture as well as the degree of sensitivity of outside agents. This chapter will examine some of the possible outcomes of rapid culture change as it affects the economy of pastoral nomads.

A review of the literature dealing with pastoral nomads in both the developing and least developed world suggests that several possible futures await pastoral peoples. These potential directions are linked to the nomad's role as an exploiter of agriculturally marginal ecological niches. Different degrees of change in the pastoral community's relationship to this niche are viewed as the basis for future prospects.

There are four possible scenarios, each possessing varying degrees of likelihood: (1) *Niche stability*, the preservation of the traditional way of life on its own terms and in its own niche, is the least likely prospect. (2) *Niche expansion* involves the addition of new features to an essentially unchanged lifestyle in such a manner that group vulnerability is reduced and viability is enhanced. (3) *Niche contraction* includes sedentarization pressures, range and stock contraction, retarded recovery following natural disasters, and varying types of culture shock and trauma, all of which reduce viability. This process, in varying degrees, has dominated the last several decades of development planning. (4) *Niche alteration*, on the other hand, describes a more adaptive process whereby less dramatic and abrupt changes occur and new techniques are selectively added to improve the effectiveness of traditional resource-use principles and systems. Despite the difficulties inherent in implementing this alternative (Myrdal, 1974), adaptive alteration is viewed as the most suitable course for development.

Niche Stability

Preservation of a stable and viable niche for traditional pastoral nomadic exploitation would require quite extraordinary circumstances. Retention of all elements of the traditional lifestyle in the same niche that had been traditionally exploited might occur in two contexts. Government adoption of a laissez-faire policy toward isolated nomadic groups could result in the preservation of the traditional regime *in situ* or its reestablishment following a natural disaster. The traditional rules and resource-use constraints of the indigenous population would thus be permitted to operate without significant contact with and/or pressure from the government, whose development efforts would be devoted to sectors of the economy that are deemed more profitable or potentially more important. Settlement projects, irrigation schemes, or other employment opportunities might well serve as the focus for a shift of surplus population out of the nomadic district; in so doing, pressure on local resources would be sufficiently reduced to make the traditional niche viable.

Another possibility would be direct government subsidies to nomadic groups, thereby permitting the retention of traditional patterns of resource use. This might occur in situations where the nomadic population is in the majority and a government's power is dependent on their goodwill. The existence of such circumstances is exceptional—and probably has been throughout human history. At present only two countries, Mauritania and Somalia, can characterize a majority of their population as nomadic. In both instances, the recent drought had a devastating effect on the pastoral population (I. M. Lewis, 1975; Rosenthal, 1973; Sheets and Morris, 1974); recovery prospects remain uncertain. Both countries have a commitment to economic development that views pastoralism as a regressive type of livelihood requiring drastic and rapid change (Box, 1971; Konczacki, 1967). Mauritania, at least, has the financial resources—from iron-ore revenues—to begin implementing its vision (International Monetary Fund, 1970). Paradoxically, in many of Africa's LDCs the one way of making a living that is most capable of exploiting the bulk of its land surface is the least regarded of development opportunities.

As a result, the culturally defined environmental niche that nomadic people occupy is particularly vulnerable to major change in modernizing regions. For many nomads, survival is a precarious business in the best of times. When faced with attractive alternative activities, they may well choose a new option. Thus, many herders, traumatized by their experiences in the recent Sahelian drought, may decide that a return to the herding districts is not practical even should government assistance be forthcoming (Laya, 1975). Moreover, niche stability would imply the preservation of all elements of the traditional lifestyle in the same niche that had been traditionally exploited. Yet environmental devastation and herd loss, coupled with degraded pastures, may well cause the destruction of the traditional resource base. When a normally resilient system has been stretched to its maximum capacity by human use, random environmental shock, such as a severe drought, can cause the collapse of the system (Holling, 1973). Longer-term patterns of climatic change could leave formerly productive grazing districts beyond the reach of seasonal rainfall patterns (Winstanley, 1973; Bryson, 1973).

Government hostility to pastoral peoples (who are often ethnically different from the sedentary population dominating the bureaucracy), changing economic structures, deteriorating pastoral resources, and the commitment of most governments to direct intervention in the development process make the retention and stability of the traditional nomadic niche only a remote possibility.

Niche Expansion

A positive response to change would be niche expansion. Here the basic nomadic lifestyle remains the same while new features are added to it to improve the flexibility and decrease the vulnerability of the group. Niche expansion often occurs when an important economic opportunity is introduced from the modern economy. A good example would be the many employment opportunities to work in oil fields and construction at Sharm-el-Sheikh, sponsored by the Israeli Ministry of Defense (Glassner, 1974).

The Bedouin of the region find this type of employment attractive because it is devoid of pejorative connotations and offers some of the swift-paced action of a frontier settlement. Wage labor is an additional source of income that, in many cases, is incorporated into the traditional nomadic lifestyle. Wages earned in the modern sector are remitted in various forms, including family support, bride price, investment in animals, and a variety of other social obligations. Use of traditional fighting prowess might well mean a selective enlistment of nomads in the military, as is the case in Jordan, while use of mobility to evade customs regulations can be an important source of income. Berman (1971) describes one such instance in the Beersheba area; in many countries where frontiers are long and unguarded, the movement of animals to distant markets escapes the attention of tax collectors and statisticians.

All such examples represent ways that the traditional nomadic community can expand its activities and tap new sources of life support. In a number of nomadic societies, especially those living in the most marginal settings (e.g., the Tuareg of southern Algeria [Nicholaisser, 1963] or the Tibbu on the

Libyan-Chad frontier [Kramer, 1975]), exploitation of a multiplicity of agricultural, pastoral, and commercial activities is a standard form of adaptation. The extension of these activities to employment in distant urban centers is simply an adjustment in scale rather than the evolution of a new pattern of behavior.

The crucial limitation in niche expansion is labor. Where family resources are sufficient, new activities are accommodated fairly easily, although the burden of maintaining traditional livelihood activities may disproportionately fall on women and the young. Where labor is insufficient, difficult choices have to be made in selecting what appear to be the most productive alternatives.

Additional possibilities for niche expansion occur with the introduction of technology into the traditional sector or areas occupied by it. The introduction of new plant species better suited to arid conditions could upgrade existing pastures. The use of shrubs with a high photosynthetic efficiency potential to increase available browse has been suggested by Björkman and Berry (1973). Transfer of these shrubs from the Mohave Desert to arid rangeland located in the LDCs of the Sahel or increased attention to the expansion of local plants with similar characteristics might permit the grazing of larger numbers of goats and camels and, by so doing, serve to expand the niche presently occupied by these hardy animals.

Provision of bore wells and pumps are more direct technological responses to the need for niche expansion. Their employment has encouraged niche expansion, not always with desirable results, in the African Sahel. Local overgrazing around wellheads and along tracts leading to wells (de Fabrègues, 1971) has been one consequence of increased well introduction. Provision of improved water supplies in the northern Sahel, in conjunction with an above-average series of rainy seasons, led to a northward movement of Fulani and other cattle herders. The expansion of cattle nomads occurred, at least to some extent, at the expense of camel herders, who found their niche invaded on its southern margins; simultaneous further expansion northward into the Saharan fringes by camel tribesmen was made possible by abnormally good summer rainfalls. When prolonged drought occurred, the overexpanded cattle niche was unable to adjust with sufficient rapidity. Large numbers of cattle died in overgrazed zones around the well sites (Johnson, 1973) or in a vain attempt to trek to better grazing farther south (Laya, 1975). In most instances, losses among cattle exceeded 50 percent of predrought stock, a mortality rate far in excess of that for goats or camels (Temple and Thomas, 1973). The large and much-publicized losses were a direct result of overly enthusiastic niche expansion based on overly optimistic assessments of short-term environmental fluctuations.

Development of supplemental flood farming represents another potentially viable type of niche expansion. Experiments with this technique have been undertaken in pilot projects among the Tuareg of Niger (National Academy of Sciences, 1974). By building low stone walls across seasonal streams, small impoundments are created. When floods occur, the water is forced to sink into the ground, where it serves as a source of moisture for small grain crops. While yields are invariably small and unpredictable from one year to another, use of such agricultural systems brings into production land that would otherwise remain fallow and water that would normally flow rapidly out of the local system. When combined with pastoral activity, the system supplements the nomadic economy by producing more grain at the point of immediate consumption.

Niche expansion would be most likely to occur where the new opportunity or innovation is sufficiently alien or removed from conventional experience to escape traditional stigmas or prejudices. The more modern and progressive an innovation, the more likely it is to be adopted. Moreover, simple devices of direct benefit to the group are more readily integrated into the existing culture. The popularity of transistor radios is a case in point. Shortwave transmitters of limited range might well represent a similarly popular device whose ability to link nomadic groups in a regional information network stressing pasture and water conditions would be analogous to the political-information possibilities of the transistor radio. The result would undoubtedly entail improved efficiency in utilizing distant pastures and a balancing of available supply with the demands of the local herding population; it would also support an expansion of herding activities into niches that might otherwise remain underutilized.

In addition, it appears that successful niche expansion occurs most often on an individual basis rather than as a group process. That is, the group may make a specific decision about allocating its labor resources, but only certain individuals may implement the choices made. Often it is the younger men who introduce the innovation or accept new opportunities. Representing the more flexible members in the group, they are often able to acquire educational and mechanical skills that have economic value in the growing urban areas. While migration to towns is a frequent occurrence (Little, 1965), this seldom reflects a complete severance of ties with the rural community. Rather, labor shifted away from the rural environment continues to funnel financial support back to rural family members engaged in traditional activities. This reverse-flow process is rarely examined as an aspect of modernization, yet it frequently involves a significant expansion of group activities into new niches. In the course of this process, extremely marginal aspects of the old niche may be abandoned due to a lack of labor—which is now invested in a modern, presumably more productive, set of activities.

Generally, such niche expansion involves a spontaneous change on the part of the group to take advantage of perceived opportunities. It is an indigenous and authentic pattern of change, although it may well represent an accommodation to impulses generated by outside forces. Governmental taxation requiring individuals to work outside the traditional context is a typical pressure tactic used to effect change. Frequently, however, such change integrates the old and the new for the economic benefit of the group— at least in the short term. The long-term implications of such change are unknown. The possibility of an eventual conflict between traditional and modern values that may ultimately be as destructive of traditional systems as an abrupt niche contraction is very real (Keenan, 1972).

Indigenous niche expansion in response to change is occurring throughout the least developed world. The prospects for success are modest and relate more to the rapidity of change and to the attitudes of planners and government officials than they do to the capacity of local culture systems to successfully adapt.

Niche Contraction

The obverse of niche expansion is niche contraction. Indeed, the two types of change are functionally linked since a shift of young men into wage labor in the towns (niche expansion) may make it impossible to continue to herd large numbers of camels at great distances from the family campsite (niche contraction). Often niche contraction occurs when changes in the traditional lifestyle create new adaptations that carry with them an increase in potential vulnerability resulting from a reduction of available options and a narrowing of choices. These tend to make the adaptation more specialized and potentially less viable; they frequently include the abandonment of traditional principles of resource use that have survival value. This is not to suggest that the results of niche contraction are always unsatisfactory for the nomads themselves and the agency sponsors. However, whenever a herding system that keeps several types of animals and engages in supplemental agriculture is converted to irrigation farming or urban wage labor, the result is bound to be less diversity in the overall system and an increase in potential instability. Greater dependence on a narrower range of resource-use options and larger-scale economic linkages invariably increases exposure to unforeseen future perturbations in that larger integrated system.

Niche contraction occurs in a number of contexts, the most common of which is associated with sedentarization of the nomadic population. This type of contraction is the result, either directly or indirectly, of government modernization plans and is variously motivated. Strong antinomadic bias on the part of sedentary and urban communities—stemming from an era in which nomads dominated the settled communities both politically and militarily—and a desire to increase accessibility to social services at central locations are the most common factors involved. This is by far the dominant source of pressure on nomadic societies. The sedentarization process is most advanced in those countries with the economic potential to offer and/or the political power to enforce a shift into new livelihood activities (Awad, 1959; Bates, 1973; al-Kasab, 1966). Sedentarization is not without its ecological problems. Overgrazing in the vicinity of new communities is a frequent occurrence (Heady, 1972) and health levels generally decline during the initial settlement phase (Omololu, 1971; Hernandez, 1974). Under the stress of rapid drought-induced settlement, these nutritional difficulties are apt to be twice as common among the formerly nomadic, as opposed to the sedentary, population (Greene, 1975).

In wealthy oil states such as Libya, massive investments in agricultural infrastructure and in new farming opportunities can create numerous outlets for a nomadic population (Libyan Arab Republic, 1974). These opportunities are seldom available in the LDCs. Economic resources are limited, agricultural land is scarce or already occupied, and water supplies are either not abundant or have yet to be discovered and developed. Prospects for productive absorption of surplus nomadic population in urban activities are generally unpromising. In their traditional setting, pastoral nomads at least make use of a resource that cannot be tapped productively by other livelihood systems. While sedentarization seems inevitable for a substantial portion of the nomadic population in the LDCs (since many nomads, especially after natural disasters such as the recent Sahelian drought, have no desire to return to nomadic life), total settlement of the entire nomadic population would be counterproductive. Complete sedentarization would result in the abandonment or reduction of the resource base being used and contraction in the range of niches currently providing stability to the national socioeconomic system.

Contraction can also occur when extreme conservation measures are applied to the amount of stock carried on rangeland. Often the professional rangeland manager and the pastoral nomad will have two different perceptions of how much stock can be supported in a given district. This difference is basic to the two cultures and reflects totally different sets of end goals. The outcome of the conflict between the two systems can often be destructive to the nomadic culture. The Navajo of the American Southwest, a least developed indigenous portion of the larger North American economic system, are a case in point. Adoption of sheep herding as a device for exploiting their tribal territory led to overstocking. Concern about range deterioration culminated in the range acts of the 1930s. These acts led to the reduction of Navajo herds to levels that were, from the Navajo perspective, insufficient to guarantee a reasonable economic return. A similar need to control stock numbers on African rangelands is essential if development is to take a course that favors ranching schemes and restricted pastoral movement (Talbot, 1972). Yet the need to control herd numbers can have a serious impact on the local cultural system when it does not coincide with the objectives of the planner. Downs (1964) has written that the coercive measures used in massive stock-reduction programs left the Navajo leery of Anglo-American culture, an attitude that exists to this day. The drastic upheaval left the Navajo in a state of cultural anomaly, contracting their ability to participate effectively in development programs and reducing the subsistence base available for basic life support.

Cultural breakdown can occur whenever outside culture groups interact with traditional groups in an insensitive manner. Keller (1972) has explored the damage done to Navajo kinship structures when the traditional matrilineal society came into conflict with the U.S. government's patrilineal operations. When the government declared that the male was the head of the household for the purpose of welfare aid, it weakened the entire clan structure in terms of sex roles and the traditional division of labor. Berman (1971) links the decline of the sheikh's power with the introduction of modern government justice, which has superseded tribal justice, thereby weakening the group's cultural integrity. Such culture-disrupting practices, whether intentional or an accidental derivative of the development process, can be expected in most of the LDCs. The loss of control over local resources and the reduced effectiveness of traditional systems is, in part, responsible for the disastrous herd losses during the Sahelian drought; in the absence of effective nomadic political control of access to bore wells, local overconcentrations of herders occurred (Bernus, 1974b) and the disaster was magnified. In such circumstances, the consequences of disruptive change can only be viewed as a niche contraction since they increase the vulnerability of the nomadic group and decrease its ability to effectively control and manage its own essential life space.

Groups under stress can suffer both cultural and physical breakdown. When a culture unable to adjust to rapid change begins to disintegrate, its people are left in a state of limbo. Without cultural guidelines, they may develop an apathetic and mistrustful frame of mind. This cultural anomaly may be passed down through generations; the original injury may thus have widespread effects.

Another consideration is the physical harm that can occur during cultural stress. People under stress are more prone to illness and accident and may produce offspring with a lower chance for survival. If the crisis creates shortages of food, or if the feeding habits of a people are seriously disrupted, the nutritional health of the people will suffer. This can result in higher infant-mortality rates and children who are more vulnerable to disease and hardship (Stott, 1969). All of these factors can seriously contract a group's environmental niche by debilitating and decreasing its population.

Contraction of the nomadic niche is also a feature of negative phases in normal environmental fluctuations. Thus, a series of drought years serves to prune the size of nomadic herds as part of a long-term oscillating equilibrium involving the herder, his animals, and the natural system. This function is accounted for in the nomadic system by the encouragement given to herd increase during cyclical improvements in grazing conditions. Large herds ensure that some animals will survive and reestablish original herd levels following a natural disaster. However, under present conditions recovery from such drought-induced niche contractions is difficult and often impossible. Population growth in both nomadic and sedentary sectors, alienation of dry-season grazing land to agricultural activity, stocking at rates that stretch the grazing ecosystem to its natural limit, disruptive technological innovations (Gallais, 1972) and a variety of other factors are apt to destroy the recovery potential of both the natural and cultural systems. When herd losses are too severe, it is probable that large elements of the traditional kinship structure will lack the necessary resources to reestablish herds, which are the basis of nomadic prosperity. The normal weeding out of poorer, less skilled, and less fortunate herders will be more comprehensive than usual under these conditions, and the recovery potential of the more prosperous herders will be substantially reduced. While losses of hardier animals, such as goats and camels, are likely to be overestimated, losses of more vulnerable cattle are probably accurate and undoubtedly exceed 50 percent (Temple and Thomas, 1973). With LDCs experiencing severe financial limitations on their own available relief and development resources, recovery for much of the nomadic community is certain to be a slow and painful process—if it is to be realized at all. Thus, a drought that fifty years ago could have been accommodated within the nomadic system may prove too severe for the present pastoral community. An altered external condition may convert a temporary niche contraction into a permanent condition wherever local pastoral adaptability is limited or recovery assistance is lacking.

Niche Alteration

Niche alteration involves a more positive adaptive process than either niche stability or niche contraction. This statement assumes that changes in lifestyle and technology will occur within the pastoral regime, but that fundamental principles supporting the traditional nomadic system can be preserved. A basic assumption in niche alteration is that traditional culture contains many positive and adaptive features (Rigby, 1972). Some of these changes are likely to be spontaneous, but all of them require sympathetic treatment from development planners if they are to be successful (van Raay, 1975). Guided change that preserves ecologically astute resource-use knowledge while assisting adaptation to the modern era is an essential precondition for niche alteration. Ranching schemes that retain the basic flexible pastoral adjustment of nomadic peoples, with more controlled livestock breeding and feeding systems, might be one way of accomplishing this objective. New agricultural opportunities could be introduced to supplement pastoral activities, decrease the vulnerability of the group, and add an additional source of income.

Major alterations would involve comprehensive planning within a context that retains local customs and leadership patterns. The Mongolian experience with cooperative ranching systems is a good example of one change pattern that involves a substantial alteration in the traditional way of life. Agrarian reform began in the 1920s. Land was confiscated from the landlords and redistributed to small landowners. Wells were nationalized and new watering places were constructed. By the 1930s, collectivization of the land into large cooperatives began, together with the steady and rapid sedentarization of the Mongolian nomads. By 1959 the sedentarization process was complete. People followed herds into seasonal pastures yet had permanent homes with adjoining allotments in the collectivized state farm. The aim was to develop a system of corral-type ranching utilizing winter hay instead of migratory grazing. All existing accounts (Lattimore, 1962; Petrov, 1970; Zhdanko, 1966) state that the program has been largely successful. This can be attributed to the use of local leaders as political intermediaries, as well as the retention of the basic pastoral identification of the Mongolian nomads even under new forms. Other forms of niche alteration might well retain greater fidelity to the traditional lifestyle. This could be accomplished by retaining basic nomadic mobility patterns while building supportive infrastructures that remove some of the risk inherent in the nomadic adaptation. Selective technological introductions would play a key role in this type of development. Numerous suggestions could be made, but the following example, based on the Sahelian drought experience, provides some insight into the possibilities available.

Most of the livestock that died during the drought were lost because of excessive concentrations of animals close to major water sources. Detailed accounts, complete with lurid photos of dead animals clustered around wells (Rosenthal, 1973) and graphic interviews with nomads whose animals died while attempting to move to new water and grazing districts after local supplies had been exhausted (Laya, 1975), suggest some of the dimensions of the problem. Uncontrolled access to water sources destroyed vegetation around the wells and starvation necessitated a search for new grazing areas. Only when forced away from preferred well sites did the constraint of water availability become crucial. Ironically, it was the time-honored impulse of the nomad to gather around known water sources (Johnson, 1973) that proved to be the undoing of many herders. But it was the basic imbalance in the supply of grass and water—first a lack of grass near the water source and then an absence of water in grazing zones away from the well site—that resulted in catastrophic animal losses.

Development of escape corridors along traditional nomadic routes of movement to secure drought-period resources could constitute an important solution to the problem. These routes are well known (Bernus, 1974b); an infrastructure that would be activated in the event of drought could be established along them. The broad outlines of the system would involve the establishment of intermediate watering points along the escape corridor between major watering points and bore holes. These capped wells would be activated only during emergencies. No permanent pumps would be installed. Rather, pumps would be mounted on small overland vehicles and moved from one well site to another along the corridor. As nomads began to cluster at the major well sites, tribal leadership would be employed to organize groups of herders and their animals. They would then move down the escape corridor, accompanied by a pump truck. Surplus animals at the major well site could be converted into "cattle credits," with some animals surrendered for slaughter and others forming part of small breeding herds used to replenish stock after the drought. Animal losses incurred during the march out of the afflicted districts could be recovered by converting cattle "credits" into real animals at a later date. Adequate forage along the march route could be assured by setting aside small tracks of rangeland; they would have to be located close to the corridor to be of use, and of necessity would be restricted in their proximity to corridor watering points. Moreover, large tracts of reserve fodder land could slow down herd movement when the objective of the exercise would be to rapidly move animals to more favored districts. Stored fodder could be in the form of cereal grains so that they could also be consumed by the nomads themselves if the need was great enough. If linked to a system of shortwave radio transmitters, contact with mobile groups could be assured and a steady flow of men and animals could be maintained. Existence of a system of this type would eliminate the total destruction of herds, especially among cattle herders, who were apparently unable to escape when they were caught too far north by the Sahelian drought in a short-term response to a period of environmental prosperity.

Niche alterations of the type previously discussed could be developed in a variety of ways: health-delivery systems compatible with a mobile population; educational opportunities scheduled to coincide with the dry-season return to home wells; increased use of modern communications devices to summon aid and/or direct movement; and the application of esoteric, remote sensing devices (e.g., aerial photography) to problems of short-term pasture identification are all methods of adaptively and creatively assisting niche alteration. Their use requires the adoption of an indigenous perspective on resource exploitation and runs counter to many of the trends of contemporary development practice and theory. However, it is an alternative development strategy of considerable interest to LDCs because it attempts to build upon local expertise by integrating new technology into a comprehensible local context.

Pastoral communities are of vital concern to many LDNs because they constitute a large percentage of their inhabitants, differ from the rest of the population in many socioeconomic characteristics, are frequently politically powerless and peripheral peoples, and yet have the ability to make rational use of very marginal dry-land resources and to adapt creatively to economic change. They present unique opportunities for creative indigenous development, but the present pattern of change in most LDNs makes their future uncertain.

In a world of rapid change, four scenarios of the future of pastoral peoples can be identified. The impetus for change rules out the prospect that niche stability and an unaltered nomadic lifestyle represent a viable development option. Niche expansion, by increasing the number of options available to a group while retaining most elements of the traditional system, increases its flexibility and thus its viability in the short term, although long-term implications remain unclear. This scenario is most likely to occur where new opportunities create little traditional resistance because they are foreign enough to be outside the traditional sphere. Niche expansion generally occurs on an individual basis as a spontaneous product of change processes within nomadic society, often in response to change stimuli stemming from outside sources.

Niche alteration also increases viability by building in more flexibility and thus ensures a group against excessive losses. It involves comprehensive governmental planning and is most successful when the essence of a culture is maintained and the transition is effected by traditional leaders working in conjunction with outside agents. Selective application of new technology is most appropriate here, but it may well require a level of resources and a commitment of will that is beyond the capacity of most of the world's LDCs.

FOR FURTHER READING

Bradley, P. et al. 1977. *The Guidimaka Region of Mauritania: A Critical Analysis Leading to a Development Project.* London: War on Want.

Datoo, B. A. 1978. "Toward a Reformulation of Boserup's Theory of Agricultural Change." *Economic Geography* 54, no. 2: 135–144.

Farvar, M. T. and J. P. Milton. 1972. *The Careless Technology.* New York: Natural History Press.

Holling, C. S. 1973. "Resilience and Stability of Ecological Systems." *Annual Review of Ecology and Systematics* 4: 1–23.

Irons, W. and N. Dyson-Hudson. 1972. *Perspectives on Nomadism.* Leiden: E. J. Brill.

Johnson, D. L. 1969. *The Nature of Nomadism: A Comparative Study of Pastoral Migrations in Southwestern Asia and Northern Africa.* Chicago: University of Chicago, Geography Department, Research Paper No. 118.

———. 1974. "Changing Patterns of Pastoral Nomadism in North Africa." *Spatial Aspects of Development.* Edited by B. S. Hoyle. London: John Wiley, pp. 147–166.

———, ed. 1977. "The Human Face of Desertification." [special issue] *Economic Geography* 53, no. 4.

Lattimore, Owen. 1962. *Nomads and Commissars.* New York: Oxford UniversityPress.

Laya, Diuldé. 1975. "Interviews with Farmers and Livestock Owners in the Sahel." *African Environment* 1, no. 2: 49–93.

Nelson, Cynthia, ed. 1973. *The Desert and the Sown: Nomads in the Wider Society.* Berkeley: University of California Press/Berkeley Institute of International Studies.

O'Keefe, P. and B. Wisner. 1976. "Taking the Naturalness Out of Natural Disasters." *Nature* 260, April 15.

———. 1977. "Global Systems and Local Disasters: The Untapped Wisdom of People's Science." *Disasters* 1, no. 1.

Sheets, H. and R. Morris. 1974. *Disaster in the Desert*. Washington, D.C.: Carnegie Endowment for International Peace.

7.

Good health is the essence of development; most people in LDCs do not have it. Malnutrition and disease are primary barriers to development in many of the least developed; in fact, mortality rates are generally high and life expectancy low.

Traditional approaches to the health problem may not be most appropriate for any developed country; they seem particularly inappropriate for the least developed. Doctors and other health-care personnel are in chronically short supply; they are heavily concentrated in urban areas, where modern medicine is available to a small percentage of the total population. For most inhabitants of rural areas and small towns, health care is sometimes nonexistent. S. Haraldson and M. Y. Sukkar argue that even massive expansion of conventional medical personnel would not rapidly alter the situation. However, a community-health program staffed, in part, by mid-level medical personnel and backed by community-oriented educational programs could begin to improve the situation. The authors investigated nomadic communities all over the world. Based upon the national-health program in the Sudan, they suggest potential ways of encouraging a change in attitude toward health programs.

It is noteworthy that Tanzania has recently completed an ambitious experiment making use of radio, adult-education approaches, and local personnel in a nationwide campaign to improve rural sanitation through the construction of pit latrines. A first assessment suggests that the multimode approach was highly successful.

Alongside this major effort to prevent the spread of disease can be ranged the successful effort to eliminate smallpox (the last case of which may have been discovered in Somalia), the partly successful effort to reduce the spread of measles, and the ongoing efforts to reduce river blindness and schistosomiasis. These efforts, combined with new ways of providing health services, auger well for LDNs. They suggest that health need only be loosely coupled with development. Major advances can be made in the absence of accompanying economic growth.

NUTRITION AND HEALTH CARE: NONTRADITIONAL ALTERNATIVES*

S. Haraldson and M. Y. Sukkar

Due to a lack of even the simplest health-care measures, vast numbers of people throughout the world are dying of preventable and curable diseases frequently associated with malnutrition. In the field of vital statistics, there are striking differences between the underprivileged world and the developed world. According to 1971 data, the average life expectancy at birth is forty-three years in Africa and fifty years in Asia, as compared with seventy-one in

*The editors must take responsibility for any errors or inconsistencies arising from the final amalgamation of the two original papers.

Europe and North America (United Nations Department of Economic and Social Affairs [UNDESA], 1971c).

There is a continuing downward trend in the infant-mortality rate throughout the world, including the developing countries. But there is still a dramatic difference in infant-mortality rates within individual countries and among a number of developing countries and the rest of the world (Bryant, 1969). The differences are even more marked when one considers deaths occurring among children between the ages of one to four. The infant-mortality rate today varies from 10 out of 1,000 newborn babies in the most developed countries to around 200 in some LDNs.

The principal causes of morbidity in the developing world are malnutrition, vectorborne diseases, and communicable, gastroenteric, and respiratory diseases—themselves the result of poverty, squalor, and ignorance. To this list must be added the diseases among mothers related to deprivation, unregulated fertility, and exhaustion—with their consequent effects on the newborn child. These conditions are linked to such social problems as overwork among women and population growth and urbanization. Their alleviation necessitates an integrated effort in which the health services must play a major role (Elliot, 1974).

Data on nutritional deficiency, low birth weight, and immaturity indicate that the deficient nutritional state of the population is perhaps the single most important factor influencing excessive mortality in developing areas. Mothers who have themselves suffered deprivation give birth to low-weight infants who often die from infectious diseases because of their increased vulnerability; those infants who survive continue because of nutritional deficiency to be more susceptible to the hazards of the environment. They continue to live "with the gas turned down" and often show signs of physical and intellectual impairment.

Insufficient or inadequate health services, as part of a general state of underdevelopment, may be a consequence of a shortage of resources or, in some cases, may be due to incorrectly utilized and geographically maldistributed resources. Maldistribution occurs in areas with scattered populations and a low population density. Since the accessibility rate of any service unit may be excessively low, the utilization and profitability rates of the unit consequently become prohibitively low. There are also places that are underserved due to sociocultural inaccessibility and interracial tensions. Finally, the acceptability of offered services may be low because the services do not correspond to local demands, values, and expectations.

Counting in average per capita expenditures for health services, there is a variation of a factor 1,000–100 between industrialized countries (e.g., the United States, Scandinavia, and Canada) and poor countries (e.g., Ethiopia, Somalia, and Kenya). For example, in 1969 the per capita expenditure for health in Ethiopia was forty cents, while for a number of Western countries it was around five hundred dollars. Naturally, this situation does not favor less accessible rural-population groups and preventive work, which may not provide as dramatic and immediate results as curative work in urban areas.

Malnutrition

Obesity is the most common nutritional disorder in Europe and North America (Davidson and Passmore, 1969), but it is malnutrition that leads to early death, decreased physical growth, and probably even mental retardation for vast numbers of children in the less-developed parts of the world. The magnitude of the problem of malnutrition in the Third World is difficult to estimate. Mortality statistics are unreliable in the assessment of the nutritional status of the population. Deaths reportedly due to infectious disease may also have malnutrition as a predisposing or associated factor. Studies in the Americas (PAHO, 1973) have shown that 7 percent of all deaths of children under five years of age had malnutrition as the underlying cause and 46 percent had malnutrition as an associated cause. The interaction between malnutrition and infectious diseases in childhood is a complex issue. Poorly nourished children frequently succumb to infectious diseases prevalent in the environment. Detrimental feeding practices usually superimpose an additional problem. For example, the withdrawal of food rich in protein and fat and its replacement by a diet high in sugar is a common practice among mothers in the dietary management of children with gastrointestinal infection. (For a review of malnutrition problems, see WHO, 1974a, pp. 3–7, 95–102.)

Protein-Calorie Malnutrition in Early Childhood

The problem of protein-calorie malnutrition (PCM) in the less-developed countries takes different forms, depending on the various factors operative in its etiology and the age at which the child is first affected. Nutritional marasmus tends to affect children under one year of age, while kwashiorkor more commonly affects children between the ages of two and four. Marasmus is a chronic condition that continues for several months before it proves fatal as a result of the absence of adequate medical and nutritional care. Kwashiorkor is more acute and usually appears after the child is weaned off the breast as a result of a second pregnancy. It may rapidly lead to death or show a quick response to appropriate treatment. These two clinical entities are not always differentiated in their classical orms; it is usual to find various degrees of protein and calorie deficiency. In all cases, however, the occurrence of clinical PCM represents a fraction of the vast numbers of children with lower grades of malnutrition.

A more reliable estimate of malnutrition has been obtained from nutritional surveys conducted in the Third World. Table 7.1 shows the prevalence of PCM in children between the ages of one and four in various regions. A total of twenty-five surveys in seventeen countries supplied data (WHO, 1974a, p. 307) for the years 1963–72.

TABLE 7.1
PREVALENCE OF PROTEIN-CALORIE MALNUTRITION
IN CHILDREN
(IN PERCENTAGE OF SURVEYED POPULATION)

Region	No. of Children	Severe Forms Range	Median	Moderate Forms Range	Median
Asia	39,494	1.1–20.0	3.2	16.0–46.4	31.2
Africa	24,739	1.7– 9.0	4.4	5.4–44.9	16.5
Latin America	108,715	0.5– 6.3	1.6	3.5–32.0	18.9

Source: "Malnutrition and Mental Development." *WHO Chronicle* 28 (1974):307.

Based on these studies, it was estimated that some one hundred million children between the ages of one and four are suffering from moderate or severe PCM; the actual statistics may be much more serious (WHO, 1974d).

In the final analysis, PCM in children may be looked upon as the end result of one or more of the following factors:

1. An absolute shortage of food supplies.
2. Uneven distribution of available food supplies.
3. Inadequate intake of utilization of food due to illness.
4. Detrimental feeding practices.

The steps taken to deal with nutritional problems will therefore depend upon an assessment of the various operative factors in any particular setting. Baseline information on the nutritional status of the population, on food production and its potential, and on sociocultural factors bearing on nutritional practices are required for the formulation of policies likely to have an impact on the problem (Sukkar et al., 1971 and 1975b). Among LDNs, such information is unavailable or unreliable and is unlikely to be used in a systematic manner for the formulation of an action plan.

Nutritional Education

Although nutritional education is part of the general field of health education, it warrants individual attention because of the multidisciplinary nature of human nutrition. (WHO, 1974b; Davidson and Passmore, 1969). In the case of the Sudan, for example, there seems to be universal agreement that the country can be both self-sufficient in food production and capable of exporting food to other parts of the world. In spite of this, there is adequate evidence of malnutrition in various parts of the country (Sukkar et al., 1971, 1975a and b).

Although natural resources for food production are available, there seems to be a great gap between this potential and its fulfillment. The gap is felt more acutely by professionals and decision makers than by farmers, who continue to eke out a subsistence level of production by following traditional and basically primitive methods of cultivation. Decisions made at the national level are therefore aimed at massive agricultural projects usually requiring some form of foreign capital. It is important, however, to recognize that change is affecting the people who are both the producers and the users of these products. It follows, therefore, that there is a need to encourage farmers to become aware of the agricultural potential of the land and to become conscious of their own abilities in the application of new knowledge. Bearing the above objective in mind, the various aspects of research and education relevant to the field of nutrition in relation to least developed motives may be summarized as follows:

1. Collection of baseline information on the nutritional status of the community.
2. Identification and improvement of suitable food products appropriate to a geographical region or community.
3. Innovation and adaptation of technology in food preservation, storage, and packing.
4. Agricultural extension to boost production of new varieties.
5. Agricultural extension to develop animal production along scientific lines, with the introduction of suitable species.
6. Introduction of relevant agricultural-education programs in schools.
7. Innovations in more effective methods of agricultural extension and implementation of school programs.
8. Demonstration of the applicability of research results in rural school programs at the community level.
9. Development of educational objectives for various groups of recipients— including teachers, parents, farmers, community workers and children—in order to increase food production and gain a better awareness of the maximum utilization of food.
10. Formulation of suitable educational programs for various groups of recipients based upon specific objectives.
11. Ensuring that educational programs make full use of locally available food and feeding practices.
12. The use of mass media, local leaders, resource persons, and other educational aids in the implementation of various educational programs.

The main objectives of this type of activity are the cultivation of popular participation and the creation of a sense of public awareness of various nutritional problems and possible solutions existing within the local resources and capabilities of the community.

Health Care

Despite the fact that health services have obviously been strengthened in some developing countries, the basic health needs of vast population groups have not been met in a satisfactory way. It is estimated that in many countries only 10 to 20 percent of the rural population actually have access to health services. This situation is made even more serious by the fact that rural and underprivileged people are not only particularly exposed but are also prone to disease and catastrophes. Poverty, ignorance, and a hostile environment add to and exacerbate the scarcity of services. Furthermore, health services and environmental health have not kept pace with population increases; in some areas of endeavor, such as rural water supply, conditions are deteriorating (Newell et al., 1975; Amundsen and Newell, 1975; WHO, 1975).

Unfortunately, the strategy thus far adopted by many developing countries, namely, modeling their health services on those of developed countries, has not been conducive to meeting needs of this magnitude. This wholesale adoption of the welfare health-care model has tended to create relatively sophisticated health services staffed with well-qualified personnel. The original intention was to expand these services progressively as resources increased until the entire population was covered. This has not occurred. Instead, services have become predominantly urban-oriented, mostly curative in nature, and accessible mainly to the already privileged groups in the population.

As recently as fifteen to twenty years ago, most top-level health experts and health planners were unwilling to compromise in the field of manpower; they obstinately insisted on a Western professional standard of personnel and services for all countries, including the poorest ones. To hope to leap from practically nothing to health services equivalent to those of industrialized countries, however, was an unrealistic dream—as is now well known (Amundsen and Newell, 1975).

Experience shows that conventional health services, organized and structured as an emanation of Western-type models, are unlikely to expand sufficiently to meet the basic health needs of all people. The human, physical, and financial resources required are too great; the necessary sensitivity to the specific problems of neglected communities is lacking; and such services may not always be acceptable to population groups with traditional cultural and social patterns.

Traditional health-service assistance to Africa during the last hundred years focused mainly on individual curative care, with little intervention to determine the underlying causes of disease. Thus, the development effect of well-intentioned efforts may in many cases have been negligible. None of the poor countries of the world has reached the minimum standard once recommended (for Africa) as a short-term goal, namely, one health center for an average population numbering ten thousand; in most cases, there is one center for every fifty thousand to one hundred thousand persons.

The relative emphasis on specific disease programs may also have hindered the development of basic health services over the last twenty years. Resources have mainly been directed to one or a handful of priorities. When eradication programs ultimately reach their maintenance phases, it is difficult to hand them over to national health services, which lack the necessary infrastructure. Problems of this kind have proven to be obstacles in carrying out large-scale programs (e.g., the fight against malaria).

Yet concise statements of priority goals within health-care systems are rarely made. Realistic criteria for the development of priorities are formulated even more infrequently. For example, little has been said about the balance between, on the one hand, curative, preventive,and promotive activities and, on the other, policies for the allocation of resources to these sectors. Curative services usually absorb a disproportionate share of resources, money, manpower, and facilities. Priorities, such as those between primary-care services and referral-care services, are seldom defined, nor are priorities within the main sectors themselves often clearly delineated. A balance is seldom established, on an objective basis, among personal health services, environmental health services, and community-oriented activities. As a consequence, personal curative services tend to receive undue emphasis even when better results might have been achieved through the utilization of an alternative approach making use of the same limited resources. Finally, it has not been accepted that general socioeconomic development is often a more reliable, albeit slower, way of achieving control over diseases.

Health Care among the Least Developed Nations

The destitution of LDNs is demonstrated by the poverty of their health-service resources and allocations, as well as their sparse networks of health-services infrastructure. Dispersed rural populations and large migratory groups in many LDNs add to this problem.

The health and nutrition of populations inhabiting LDNs is poorly monitored; this in itself is a reflection of their underdevelopment. Yet this crucial monitoring task must be undertaken if we are ever to fully understand the plight of these people. Such measures as infant-mortality rates and life expectancy at birth can only be estimated on the basis of small local studies and observations. Complete censuses and accurate registration of births and deaths, as well as morbidity statistics, do not exist. Thus, in many cases intelligent guesses may take the place of facts.

In order to compare health-related conditions in LDNs with those of other developing countries, several African countries where such information is available are listed in tables 7.2 and 7.3. Although most figures may be characterized as less reliable, a considerable gap seems to exist between the two groups of nations when the following three parameters are utilized: the average population per physician is about three times greater among the LDNs; the incidence of infant mortality is 32 percent higher; and life expectancy at birth is about seven years shorter.

One can thus conclude that important differences probably exist between LDNs and other underdeveloped countries. It is interesting to discover, first, how LDNs differ from other underdeveloped countries and, second, to find

TABLE 7.2
HEALTH AND DEMOGRAPHIC INDICES OF
LEAST DEVELOPED NATIONS IN AFRICA

Nations	Pop. (thousands) Est. Year 1972[a]	Physicians 1971[b]	Average Pop. per Physician	Infant Mortality[b]		Life Expectancy at birth[b] (Years)	
Burundi	3,403	76	45,800	150	(1965)	M 35.0	
						F 38.5	(1965)
Central African	1,670	55	30,000	190	(1959–66)	M 33	
Empire						F 36	(1959–60)
Chad	3,791	63	60,200	160	(1963–64)	M 29	
						F 35	(1963–64)
Dahomey	2,869	93	30,900	110	(1961)	37.3	(1961)
Ethiopia	25,933	350	74,100	84	(1963)	38.5	(1965–70)
Guinea	4,109	129	31,900	216	(1955)	M 26	
						F 28	(1955)
Kenya	12,067	1.7	6,400	55	(1970)	M 46.9	
						F 51.2	(1969)
Malawi	4,660	53	87,900	120	(1953)	38.5	(1965–70)
Mali	5,257	124*	42,400	120	(1960–61)	37.2	(1965–70)
Mauritania	1,218	68	17,900	184	(1964–65)	41.0	(1965–70)
Niger	4,243	69	61,500	200	(1959–60)	41.0	(1965–70)
Rwanda	3,896	67	58,100	133	(1970)	41.0	(1965–70)
Sudan	16,489	1.1	14,000	94	(1956)	47.6	(1965–70)
Togo	2,092	90	23,200	127	(1961)	M 31.6	
						F 38.5	(1961)
Uganda	10,462	1.1	8,900	160	(1959)	46	(1965–70)
United Rep. of				160-			
Tanzania	13,996	517	27,100	165	(1967)	40.5	(1967)
Upper Volta	5,611	5.9	76,900	182	(1960–61)	M 32.1	
						F 31.1	(1960–61)
17 LDNs	121,766	5,962	20,400	(144.1)		(37.5)	

SOURCES: [a]WHO Health Statistics Annual, 1972.
        [b]Demographic Yearbook, UN, 1974 and 1969.
        *In government services.

TABLE 7.3
*HEALTH AND DEMOGRAPHIC INDICES OF
SELECTED DEVELOPING NATIONS IN AFRICA*

Nations	Population (thousands) Est. Year 1972[a]	Physicians 1971[b]	Average Pop. per Physician	Infant Mortality[b]	Life Expectancy at Birth[b] (Years)
Algeria	15,270	1,698	9,000	86.3*[c] (1965)	50.7 (1965–70)
Angola	5,798	533	10,900	103.3 (1971)	33.5 (1965–70)
Congo	981	112	8,800	180.0[c](1960-61)	41.0 (1965–70)
Egypt	34,839	18,802	1,900	103.3 (1971)	M 51.6
					F 53.8 (1960)
Ghana	9,087	715	12,700	63.7 (1971)	M 37.08 (1960)
Liberia	1,016	110	9,200	159.2 (1971)	M 45.8
					F 44.0 (1971)
Libya	2,084	1,336	1,600	—	52.1 (1965–70)
Morocco	15,704	1,096	14,300	149.0 (1962)	50.5 (1965–70)
Mozambique	8,519	510	16,700	92.5 (1969)	41.0 (1965–70)
Nigeria	58,020	1,300	44,600	58.0 (1969)	M 37.2 (1965–70)
					F 36.7 (1965–70)
Senegal	14,022	277	50,600	62.7 (1972)	41.0 (1965–70)
Tunisia	5,336	1,004	5,300	76.3 (1971)	51.7 (1965–70)
Zaire	22,860	758	30,200[c]	104.0(1955-67)	M 37.64
					F 40.00 (1950–52)
Zambia	4,420	527	8,400	259.0 (1950)	43.5 (1965–70)
Zimbabwe Rhodesia	5,690	836	6,800	31.9 (1971)	51.4 (1965–70)
Fifteen Developing Countries	203,646	29,614	6,900	(108.7)	(44.2)

SOURCES: [a]*WHO Health Statistics Annual*, 1972.
[b]*Demographic Yearbook*, UN, 1974.
[c]*Demographic Yearbook*, UN, 1969.
*African pop. only.

out if LDNs constitute a homogenous group with common problems and common causes of underdevelopment. If this proves to be the case, it may be possible to formulate common solutions so that one country can learn from the experiences of another (UNDESA, 1971a and b).

New Ideas and Methods

The state of affairs of LDNs has been of serious concern to WHO and other international organizations. Consequently, there is now increasing interest in the problems of neglected population groups of the world. New and nontraditional approaches are being objectively studied and considered as alternatives to previously tested and apparently less successful systems and methods.

One of the purposes of this chapter is to provide a "state of the art" view of alternative and nontraditional approaches to the challenge posed by a majority of the world's population still deprived of even minimum health care (Haraldson, 1975; Navarro, 1973; WHO, 1974c).

At the outset, it may be worthwhile to ask what the concept *health* means to a target population and what the latter's expectations and priorities are. Although physical diseases and symptoms always demand solicitude, a lack of social and mental well-being may be more important "sicknesses." They are, however, less easily identified and influenced. There are many areas where physical ill health is less alarming than a nonspecific feeling of malaise resulting from a lack of security and well-being or a loss of cultural self-confidence and identity. From a conventional medical viewpoint, these values or deficiency conditions may be subtle and difficult to isolate. More visible and obvious physical symptoms may attract greater attention and interest.

The deployment of measures that may not be directly related to health but have important health implications is often neglected. Sometimes the favorable "effect" flows from contemporary, nonmedical, general socioeconomic development. The current health situation of industrialized countries is surely more a result of general socioeconommic conditions than health services. Improved housing and working conditions, nutrition, education, hygiene, and sanitation are all essential factors in the development of national and individual health (UNICEF/WHO, 1969).

The underdevelopment of health services is part of a complicated pattern of general socioeconomic underdevelopment (Campbell and Katz, 1975; Taylor and Hall, 1967). For example, lack of water is a common consequence of poverty; and water is of basic importance to health. Ignorance and superstition are kept alive by a lack of educational facilities. Therefore, general socioeconomic development leading to improved water supply and educational facilities will often result in improved health conditions as side effects. An adequate approach to health development must of necessity be multidisciplinary and must recognize the value of development within nonmedical fields.

As a result of hard-won experience, a range of deficiencies in less successful health programs have been identified, analyzed, and added to a list of future improvements. Such decisive factors include: the need for a thorough coordination of all efforts; securing the participation of the local population; adequate and realistic manpower planning, utilizing front-line health workers as cornerstones; and a continuous planning and evaluation of health services and priorities based on reliable statistics.

COORDINATED EFFORTS

An effective health approach requires the coordinated effort of all sectors capable of contributing directly or indirectly to the promotion of health and well-being. This is so not only at the central level but also at the intermediate and, above all, the peripheral level. Moreover, health should be considered as an integral part of development, with clearly defined goals, policies, and plans (Haraldson, 1970, 1973a, and 1975).

Unfortunately, in many developing countries this approach is not followed. As a consequence, overall health goals and policies are missing, which largely precludes health planning. Even when policies and goals have been established and the principle of multisectoral action has been accepted, national or international agencies still have difficulty in crossing sectoral lines in order to implement policy.

People in many rural areas are isolated and scattered. Providing for public services of a conventional type, including health and other social services, is therefore difficult and expensive (Banarji, 1974). New designs and modeling are essential given this situation. One must accept the fact that, due to geographical distances, the utilization rate of any service unit will be low; consequently, the profitability rate—counted as cost per visit—will necessarily be prohibitive and will initially act as a deterrent.

Local Participation in Health Services

Many health-care delivery systems have not been sufficiently accessible and/or acceptable to people in need. Primary health-care interventions must be made available to people at a reasonable distance from their homes.

The acceptance of many health measures may involve a change in living habits; hence the community itself must decide on specific measures and help in carrying them out and evaluating them. A great deal of basic health care and sanitary interventions can be undertaken by ordinary people who possess adequate training with technical advice and supervision.

It follows that there must be a clearly defined relationship between front-line health-care activity carried out by the government and that carried out by the people themselves. The relative contribution of each partner should be determined by the political and socioeconomic situation in a particular country or geographical area.

Organizing the delivery of health-care service in such a way that part of the service "belongs" to those whom it should serve has enormous advantages. It can result in the tapping of local resources for health-care delivery and can bring about a different view of its nature. Ideally, this component of health-care delivery should be under the control and administration of the consumers themselves, but such a structuring of responsibilities within the health-care delivery system need not detract in any way from the primary principle that health-care delivery must be conceived and planned as a whole. A thorough coordination and cooperation between the two components is a sine qua non.

Nevertheless, obstacles to achieving a close cooperation between consumers and health services offered by the government do exist. They include:

● Political systems that do not encourage local self-government in health and development in general
● The rigid, centralized organization and structure of many conventional government health services
● Competition between local, traditional systems of health care and the modern system
● The system of beliefs, superstition, and social stratification in rural communities

Manpower

The developing world lacks human, material, and financial resources with which to meet health needs. In addition, the situation is often complicated by faulty utilization of available resources, geographical maldistribution, uneconomical proportions (malproportions) among the number of health workers at different levels. The distribution of professional personnel within developing countries is virtually inversely proportional to the distribution of people. For example, in 1967 in Ethiopia there were a total of under four hundred trained physicians (for twenty-five million people), more than 50 percent of whom worked in Addis Ababa, where 3 to 4 percent of the total Ethiopian population lived. This phenomenon is not confined to physicians. Outside the main cities and towns there are very few professional health personnel. It is not uncommon for populations of fifty thousand or over to be served by one physician. Maldistribution of health personnel also exists in countries where a large number of professionals are trained. Most educational systems produce professionals in accordance neither with the country's needs nor with the expectations of the trainees.

Training programs, both undergraduate and postgraduate, are frequently unrelated to, or not commensurate with, local health needs. Graduates in general have difficulty in adapting themselves to the activities necessary to meet basic national needs and prefer to perform curative hospital work for which they were trained. Higher education tends to develop a communication gap between professional personnel and primary health workers, as well as between professional personnel and lay people.

The term *primary health worker* covers nonprofessional health personnel, who carry out front-line curative and preventive tasks within health-care delivery systems. Professionals are in the main unwilling to work in rural areas, where health services are most needed, yet they paradoxically often resist the delegation of functions to auxiliary health workers in the delivery of primary health care. The medical profession often opposes new types of health personnel on the grounds that the provision of medical care is too important to be left in the hands of less-trained or differently trained personnel. This opposition may be disruptive since primary health work needs the active support and encouragement of physicians or other health-service staff in order to function effectively.

One of the major factors hindering the development of health services in rural areas has been the absence of clear thinking about the kinds of health personnel needed to provide necessary services at the village level. Most preventive measures, and a large number of medical procedures, are simple and do not require extensive professional training. In recognition of this fact, there is now a trend toward establishing a body of primary health workers who can be trained more rapidly, less expensively, and in greater numbers than doctors or nurses. It is particularly important to use them for primary care in rural areas (Elliot, 1975; Fendall, 1972a).

Some fifteen years ago, a perfectionist attitude still dominated international discussions of health services in poor countries. The latter, the argument ran, should not have services second to those of rich countries; one should wait for professional personnel rather than compromise. This attitude hampered development for years until it was finally realized that no improvements were forthcoming. The only realistic solution to the present situation (viz. large population groups of the world that are medically underserved) was to accept auxiliaries and, at the same time, create a network of services based on these categories, supervised by professionals and with adequate communication and transport facilities.

After a few decades of status-quo conditions, snobbery has successively given way to fresh approaches. One now is ready to discuss alternative solutions at all levels. Furthermore, in many cases the compromises have proved to be better alternatives, ones that are more appropriate to local needs and conditions, especially in relation to available financial resources.

Primary health workers can be recruited from among the villagers and may be trained in or near the village so that they truly belong to the people. They can be employed full time or part time. This kind of auxiliary health worker has been successfully working in some countries for a number of years: the barefoot doctor of China, the aide-post orderly of Papua New Guinea, and the village health aide of the Alaskan Eskimo. All are occupied part time with health services and devote the rest of their time to traditional village occupations. All are initially selected by their fellow villagers for training and thus possess the necessary "double loyalty."

However, the development of a system of primary health workers, while offering the promise of a primary health-care alternative, may raise a new set of difficult problems in relation to their selection and administration, their links with other parts of the health services, and their logistic support. For example, their generally limited basic education and short period of preparation require continuous on-the-job training and the full moral and professional support of the whole health-service system. Unfortunately, existing health establishments have not always met their obligations toward primary health workers (Fendall, 1972b).

Again, because primary health workers often work in remote areas not served by well-developed communication and transportation links, it is difficult to ensure that they are properly equipped and that patients have easy means of referral to other levels of care. Similarly, because of the remoteness of their posts, it is more difficult to supervise and evaluate their work.

Developing countries and areas in which flying-doctor services have been introduced have also had to cope with financial and technical difficulties. Moreover, these services are not ordinarily designed to provide primary health care and appear to be effective only as a referral link where primary health care is available separately. They may be spectacular, but they do not correspond to a realistic cost/benefit type of thinking, and usually assist only in terms of curative services.

While many communication problems may be solved through the introduction of two-way radio systems, the cost-per-unit service is often prohibitive. However, with a well-planned maintenance program and proper training of health personnel in this special field, radiotelephone can be an inexpensive and valuable communication facility in health services, as has been demonstrated in arctic Alaska.

Unless front-line workers are provided with support (supervision, training, logistics) and commentary functions (referral) from the rest of the health system, rural populations may also reject a service that is isolated and clearly insufficient unto itself. Furthermore, traditional healers and medicine men are often antagonistic toward primary health workers and consider them a threat to their own power and livelihood.

The technical aspects of the work of primary health workers are of critical importance, for they serve as the entry point to the health system for the majority of the population. If they offer inappropriate treatment and do not refer patients when they should, the system will not function properly. And yet these individuals, basic components in the day-to-day functioning of the system, receive only brief initial training. Consequently, their tasks must be clearly defined and their training programs must be made efficient. The specification of tasks and the development of training programs place a heavy burden on countries short on skilled manpower.

Infrastructure and Resources

A common feature of health services in poor countries is the lack of a sufficient infrastructure, one which can offer a reasonable accessibility rate for the population it is meant to serve. In some places (e.g., Ethiopia) practically nothing below the provincial level exists.

A rural infrastructure consisting of one unit—usually a health center for ten to twenty thousand people—has been suggested as the minimum requirement for taking over malaria- or leprosy-control projects in their maintenance phase and for the continuation of adequate control. The lack or inadequacy of existing infrastructure has resulted in the failure of malaria programs in several countries (e.g., Somalia). Even for day-to-day curative services, a density of services at this level would be a realistic prerequisite. Instead, most poor countries have one unit for a population of anywhere from fifty to one hundred thousand. Thus, the long-term systematic control of such diseases as tuberculosis, leprosy, malaria, venereal disease, and malnutrition remain in the realm of wishful thinking in most areas. Much money has been wasted on initially promising projects that successively die out when it comes to a takeover of work by local health services and personnel.

What has hampered the growth of infrastructure in poor countries is not merely the shortage of funds but the favoring of densely populated areas and urbanized centers as well; here the utilization rate, and consequently the profitability rate, are regarded as acceptable in relation to available funds. But what has hampered the sound development of rural-health infrastructure even more is an "exclusive" attitude toward the staffing problem, a stubborn desire for service units staffed by professional personnel, university-trained physicians, and registered nurses.

Notwithstanding shortages of resources, the paradoxical phenomenon of underutilization of available services exists in developing countries. The multiple factors responsible for this phenomenon differ from situation to situation. In many cases underutilization stems from such factors as job dissatisfaction of health personnel, exhausting workloads or unrealistic staffing, negative attitudes, disregard of traditional systems and personnel, an inadequate awareness of the need for community experience and involvement, unsatisfactory physical and social accessibility, and poor transportation systems. It is also true, however, that people are often not informed about available health services or are not aware of the types and significance of existing health measures.

If the population does not have confidence in the local health institution, patients may ignore that institution, preferring to seek care in urban hospitals or from traditional practitioners. This "bypassing" phenomenon leads to an underutilization of local health units and, at the same time, places added strain on more expensive services, such as hospitals, which should more properly be providing secondary rather than primary care. Factors responsible for this important phenomenon may include inadequate or inferior quality of service, failure to meet the expectations of the community, staff arrogance, and discrimination.

Health Planning

Although health planning has increasingly been adopted in developing countries, its implementation has been successful only in a few cases. The weakness of many health-planning endeavors is the result of the absence of a comprehensive health policy, a political will to provide the necessary resources for implementation, and an effective structure to implement decisions (WHO, 1973a).

There may, however, be a host of other reasons to explain this failure. Often health plans are designed in such a manner that they cannot be integrated into the country's socioeconomic development programs. Information and effective machinery for national-health planning and evaluation are often lacking. Many health administrations do not have a planning system or competent planners, especially at regional levels. This may lead to the formulation of haphazard plans that are neither realistic nor attractively designed to appeal to the cost/benefit and cost/effectiveness-minded economists of national planning bodies. This is a serious shortcoming since economic development usually receives the undivided attention of planners and decision makers while social sectors and health in particular are relatively neglected.

Another consequence is that plans are frequently directed toward the realization of intermediate objectives, prestige hospitals, and training centers, which may fail to achieve the objective of a change in the community's health status. An obvious step—the identification of the general population's needs at the local level prior to the commencement of planning—is not always followed in practice. Frequently planning is based on statistical evidence that may either be faulty or nonrepresentative. Finally, a systematic evaluation of the effects of a plan is difficult to undertake and is consequently seldom done.

Health-care delivery systems—public and private; national and international; curative and preventive; peripheral, intermediate, and central—must be considered as a whole. Overcentralization of authority and executive responsibility may prevent the adequate delivery of services at the periphery. This tends to lead to an overconcentration of personnel, institutions, and facilities, and therefore to a maldistribution of resources. Furthermore, central authorities become too mentally and geographically removed from, and thus out of touch with, community needs and expectations.

While integration of specialized programs in the general health services is progressing for some programs, others tend to remain autonomous. The fragmentation of a health service into disparate parts, designed to serve either a small segment of the population or a single purpose, militates against the goal of comprehensive and optimal utilization of limited resources and a firm health policy. Although the trend is still to develop separate services—industrial health, malaria control, nutrition, school health, prison health, and family planning—in reality these services would operate more effectively if they were amalgamated into a single, comprehensive service with an adequate infrastructure.

The interaction between the public and private sectors of the health-care system has not been fully studied, nor has its importance been properly appreciated. The private sector includes individuals and institutions with different skills and resources, ranging from the specialized hospital to the private general practitioner, the pharmacist, the village midwife, or even the local healer. All these services are part of the health-care system. National-health authorities miss real opportunities in not taking advantage of those resources that already exist and can be directed toward meeting the goals of the national-health service.

Resources within communities may not have been identified, but in many cases the operators of health services have been unwilling or unable to seek out these resources and mobilize them. Often ignored, for example, are indigenous systems for providing health care, including traditional birth attendants.

If the private sector is dominant within health services, there is a danger that underprivileged sections of society will be deprived of indispensable health care. Essential health-care services should not largely depend upon the purchasing ability of the individual. It is therefore a national responsibility to provide health care that is free or within the financial means of the individual. Most governments are aware of this responsibility yet often fail to suggest an approach that could progressively build up the community's capacity to provide such care.

Health Education

High morbidity and mortality, particularly among infants and children, are not only an index of a community's low health level but are also a sign of inadequate health education. A great number of diseases could be prevented with little or no medical intervention if people were adequately informed about them and were adequately motivated to take necessary precautions. Prominent among these are most childhood and nutritional diseases, as well as diseases preventable through immunization. Health education is especially needed where the network of services is weak and where people must learn to guard themselves against disease and seek help only in case of need.

The main role of health education is to give people the self-respect arising from the knowledge that they can prevent disease and thus change the course of their lives through their own efforts. Health education has frequently not been patterned on existing economic, human, and cultural resources. This condition has often contributed to its failure (UNICEF/WHO, 1971).

While a nucleus of health-education specialists may be necessary for planning and guiding health-education activities in a country, it is surprising how much can be accomplished by using the following frequently mentioned and just as frequently ignored human resources: teachers, agricultural workers, community-development agents and—depending upon the culture—religious leaders, youth groups, traditional healers, and untapped resources. Problems of environmental health, especially water sanitation and sewage disposal, should be mentioned as examples of the effectiveness of health-education specialists in educating the public, especially where illiteracy is prevalent (see chaps. 8 and 11; WHO, 1973b). The Australian experience in the 1960s can be cited as "opening up" primitive isolates in the territory of Papua New Guinea. It is an example of a successful, realistic approach wherein health education was naturally integrated into the wider concept and field of community development.

Reporting, Statistics, and Evaluation

Considerable confusion still exists between the terms *statistical data* and *information*, with the result that many statistical services fail to provide health administrators with appropriate information for sound planning and decision making. If national systems are to be geared to solving the real problems of communities, a radical reform of data-collection objectives and methods is required. The routine collection of data of doubtful validity or utility serves no beneficial purpose either for the decision makers or for the community being served; it results in wasteful expenditure of resources. Information services should be structured on the basis of the priorities of the health system and should employ a strict problem-solving approach.

A continuous evaluation of methods and results is required. Such evaluations should be based upon simple criteria used to evaluate health services or the impact of a particular health measure. These might include:

- Life expectancy at birth
- Infant mortality rate
- Nutritional status of the population
- Prevalence and incidence of infectious diseases (e.g., leprosy, tuberculosis)
- Per capita cost of the program
- Coverage of the target population of services offered

The crude mortality rate may be less useful since its fluctuation may reflect changes in the age structure of the population and occasional epidemics. Age-specific and disease-specific mortality rates may be more useful, but they are also too sophisticated in countries with less reliable services. Unfortunately, such essential values as quality of life, happiness, satisfaction, self-confidence, and well-being are for the most part nonmeasurable.

Apart from evaluating these components of the effectiveness of a program, the per capita expenditure for the program will reflect its efficiency—providing that the right targets have been selected as priorities. Any percentage of financial resources that can be transferred to an activity where the output will be greater is being incorrectly used. One must be stern and uncompromising on this point and not be swayed by "popular" targets and effects. The real profitability, namely, the lasting development effect, should be the guiding principle.

The effect of a health program should also be measured in terms of its coverage, that is, the extent to which services are accessible and utilized. This represents the geographical or qualitative coverage that can be presented as the percentage of a target population actually making use of the service. A geographical redistribution of disposable resources can have a considerable effect—without any extra financial expenditures—through the abolition of a maldistribution of services. This inexpensive solution should be considered at an early stage, especially by governments that cannot count on increased health budgets.

In conclusion, one can say that the current global health situation is serious enough to justify and necessitate drastic changes in the traditional design—especially in rural areas—of health services. Old methods have apparently failed. A fresh, unbiased, and critical review of conventional and accepted methods is needed, one aimed at newer, nontraditional alternatives.

Several solutions increasingly being recommended and tried, and forming the core of an alternative approach, can be outlined as follows:

- Participation by local communities and the consumer population in the planning and operation of sanitation and health services—aimed at developing a reasonable network of rural health services
- Selection of local people by their communities for auxiliary training as primary health workers
- Design of an intensive consultation and supervisory service for rural health-service units, including regular in-service training and advice and assistance in complicated diagnostic and therapeutic cases
- Development of a reliable communication system (e.g. radiotelephone)
- Development of a weather-immune transportation system for emergency and referral cases, personnel, drugs, and equipment
- Introduction of simple information systems and statistical health-planning and evaluation services

The backbone of successful health-service systems has frequently been the primary health worker stationed in his own village (which selected him for training), who offers the villagers either minimum health care or basic health services and serves as a link in the wider service system that supports his work.

Village auxiliaries who work in this manner are acting not as isolated health workers but rather as the extended arm of more qualified services and personnel. An essential and indispensable feature of these successful systems seems to be the "double loyalty" of the health aide to his own people or tribe (who originally selected him for training) and to the professionals and supervisors who first offered the possibility of training and continuously provide the health aide with moral support and advice.

Auxiliaries are inexpensive to train and to remunerate, they are willing to be stationed in rural and remote areas, and they often possess in-depth knowledge of local social and cultural patterns and values, as well as language comprehension.

Despite the magnitude and gravity of the problems faced by many nations—including widespread poverty, ignorance, and lack of resources—it is believed that much can be done to improve the health of the people in least developed nations. Successful or potentially successful programs that meet basic health needs do exist in some countries. They range from new health systems introduced in the wake of radical changes in political and social systems (e.g., China, Cuba and, to a certain extent, Tanzania) to innovative alternative programs covering limited areas (e.g., Venezuela).

The system outlined earlier, or parts of it, has recently been launched in some countries: the "simplified medicine" of Venezuela; the Ujamaa village system of Tanzania; Eskimo "village health aides" in Alaska; "aide-post orderlies" in Papua New Guinea; and "barefoot" doctors in China. Reports presented to WHO suggest that these projects are successful or hold out the promise of future success. They appear to be not compromises but realistic solutions to the rural health problem.

FOR FURTHER READING

Bryant, J. 1969. *Health and the Developing World*. Ithaca: Cornell University Press.

Eckholm, Erik P. 1977. *The Picture of Health: Environmental Sources of Disease*. New York: Norton.

———. 1977. *Losing Ground: Environmental Stress and World Food Prospects*. New York: Norton.

Gish, Oscar. 1975. *Planning the Health Sector*. London: Croom Helm.

Griffeth, D. et al. 1971. "Contribution of Health Care to Development." *International Journal of Health Services* 1, no. 3: 253–270.

Horn, Joshua. 1970. *Away with All Pests*. New York: Monthly Review Press.

Jelliffe, E. F. P. and D. B. Jelliffe. 1975. "Human Milk, Nutrition and the World Resource Crisis." *Science* 188:557–561.

Kuhner, A. 1971. "The Impact of Public Health Programs on Economic Development." *International Journal of Health Services* 1, no. 3: 285–292.

Malenbaum, W. 1973. "Health and Economic Expansion in Poor Lands." *International Journal of Health Services* 1, no. 3: 161–176.

Marshall, Carter. 1974. "Health, Nutrition and the Roots of World Population Growth." *International Journal of Health Services* 4, no. 4: 677–91.

May, Jaques. 1958. *The Ecology of Human Disease*. New York: MD Publications.

———, and Donna McLellan. 1961–1975. *Studies in Medical Geography*. 14 vols. New York: Hafner.

Montoya-Aguilar, C. 1977. "Health Goals and the Political Will." *WHO Chronicle*, no. 31: 441–448.

Navarro, V. 1976. "The Under-development of Health or the Health of Underdevelopment." *Medicine Under Capitalism*. New York: Prodist.

Ravelle, R. 1974. "Food and Population." *Scientific American* 231, no. 3: 161–170.

Turshen, Meredith. 1978. "Women and Health—Lessons from the People's Republic of China." *Antipode* 10, no. 1: 51–63.

Wolstenholme, G. E. and M. O'Connor, eds. 1971. *Teamwork for World Health*. Ciba Foundation Symposium, London: J. & A. Churchill.

WHO. 1974c. *Alternative Approaches to Meeting Basic Health Needs*. Document, J. C. 20/UNICEF-WHO/75.2.

———. 1975. *Health by the People*. Geneva: WHO.

———. 1976. *Food and Nutrition Strategies in National Development*. Technical Report Series, no. 584. Geneva: WHO.

———. 1976. *Methodology of Nutritional Surveillance*. Technical Report Series, no. 593. Geneva: WHO.

8.

Water is in demand everywhere yet no one is without water. The solutions to this basic paradox are critically examined by I. Burton and A. Whyte. A billion members of the world's population make daily arduous journeys to reach water-supply centers, many of which are highly mineralized or locally polluted. A major global effort is under way to bring this precious substance a bit closer. But even the most optimistic projections for the current decade still predict that fifty million more people will be denied easy access to safe water sources since the effort first began.

Even where water is distant or polluted, people still exercise a degree of selectivity, balancing their conceptions of cleanliness with the effort required and the social relationships that must be maintained (White, Bradley, and White, 1972). Can daily human efforts to obtain needed water be integrated into an alternative approach for producing water?

Alternative approaches do exist. Burton and Whyte assay their weaknesses and future potential, arguing in favor of an integration of these approaches and some small-scale experiments in their application. Such efforts are particularly appropriate for LDNs, where access to water is more of a problem than in developing countries. But as M. R. Mujwahuzi notes in chapter 10, even in Tanzania, where the "human right" concept of water access is a national goal and self-help is encouraged, the integration of self-help with the standard delivery system has not succeeded to date.

The water-supply issue poses a basic test in the development of alternative approaches. If these approaches cannot succeed in this sector—where human need is undisputed and present progress is demonstrably inadequate—then the hope for alternatives is probably misplaced.

USER-CHOICE IN COMMUNITY WATER SUPPLY: PANACEA OR PALLIATIVE?

I. Burton and A. Whyte

Water Supply and Development

Over one billion people living in rural areas of developing countries do not have access to a safe and adequate supply of water. This simple truth represents a major blot on human achievement. It has given rise to ringing declarations of intent to provide "safe water for all" and to outbursts of anger and frustration. A solution to the problem surely is not beyond the technological capacity of an age of nuclear power and space travel. Nor is the cost of a solution very large in relation to existing wealth or expenditure levels in other areas, notably military hardware. And yet the problem and the accompanying frustration remain. Recently, the notions of user-choice and community

117

involvement have been described as part of a new approach that holds out greater hopes for the future (Whyte, 1976). This chapter provides a background perspective on the user-choice idea in order to show how it relates to conventional thinking and recent experience. Next it explores some of the problems that arise in adopting a user-choice approach and cautions against its easy acceptance as a panacea for present frustrations.

Water Supply and the Least Developed

Who are the least developed? Who are "the poorest of the poor"? In the context of this volume, *least developed* refers to a group of nations so designated. In relation to water supply, however, this chapter adopts the view that least developed refers to *situations* in which people are forced to rely on sources of water that may make them ill or cause them to expend a disproportionate amount of time each day to fetch water from distant sources. Redraw the political map of Africa or of the Himalayan region and many LDNs could be made to disappear in an aggregation of statistical data. Least developed situations involving lack of access to safe and adequate supplies of water would nevertheless remain in those places as well as many other countries—including Brazil and Canada, which are not usually considered to be among the least developed.

Why do people lack water? In an absolute physical sense, no one lacks water. Everyone has access to water of some sort, for without water a person cannot live for more than a few days. Moreover, human settlements always have had water. The situation in which we now find outselves is of our own making. It arises not from the parsimony of nature but from the very processes of development designed and intended to improve the human condition.

The growth in density of rural populations and their aggregation into larger villages have resulted in a contamination of the environment such that previously safe sources of surface water are now a source of disease. At the same time, permanent human settlements have spilled over into semiarid areas characterized by long, pronounced dry seasons during which perennial sources of water are few; those in less-favored places may be forced to walk several miles each day to obtain water. The process responsible for making water sources unsafe and distant has been exacerbated in some regions by periods of drought, overgrazing, and the extractive use of groundwater, which lowers the water table and allows wells to run dry. The fruits of development have been obtained at the expense of reducing some members of the human family to a condition that Paleolithic man would have considered unacceptable. Not to have good-quality drinking water within easy reach is certainly to be counted among the least developed.

The Role of Water

Unfortunately, the problems created by development are not easily solved by inputs of capital and technology. Having upset the balance of traditional systems of livelihood, the problems cannot simply be solved in a technical fashion. The reason for this is that the use, source, transport, and disposal of water permeate the fabric of rural life. Attitudes toward water are strongly anchored in traditional beliefs, often possessing religious significance. Rules vary from group to group; thus, a satisfactory solution in one area may prove disastrous elsewhere. A change in water supply can affect the whole village organization, the relation of women to men, and the traditional structure of power and authority. Much more than health and convenience is at stake. The improvement of rural water supplies clearly requires a sensitive interdisciplinary approach. What it has received in the past has largely been dominated by the concerns of finance and technology. These are important, but they are not everything.

Water Supply: Human Right or Economic Good?

Since the problem of rural water supply evolved as part of the larger process of economic development, it is not surprising that economic-development thinking has dominated the search for solutions. For two decades—roughly from 1950 to 1970—improvements in water supply were required to satisfy the economic tests of efficient allocation of scarce resources. Water-supply projects would not be built unless it could be shown that there were substantial benefits to justify the expenditure, or unless the people themselves were willing to pay for the improvements in cash.

Given the fact that scarce financial resources were considered to be a major constraint on development, it made sense to invest in those areas where a return on capital would be forthcoming. To invest in nonproductive services was considered to be a misallocation. A long debate ensued in which the proponents of rural water-supply programs argued that those investments were indeed productive because the improved health of rural populations meant that they could work more effectively and thus produce more crops. This led to attempts to quantify and demonstrate public-health and productivity benefits resulting from an improved water supply. The literature has been well summarized by Saunders and Warford (1976). The studies conducted were often costly and time consuming. Flaws in research design (due to cost and time limitations) were such that no convincing evidence for the supposed benefits could be attributed with certainty to water supply. Other secular processes already in motion made it difficult, if not impossible, to state what would have occurred without the improvement. Some of the results even cast doubt on the benefits. Diseases are spread in several ways; a focus on water alone, without attention to sanitation and health education, resulted in minimal or no public-health benefit. If there is any reduction in the time spent fetching water and that resulting from sickness, the additional free time is just as likely to be invested in other social activities as it is in increasing output.

The emphasis formerly given to water as an economic good has gradually weakened. This is not to say that the validity of the idea of efficient allocation of scarce resources has been totally disproved; it has merely been disapproved in the case of such a basic need as water. It simply was not solving the problem rapidly enough. Indeed, while the slide rules and computers were busily calculating public-health benefits, the numbers of people without access to safe water continued to grow. In the early 1970s, a major change in attitude and orientation occurred. Access to safe water was now seen as a human right (G. F. White, 1974a). Arguments favoring the expansion of national and international efforts were based on the assumed impact on the living conditions of the poorest, as well as their capacity to participate in their country's development. The change in approach to economic development has sometimes been referred to as "the end of trickle-down" (see chap. 2). No longer is it acceptable to concentrate on development in the urban and industrial sectors of the economy. According to the new philosophy, if a country is to develop the necessary determination to modernize, all segments of the population and all regions must be drawn into the development process.

International Action

A recommendation of the UN Conference on Human Settlements, "Habitat," held in Vancouver in June 1976, states (p. 33):

(a) In the less developed countries, nearly two-thirds of the population do not have reasonable access to safe and ample water supply, and even a greater proportion lack the means for hygienic waste disposal.

(b) Safe water supply and hygienic waste disposal should receive priority, with a view to achieving measurable qualitative and quantitative targets serving all the population by a certain date; targets should be established by all nations and should be considered by the forthcoming United Nations Conference on Water.

(c) In most countries urgent action is necessary to:

   (i) Adopt programmes with realistic standards for quality and quantity to provide water for urban and rural areas by 1990, if possible;

   (ii) Adopt and accelerate programmes for the sanitary disposal of excreta and waste water in urban and rural areas;

   (iii) Mobilize popular participation, where appropriate, to cooperate with the public authorities in the construction, operation and maintenance of infrastructure;

   (iv) Plan water supply and the sanitary disposal of waste together in the framework of national resource planning;

   (v) Reduce inequalities in service and access to water, as well as overconsumption and waste of water supply;

   (vi) Harmonize and coordinate the interests and efforts of local governments and other public bodies concerned through the appropriate planning by the central government;

(vii)   Promote the efficient use and reuse of water by recycling, desalination or other means taking into account the environmental impact;

(viii)   Take measures to protect water-supply sources from pollution.

In the light of the expressed aspirations of the Habitat Resolution, it is clear that every effort should be made to achieve a reasonably safe and adequate supply of water for the world's human population by no later than the end of this century—or earlier, if possible. These improvements must be accompanied by concomitant improvements in rural sanitation, especially sewage disposal.

The sentiment was echoed at the World Water Conference, held in Mar del Plata, Argentina, in February 1977. Since then it has become increasingly clear that a major effort to improve rural water supply is in the making. The period 1980–1990 has been designated the International Drinking Water Decade by the UN General Assembly. National governments in developing countries have been giving higher priority to rural development, including rural water supply and sanitation, in their development plans. Bilateral aid agencies are prepared to substantially expand financial and technical assistance for rural water supply. International organizations have joined in an effort to consolidate their activities. At the initiative of the International Development Research Centre (Ottawa), a series of meetings was held between 1974 and 1977 of the Ad Hoc Working Group on Rural Potable Water Supply and Sanitation. The advisory organizations included UNICEF, UNDP, UNEP, IBRD, WHO, IDRC, and OECD, later joined by FAO. The group activity sought to develop a coordinated program of international action to lead the global assault on the problem of rural water supply. At its most ambitious, the group was modeled on the International Consultative Group for Agricultural Research, which helped to establish and support the series of international agricultural research centers around the world, which, in turn, have fathered the "green revolution" in agriculture.

The Ad Hoc Working Group established a task force of experts to develop a plan of action and itself attempted to work out a means of procedure. Many of the task force recommendations are now being implemented in collaborative arrangements between international and bilateral organizations. An increased effort will be made to provide the poorest of the poor with improved water supplies and to develop local abilities to run them. More attention will be paid to the social aspects of water and to health education. But these plans are still in the future.

Recent Progress

A 1970 assessment of the world situation (ninety developing countries excluding China) prepared by WHO indicated that during this year some 88 percent of the rural populations in ninety developing countries were without access to safe supplies of potable water. By 1980 this percentage is expected to fall to 75 percent. Such a rate of progress would still result in an estimated

TABLE 8.1
PROGRAM FOR RURAL WATER SUPPLY IN NINETY
DEVELOPING COUNTRIES, 1970–80
(Population in Millions)

Type of Supply	1970		1980		Increase 1970–80	
	No.	%	No.	%	No.	%
Access to safe water	140	12	357	25	217	155
Without access to safe supply	1026	88	1081	75	55	5
Total population	1166	100	1438	100	272	23

SOURCE: World Health Organization, Twenty-fifth Health Assembly. Community
Water Supply Programme. Progress Report of the Director-General. Document A 25/29. Geneva, April 1972.

increase of fifty-five million rural inhabitants without access to safe water
(table 8.1).

It was, in part, the discouraging estimates and forecasts of WHO that
spurred the movement for an expanded global program now taking shape.
Further encouragement has emerged from the statistics revealed in the Mid-
Decade Progress Report for 1975, prepared by WHO (1976). The latter
shows that the progress achieved up to 1975 was in excess of the rate required
to achieve the 1980 target of 25 percent. The new regional targets adopted
by WHO in 1976 indicate a net global increase from 25 to 36 percent on a
"global" basis (fig. 8.1). The 1971–75 performance rate, if extended to 2000
A.D., would result in the achievement of improved supplies for almost 70
percent of the rural populations. Linear extrapolation of the 1975–80 target
rate would, if carried out in practice, achieve improved supplies for 95
percent of all rural populations by the end of the century.

The rate of progress has varied considerably among the regional groupings
of countries used in WHO statistics (fig. 8.2). The rate of achievement has
been good in Africa and the western Pacific regions; both areas are expected
to reach a new target of 35 percent by 1980. Improvement has been slower in
the Americas; it will be difficult for the Latin American countries to achieve
the "Santiago goal" of 50 percent by 1980 without greatly expanding their
efforts.

Viewed on a world scale, the bulk of the problem lies in Southeast Asia
(fig. 8.3). Approximately 62 percent of the world population still without improved supplies in 1975 may be found in that region—over 37 percent in
India alone.

Figure 8.1

Linear Extrapolations of Rural Populations with "Reasonable Access to Safe Water," Based on 1961-70 Performance, 1970-80 Program, 1970-75 Performance, and 1975-80 Target Rate

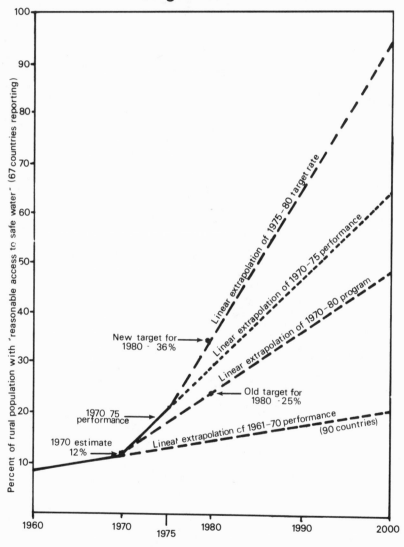

FIGURE 8.2

Progress by Region, 1970-75, and Revised 1980 Targets

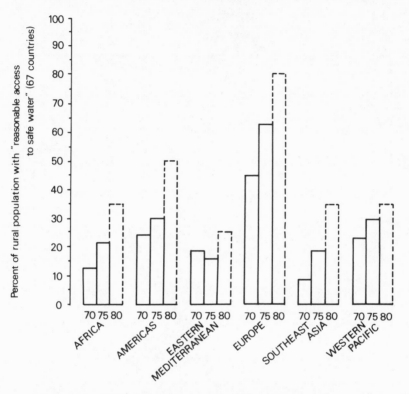

Source: World Health Organization, "Community Water Supply and Wastewater Disposal." Mid-Decade Progress Report. Document A 29/ Revision 1. Geneva, 1976.

FIGURE 8.3

Regional Distribution of Rural Populations without Reasonable Access to Safe Water, 1975 (67 Countries Reporting)

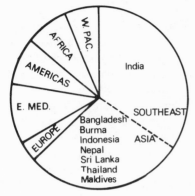

Countries Reporting

Africa:	Americas:
Benin	Argentina
Guinea	Barbados
Ghana	Bolivia
Kenya	Chile
Madagascar	Colombia
Mauritius	Costa Rica
Niger	Dominican Republic
Rwanda	Ecuador
Swaziland	El Salvador
Togo	Guatemala
Uganda	Guyana
United Republic	Haiti
of Tanzania	Honduras
Upper Volta	Mexico
Zaire	Nicaragua
Zambia	Panama
	Paraguay
	Peru
	Uruguay

Eastern Mediterranean:
Afghanistan
Bahrain
Cyprus
Ethiopia
Iran
Iraq
Kuwait
Libyan Arab Republic
Oman
Pakistan
Qatar
Saudi Arabia
Somalia
Sudan

Western Pacific:
Fiji
Lao People's
    Democratic Republic
Malaysia
Papua New Guinea
Philippines
Republic of Korea
Singapore
Tonga
Western Samoa

Europe:
Algeria
Turkey

Source: World Health Organization, "Community Water Supply and
    Wastewater Disposal." Mid-Decade Progress Report. Document
    A 29/12, Revision 1. Geneva, 1976.

The global rate of expansion of the improvement effort is better than had been expected in 1972. But the magnitude of the problem in Southeast Asia is cause for concern. If the situation in that region could be substantially improved, the world picture would also look radically different. From an international perspective, it appears that external assistance should be concentrated where the bulk of the problem lies.

The relatively slow progress of the Latin American countries is also somewhat disappointing. They have always been regarded as the leaders in the developing world, as far as water supply and sanitation are concerned. It now appears possible that Africa may catch up with them, or even be in a better position, by 1980. The Mid-Decade Progress Report suggests that the relatively slower performance of the Latin American countries in the rural sector is due to an insufficient allocation of resources. A factor that might lie behind this is that much of the rural settlement in Latin America still without adequate water supplies is either in dispersed or only semiconcentrated farmsteads (Pineo and Donaldson, 1976). After the more concentrated rural settlements (*rurban* is Donaldson's term) have been supplied, it becomes increasingly expensive to reach and supply the more dispersed settlements. Another reason for slower progress is that many of the poorest people live in shantytowns around the major cities. They lack both the feeling that they are a part of the social fabric and a communal sense of permanence, both of which provide cohesion and leadership in traditional rural villages. The phenomenon involving a declining rate of progress once more accessible rural communities have been reached might also occur in other regions. It is well known that the larger, more influential, and more affluent communities, as well as those nearer to major cities, tend to be reached first. The accelerating rate of improvement suggested by figure 8.1 should not lead to quick overoptimism. The greater costs involved in reaching poorer and more remote rural people may be operative sooner rather than later.

There are additional reasons for caution. Reliability of the data collected in the WHO questionnaire surveys can vary considerably. The Mid-Decade Progress Report states: "The data obtained from this survey should be considered as order of magnitude estimates only." The data are also subject to two types of systematic error. First, the number of people with improved supplies may be overestimated; a national program may incorrectly assume that once an improvement has been provided, it continues to be available indefinitely. An example can be cited from one African country where a number of new drilling rigs were purchased with the assistance of a capital loan from a bilateral aid agency. In compiling data on wells drilled, however, no provision was made for rig or well maintenance, nor was thought given to the problem of getting rigs into some villages that lacked all-weather access roads. Hence, there is a tendency to use the predicted number of wells as a basis for estimation and to assume that even when a well has been provided, water will continue to be available.

Second— and, to some extent, compensating for the first source of error—

it is sometimes assumed that unless a village has been supplied with a water-supply improvement through a national program, no improvement has occurred; and that, by definition, the water used must be unsafe, inadequate in quantity, or not accessible. This view ignores the efforts sometimes made by communities to help themselves or the assistance that they receive from nongovernmental bodies.

It would be consoling to say that these two sources of error cancel each other out. They probably do not. More likely, the statistics erroneously suggest that the situation is better than it is.

While there are some encouraging signs of recent progress, the record to date would indicate caution in the design of expanded and accelerated programs. The encouraging signs are of two sorts. First, there are statistics collected by WHO that, for reasons already cited, are likely to err on the optimistic side. Second, there are new actions and preparations for action by international and bilateral agencies and shifts in national priorities. But these are both far removed from actual practical experience. One observer has recently reported that "35 to 50 percent of the water taps in rural areas are out of order three to five years after their construction" (Imboden, 1977). This statement is in accord with other field reports and recent personal experiences. There appears to be no reason to doubt that many rural water projects continue to fail. There is a real danger in the desire to upgrade the quality of life for the least developed. Much money and effort might be wasted on systems that would eventually fail. In addition to financial waste, many rural people might be left with a sense of failure. A more careful appraisal and evaluation of past experience is urgently required.

Evaluating Past Experiences

Why Projects Fail

It is a common and oft-repeated story that rural water-supply improvements installed at the village level break down or become inoperative shortly after the fanfare associated with their opening has subsided. Many reasons for this are given, and all of them are undoubtedly valid in some cases. The litany may be summarized briefly.

Insufficient money is invested in the schemes, so that once they are opened proper repair and maintenance are not carried out. Those individuals in charge of maintenance are overworked or, in some cases, not properly trained. Spare parts are either difficult to obtain or out of stock; they must be ordered from overseas and paid for with scarce foreign exchange. The technology is too complex or advanced, too capital-intensive and too reliant on skills and supplies that are absent or difficult to obtain. Equipment imported from "donor" nations is not suited to "user" conditions. Pumps that served from one to four houses in the countries where they were developed are not strong enough to stand up to the heavy use and misuse they receive in developing countries; each pump must carry too big a load—including animals in addition to many families— and breakdowns occur with some frequency. In some countries, several different designs of equipment are used, imported from many different countries; this complicates the spare-parts and maintenance problems.

The village populations do not understand or appreciate the benefits of improved water supply. Once an improved source fails or presents some difficulty, they readily abandon it and revert to the traditional supply, which is often surface or unprotected water. They do not make any effort themselves to protect the new system and to ensure that it does not break down. A possible reason for this is that the improvements are seen as an externally owned and operated system. The new water supply does not belong to the community; it is an alien thing. Moreover, it may disrupt the village's social life or introduce a new and unwelcome element into the politics of the community.

All these reasons are familiar to workers in the rural water-supply field. Accounts of partial success are mingled with accounts of genuine difficulty, excuses, and apologies, a mixture that is not easily separated. Nevertheless, it is clear that there are many valid reasons why projects fail.

It is less clear why projects succeed. That some do succeed cannot be doubted if one accepts the criterion that three to five years later they are still functioning as originally intended. Generally, however, there are special explanations for the latter. One outstanding success story has been the Kandara scheme in the Aberdare Mountains of Kenya. Water is piped, by means of gravity, from a small reservoir high up in the watershed. It is used from both public standpipes and house connections by a rural population spread over a wide area. Indications, however, are that the project is expensive and has only been made possible through sustained support both within Kenya and from outside groups. The backing of an energetic local politician with influence in the national capital and friends abroad has contributed significantly to the requirements for success. In addition, the demand for local contributions has not been pressed too strongly. Many of the water users are being permitted to divert modest amounts of the piped supply to small-scale "kitchen garden" irrigated plots. Local support for the scheme is strong and enthusiastic. It has become a showpiece for foreign visitors.

These ingredients for success cannot be replicated everywhere. The scheme has not met one stringent test for success: it does not have its imitators; there is no "contagion effect." Even casual observation in rural areas of developing countries reveals that innovations that meet local needs and fall within, or close to, the capacity of the local community or individuals to adopt can spread like wildfire. Such commodities as shoes, bicycles, and transistor radios have shown that rural populations are not resistant to change once the opportunity is within reach. Similarly, the rapid spread of hybrid grains in the "green revolution" is evidence that innovations and systems that work find ready adopters.

Why is there no "contagion effect" in rural water-supply improvements? An explanation that has increasingly been put forward in recent years is that a large gap exists between externally sponsored improvements and the wishes, needs, and understanding of local communities. Some of the key elements in rural water-supply and sanitation-improvement programs are displayed in figure 8.4. These have been described in detail elsewhere (Burton, 1977). One element that is largely missing or poorly developed in existing programs is community participation. The gap between external and local groups is so strongly felt in some areas that it is possible to describe two separate systems of water supply.

There is, on the one hand, the externally designed system that is brought to the village by a national or regional government organization and planted in place with a minimum of local consultation. The village may be asked to provide labor for the project, but it is not asked for its advice or opinion; to do so might imply that the village residents possess more knowledge of some things than the external technical and planning staff. This approach could be called "the delivery system."

Unconnected to the "delivery system" is the traditional village system. Here traditional technology is used, relying solely on local materials and local skills. The operation of the system (e.g., use of well, surface storage tanks or ponds, access to springs, streams) is controlled by the community decision-making and power structure and is deeply ingrained in the social and religious life of the community. This traditional system functioned well in the past. Although it can no longer cope with present-day demands in many areas, it is still preferred by some. When new systems are first installed, they are often viewed with suspicion. When they break down or need repair, the community is often eager to return to traditional sources of water if these are still available.

As an antidote to this experience, it has been suggested that much more community involvement is required for there to be any real success.

User-Choice

An approach in this direction has been described by the term *user-choice* (Whyte, 1976). The term emphasizes the fact that in traditional systems the water *users* help make decisions about sources of water, methods of obtaining water, and ways in which the supply is to be used by a community. In delivery systems, external designers usually make all three sets of choices without consulting users. The incorporation of a user-choice philosophy in community water-supply improvements is therefore a means of dramatizing the sort of community involvement that is thought to be important for success.

The concept of user-choice does not mean that villagers are given a free hand in deciding about their water supply. Their knowledge of technical options and health implications will inevitably be limited. Nor does it mean that

FIGURE 8.4

Key Elements of Rural Water-supply and Sanitation-improvement Programs

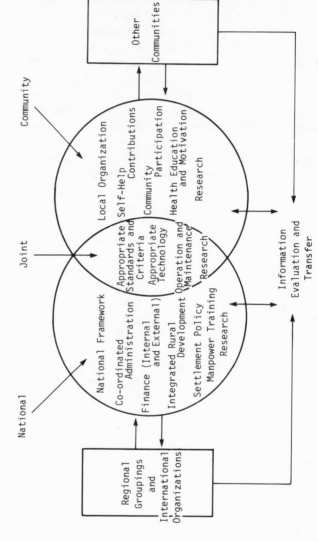

Source: Ian Burton, "Safe Water For All," *Natural Resources Forum* 1 (1977): 95-110.

villagers are simply required to provide labor for construction or payments when the water is supplied—although frequently this type of approach is misnamed "self-help" or "participatory." Rather, user-choice implies a collaborative situation in which outside expertise is combined with local knowledge and capability.

What does user-choice mean in terms of the expansion of rural water-supply programs resulting from national and international initiatives? First, it suggests that the community should be consulted concerning the source of water to be used; second, it implies that the community should have a choice in the overall design of the system; and third, it means that the community should have a choice in the operating rules and procedures.

Take, for example, the source of water. Is groundwater to be used or are surface supplies capable of development? If surface supplies are contemplated, can sources near at hand be used or will pipes have to be laid to bring the water closer? Engineers tend to favor groundwater supplies; they are less easily subject to contamination; moreover, once a well has been drilled and a pump installed, the basic elements of a system are in place. Surface supplies, on the other hand, are more subject to contamination. In many regions they yield insufficient quantities of water; long pipelines may be required to bring an adequate source of water to the community. Local communities traditionally accustomed to surface supplies may not respond with enthusiasm to groundwater supplies. Once a system has been installed, they may object to the taste of the water, which is often highly mineralized. Sometimes their objections are based upon beliefs concerning spirits inhabiting underground water.

Although a strong argument can be made in favor of adopting a user-choice approach, such an approach is not necessarily easy to achieve. The needs of a user-choice strategy are at present acting as constraints on its diffusion. In many areas these needs cannot be met without some initial changes. These conditions include:

1. *Long lead time* between the initial idea and the physical realization of the scheme. This may take weeks, months, or even as much as one to two years. This time is necessary to contact all members of the community, solicit their opinions, and obtain their agreement. It also accounts for the holding of meetings and the establishment of committees to organize the project at the local level.

2. *Availability of people to visit villages* and promote new schemes, collect necessary data, advise on health education, organize committees, and identify local manpower for training as pump attendants.

3. *Retraining of engineers and drillers* (who visit villages to install water schemes) to sensitize them to the sociopolitical nuances of water supply and to teach them how to comunicate effectively about their own area of expertise—to explain what they are doing, why, and to be prepared to ask for local guidance on some questions. Communication cannot simply be left to the project team member whose job is that of "communicator."

4. *Linkage of water supply to improved sanitation and extensive health-education schemes.* This inevitably complicates and slows down the water project. However, past experience indicates that health improvement does not come with water-improvement schemes alone. Water supplies that are "good" at the standpipe often become contaminated by the time they reach the cup as a result of inadequate sanitation and a poor understanding of the relationship between health and clean water.

5. *Fulfillment of choices.* Once alternatives are offered to a community in the context of cost and technical feasibility, they should be able to be implemented. Two sources of difficulty may arise: unless rigorous standardization is followed for technology (i.e., reduction in choice), equipment and parts may not be available from manufacturers without long delays. This is one rationale for UNICEF's warehouse of standardized equipment for water supply—it is available immediately. The other source of difficulty is simply that, despite our technological era, the choice of good equipment in rural water supply is not that great. The long, sad history of hand pumps is proof of this.

6. *Choices, once made, should be respected.* There is a strong sense in rural water development that the experts know what is best. There is therefore a reluctance on the part of the latter to let villagers make "wrong choices." However, if user-choice schemes are to be implemented, it is important to let local decisions stand (within the framework of the project). Thus, if it is agreed that a village committee will collect the fees payable and account for them once a year to the national water body, the local committee should be allowed to decide how often it will collect the money or how to deal with nonpayers. These decisions are best made at the local level and need not conform to some national plan about what is appropriate procedure.

It should also be recognized that improved water may be lower on a village's priority list than other national programs it may have heard of, such as schools, health clinics, and roads. Villagers may therefore be reluctant to invest time and effort in water development when they really want education for their children. This is where extended information and promotion programs are necessary, as well as better coordination among various national rural development programs.

7. *National government attitudes may have to change.* Some national governments view the provision of water as one means of politically legitimizing their development policies and are consequently reluctant to permit the projects to become local rather than national. Other national governments experience reluctance on the part of their own officials to downplay their own expertise in order to encourage and accommodate local decision making.

8. *External agency attitudes may have to change* in cases where local choices appear unpalatable to them (e.g., in the choice of a water source, where a local leader wants the well placed closer to his house; in the selection of the local organization to run the system, which may be undemocratic but nonetheless more acceptable to the villagers than a democratic committee). This is not to say that local choices should always be considered sacrosanct; outside agencies, both national and international, must be prepared to bend a little under some circumstances.

Although the number of successful rural water schemes is much smaller than those that failed or achieved only limited success, they do seem to point to the user-choice approach as a viable alternative. There is also increased evidence that local villagers can make rational choices when alternatives are clearly presented to them, including cost, time constraints, and other factors. Tradeoffs can be recognized, discussed, and decided upon, but it will take time, as will any form of public participation. We may, however, be moving toward a situation requiring more haste and less speed, in our present attitude to rural water development.

User-choice, or local participation, still seems to provide the widest scope for developing more successful water schemes. It is not the final solution to the problem, however. There are still some very real technological obstacles to be overcome. Nor is user-choice a simple matter of everyone in national and international agencies suddenly "seeing the light." It will take time, as well as many other preparatory changes, to work out a new scheme on a large scale—and even then it will not work everywhere. There will still be the usual failures, hopefully fewer in number.

User-choice is therefore neither a panacea nor a palliative. It is an approach that has been tried with some success in various places and has been deemed worthy of incorporation in the expanded international effort for the International Drinking Water Decade.

FOR FURTHER READING

Burton, I. 1977. "Safe Water for All." *Natural Resources Forum* 1: 95–110.

Feachem, R. et al., eds. 1977. *Water, Wastes, and Health in Hot Climates.* New York: John Wiley.

International Institute for Environment and Development. 1977. *Clean Water for All.* Washington, D.C.: IIED.

Maystre, Y. and I. Burton. 1973. *Technology Assessment and Research Priorities for Water Supply and Sanitation in Developing Countries (with special reference to rural populations and small communities).* Ottawa: International Development Research Centre.

Pineo, Charles S. and D. Donaldson. 1976. "Rural Water Supply Problems and Potential Solutions in Latin America." Unpublished manuscript prepared for the United Nations Water Conference, Mar del Plata, 1976.

Saunders, R. J. and J. Warford. 1976. *Village Water Supply: Economics and Policy in the Developing World.* World Bank Publication. Baltimore: Johns Hopkins University Press.

Stein, Jane. 1977. *Water: Life or Death?* Washington, D.C.: International Institute for Environment and Development.

Weiner, A. 1972. *The Role of Water in Development.* New York: McGraw-Hill.

White, G. F. 1974. "Domestic Water: Good or Right?" *Human Rights in Health.* Edited by K. M. Elliot. CIBA Foundation Symposium 23, new series. Amsterdam: Elsevier Excerpta Medica–North Holland Associated Scientific Publishers.

———, et al. 1972. *Drawers of Water—Domestic Water Use in East Africa.* Chicago: University of Chicago Press.

WHO. 1971. *International Standards for Drinking Water.* Expert Committee on International Standards for Drinking Water. Geneva: WHO.

Whyte, A. V. 1976. "Towards a user-choice philosophy in rural water supply programmes." *Carnets de l'enfance*, no. 34. New York: UNICEF, pp. 35–54.

9. It is difficult to measure the impact on human life of a natural disaster: a comfortable suburban home in western Europe is destroyed by a flood; a mud dwelling in India crumbles under the battering of monsoon rains; a nomadic family's whole herd is destroyed during a drought. Who suffers the greatest loss?

As R. W. Kates demonstrates, the ultimate loss—loss of life—impacts unevenly on the developing world. The annual probability of the death of an individual as a result of natural disaster is one in one million in developed countries, one in one hundred thousand in most developing countries, and one in ten thousand in Bangladesh.

The incidence of natural hazards in developed countries is uneven—and not necessarily focused most heavily on the least developed. However, drought is one hazard that has had a greater effect on the least developed than on other developing countries. For example, the 1977 UN Conference on Desertification directed much of its attention to the arid and semiarid LDCs. But the very lack of a resource base and the landlocked position of some countries provide a form of protection (viz. that of poverty) against the impacts of other natural hazards.

Statistics help in defining the problem; a multitude of approaches is necessary to outline solutions. Kates presents a view of qualified optimism. Death rates can be substantially reduced and losses and costs can be lessened or better absorbed. But these changes will demand a different kind of management, a more thoughtful development strategy, and a willingness to plan ahead to meet the threat of disaster in an economy short on manpower. His optimism may be justified. The Sahel drought of the early 1970s has resulted in a unique donor-host international club, *Le Club des Amis du Sahel*. A national symposium on drought and planning for drought was completed in mid-1978 in Botswana—and this while the rains were still good. Despite the continuing problems posed by natural hazards, there is still room for hope and support.

DISASTER REDUCTION: LINKS BETWEEN DISASTER AND DEVELOPMENT

R. W. Kates

To be poor is to be vulnerable to the harmful acts of men and the hazardous events of nature. It is only recently, however, that we could begin to specify the relative vulnerability of poor nations to natural disaster: per capita deaths perhaps a hundred times greater; relative per capita damage perhaps ten times greater than among rich nations. We have yet to assess the heightened vulnerability of the poorest of the poor. As a result of the research effort of the past decade, natural disaster can now be related to development. The global toll of disaster can be estimated, the distinction between the poor and the wealthy can be described, and one can speculate on the differences between the poor and the very poor. Drawing upon the experience of developing and

LDNs, alternative approaches to disaster prevention and mitigation can be suggested. These approaches provide a special opportunity for LDNs within their own capabilities, to improve the lives and ensure the well-being of their peoples.

The Toll of Disaster

Political rhetoric or journalistic impressions to the contrary, there is little social leveling in a natural disaster. Death, the ultimate human loss, is relatively rare; but death comes unequally in the thirty-five or so major disasters that occur each year. The annual probability of the death of an individual as a result of a natural disaster in developed countries is in the range of 10^{-6} (one or more chances in a million per individual per year), 10^{-5} in a developing nation, and 10^{-4} in Bangladesh. But no one really knows the exact frequency of disaster occurrence and the annual toll in lives, material wealth, and productive activities. The outlines of the global, regional, national, and community-loss patterns are just beginning to become evident; there have been some initial efforts at global compilations, some comparisons made among nations and disaster types, and some critical studies of individual disasters and processes.

Global Compilations

Like many other statistics, the global toll of disaster is unknown. The Disaster Research Unit (DRU) of the University of Bradford, in its recent overview of data sources (Baird et al., 1975, p. 23), concluded:

> First, there is no common definition of disaster, no universal scale of disaster measurement and consequently little compatibility between the data. Secondly, there is no accounting for disaster losses except in individual appraisals of a specific disaster situation. Thirdly, most data contains a bias which results from its specific viewpoint on disaster. Fourthly, at the present moment the best data is available from UNDRO (United Nations Disaster Relief Office) and the National Hazard Research Group. The USAID (United States Agency for International Development) provides the most information, but the internal and external consistency of the data is much in question

Some estimates are nevertheless available. Utilizing DRU study data and data of the Natural Hazard Research Group (NHRG) (Dworkin, 1974), table 9.1 compares disaster numbers, type, and region of occurrence. The first two columns represent attempts at total compilation; the remaining estimates are more incomplete, having been compiled from records of selective disaster aid. The discussion that follows relies heavily on NHRG data. In general, the latter appear more complete and consistent for the same time period than those of the United Nations Disaster Relief Office (UNDRO) and, although biased, can be more clearly recognized as such.

TABLE 9.1
GLOBAL DISASTER AND DEATHS: AVAILABLE COMPILATIONS BY NUMBER, TYPE, AND REGION

	Recorded Disasters		Disasters in Which Aid Was Given				Recorded Deaths
	(1)	(2)	(3)	(4)	(5)	(6)	(7)
	Natural Hazard Research Group	UN Disaster Relief Office	League of Red Cross Societies' Major Appeal	Catholic Relief Services	US/AID	UK/ODM	Natural Hazard Research Group
Years of Record	1947–73	1919–71	1961–70	1970–72	1968–71	1974–75 <1 yr.	1947–73
Total	833	251	112	110	104	13	848,815
Per year	31	5	11	55	26	13	27
1968–71 average	28	13	n.a.	n.a.	26	n.a.	n.a.
Disaster Type:							
Flood	269	n.a.	58	51	41	5	182,270
Tropical cyclone	169	n.a.	18	15	24	3	467,508
Earthquake	115	n.a.	19	7	19	1	129,076
Drought and famine	n.a.	n.a.	8	34	18	2	n.a.
Volcano	13	n.a.	3	3	–	–	7,220
Epidemic	n.a.	n.a.	6	–	2	–	n.a.
Other	267	n.a.	–	–	–	2	62,741
Region of Occurrence:							
Asia	⌐325	89	46	⌐45	32	⌐5	⌐706,566
Middle East	23	38	20		5		
Africa	–	33	22	31	19	6	18,994
Americas:		42	11	–	41	1	–
U.S./Canada	287	–	–	–	–	–	9,177
Latin America	121	–	–	31	–	–	88,963
Europe	102	49	13	3	7	1	20,698
Australia	13	–	–	–	–	–	4,417

SOURCES: Columns 1 and 7: J. Dworkin. 1974. Natural Hazard Working Paper, no. 26.
Columns 2–6: A. Baird et al. 1975. Disaster Research Unit Occasional Paper, no. 10.

In both this NHRG compilation and its earlier version (Hewitt and Sheehan, 1969), disasters are defined operationally as encompassing all geophysical natural events (with the exception of drought), causing at least one million dollars in damages or one hundred dead or injured. Sources include standard English-language international newspapers and reference works. The period chosen, 1947–73, is designed to cover only the phase of modern, post–World War II expanded communication. The compilation suffers from biases of definition; underrepresentation of northern Europe, Africa, the USSR, and China; overrepresentation of the United States; and from the omission of drought in order to avoid the obvious underreporting of occurrences and confusion over drought timing and territorial extent.

This latter omission further limits the usefulness of data for LDNs since they now appear to be especially drought-prone. Despite the difficulty involved in obtaining comparable data, a survey of drought references in the *New York Times* was completed for the years 1950–75. On the average, 9.23 droughts are described each year. Of these, about a third have been judged roughly comparable in damage or deaths to the criteria of the original compilation.

The trends in these data (excluding drought) are shown in figure 9.1. Over a twenty-seven-year period, the average number of disasters has remained relatively constant (about thirty per year) or, if anything, has declined somewhat. At the same time, death rates have been climbing significantly— admittedly distorted somewhat by the occurrence of the largest single disaster of the century, the Bangladesh cyclone of 1970. The areal extent of disaster, measured by the increase in the number of large-area disasters, also appears to have grown significantly.

If the number of disasters and their resulting deaths are sketchy at best, estimates of the global losses of material wealth and productive activity, as well as the costs of disaster aid or prevention, are nonexistent. With the organization of UNDRO in 1972, better compilations may be forthcoming. But these will always be approximations at best because of the distortions inherent in arriving at damage estimates.

Postdisaster estimates are usually overestimates, often by a factor of two. Such early uncorrected damage estimates for catastrophic disasters tend to find their way into international records, while small losses resulting from recurrent, localized disasters are undercounted. The absurdities of national accounting practices often turn postdisaster aid or reconstruction costs into positive gains of GNP; these may be further increased by disaster-induced inflation. Disaster-prevention costs are buried in governmental budgets or are unknown for nongovernmental production units. Moreover, many long-term social costs are never accounted for. They are concealed or go unrecognized in the "average" statistics. All of the foregoing are unintentional distortions. One must add to this list many intentional distortions. The politics of disaster can either lead to excessive claims or to a denial of losses. Nonetheless, by using the scattered estimates detailed in the next section as guide, it is

FIGURE 9.1

Global Disasters 1947-73

Five-year moving average

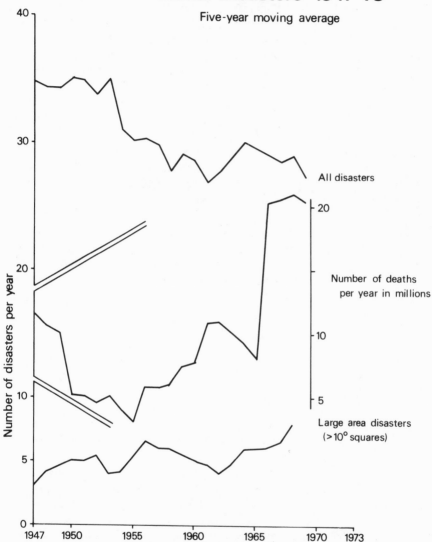

Source: J. Dworkin. Global Trends in Natural Disasters, 1974-73.
Boulder: Univ. of Colorado, Institute of Behavioral Science, 1974
NHRWP. No. 26.

possible to make an educated guess as to global losses and the cost of prevention.

Natural hazards tax the global economy by perhaps $40 billion a year, $25 billion of which is in damage losses and the remainder in the costs of prevention and mitigation. Of the $25 billion, perhaps $10 to $15 billion in damages is the result of disasters and large catastrophic losses, bringing the average disaster loss to $350 to $500 million. Similarly, the annual death toll stemming from natural hazards might be estimated at around 250,000 deaths, about half of which occur during major disasters.

Hazard Types

Interpreting the data contained in table 9.1 rather freely, one can say that roughly 90 percent of the world's disasters are due to four hazard types: floods (40 percent), tropical cyclones (20 percent), earthquakes (15 percent), and drought (15 percent). Earthquakes are generally overestimated because of the ease of their detection; conversely, drought is usually underestimated because of difficulties in its definition, timing, siting, and in distinguishing drought impacts from perennial seasonal hunger or malnutrition. The proportion of deaths resulting from floods and tropical cyclones is probably reversed: floods are more frequent and do greater damage; tropical cyclones are more deadly.

Regional and National Losses

From the deaths recorded in table 9.1, it can be safely inferred that even though developing countries account for only two-thirds of the world's population, they experience 95 percent of disaster-related deaths. The vulnerability of developing countries to death resulting from disaster is not uniform, however. For example, data on death rates and national income (table 9.2) suggest that for the more acute and intensive hazards, death rates were highest among less poor, less-developed countries.

The figures are distorted due to the exclusion of drought, which affects LDCs to a greater extent. Indeed, the number of drought reports emanating from LDCs has increased considerably (fig. 9.2). Recent work on desertification suggests that a greater vulnerability exists among LDNs (Kates et al., 1976). Nevertheless, nations more vulnerable to natural hazards are probably not the poorest; they are found in the middle range of developing countries. LDNs have the means to prevent higher death rates accompanying a growth in per capita wealth, as the concluding section of this chapter will demonstrate.

In contrast to the exceptional regional differences in death rates, losses resulting from natural disasters are more proportional to global income distribution. Perhaps three-fourths of all global hazard losses occur in wealthy countries, although the proportional burden of losses is much higher in developing countries. NHRG has compiled careful estimates of losses for

TABLE 9.2
COMPARATIVE DEATH RATES RESULTING FROM NATURAL
DISASTERS (EXCLUDING DROUGHT) CLASSIFIED ACCORDING
TO NATIONAL INCOME

Annual Death Rate (Per Million Pop.)	Per Capita National Incomes		Industrial ($1,000)	Total
	Least Developed (< $200)	Less Developed ($200–$1,000)		
High > 200	2	14	1	17
Moderate and Low < 200	10	24	19	53
Total	12	38	20	70

three major natural hazards—drought, flood, and tropical cyclone—and has compared the costs and losses for each in one industrial and one developing country. The results are shown in table 9.3. Two of the three developing countries are among the poorest nations; in all three, per capita losses are about twenty times greater than among industrial nations.

Another useful estimate is also available for the total cost of fifteen geophysical hazards in the United States. Annual damage losses represent about $230 per capita, or about 0.5 percent of the GNP; added to this figure are the costs of adjustment for damage reduction and prevention equal to about half the damage (White and Haas, 1975). Extrapolating liberally from these scattered estimates, geophysical hazard-damage losses and costs of loss

FIGURE 9.2

Drought Frequency in Least Developed Countries as Proportion of Total Reported Droughts, 1950-76

Five Year Running Average
(United Nations Definition of L.D.C.)

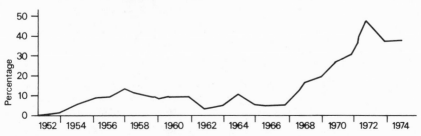

TABLE 9.3
SELECTED ESTIMATES OF NATURAL HAZARD LOSSES

Hazard	Country	Total Pop.	Pop. at Risk	Annual Death Rate per Million at Risk	Damages Losses	Costs of Loss Reduction	Total Costs	Total Costs as % of GNP
					Losses and Costs Per Capita at Risk			
Drought	Tanzania	13	12	40	$ .70	$ .80	$ 1.50	1.84
	Australia	13	1	0	24.00	19.00	43.00	0.10
Flood	Sri Lanka	13	3	5	13.40	1.60	15.00	2.13
	United States	207	25	2	40.00	8.00	48.00	0.11
Tropical Cyclone	Bangladesh	72	10	3,000	3.00	.40	3.40	0.73
	United States	207	30	2	13.30	1.20	14.50	0.04

reduction and prevention can be estimated as the following percentage of the GNP: Europe, 0.5 percent; North America, 0.75 percent; Central and South America and the Middle East, 2 percent; Africa, 2.5 percent; and Asia, 3 percent. These extrapolations are the basis for the summary estimate of global losses in the previous section.

National Experience Among Developing Countries

A collaborative effort undertaken by the Commission on Man and the Environment of the International Geographical Union provides an opportunity (White, 1974a; Burton et al., 1978) to examine in detail individual developing nations' experience with four major hazards: drought in Tanzania; floods in Sri Lanka; tropical cyclones in Bangladesh; and earthquakes in Managua. One of these countries, Tanzania, is counted among the LDNs. Another, Bangladesh, is already among the poorest, although its large population set it apart from the original group of LDNs. The experience of all four nations is relevant in identifying various ways (some, perhaps, to be avoided) of coping with disaster.

Drought in Tanzania

One of the least developed African nations, Tanzania is the home of thirteen million people, 90 percent of whom live off the land. Maize, cassava, bananas, and cattle are major food sources; cotton, coffee, and sisal are exports. Most of the country is semiarid. Extending ten degrees south of the equator, encompassing the snows of Kilimanjaro and the warm shores of the Indian Ocean, the rainfall pattern is complex. Rain falls in distinct, single wet seasons and in multiple wet seasons of both "short" and "long" rains.

In a country as large as Tanzania, drought occurs somewhere two out of every three years; one year in five, upward of half the country may be affected; one year in ten, an event with famine potential is experienced. During such years—for example, 1964–65—as many as a million households were affected. Nationally, crop and animal production declined 8 percent; the GNP fell 3 percent. Over a recent twenty-five-year period, such recurrent losses were estimated to average annually 0.75 percent of the GNP.

In addition to losses of production, there is the problem of malnutrition, the latter accentuating the vulnerability of the very young, who already experience death rates of from 30 to 40 percent. Beyond physiological effects, there are the social-psychic stresses of famine, loss of livestock and savings, and the ultimate grief of premature death of family members.

That the losses incurred are not greater is due to continuous efforts to reduce the disaster potential of drought, an adjustment falling, in the main, on the farm family. The overall list of adjustments is a long one, attesting to the adaptive qualities of the culture. The most common adjustments are prayer, planting in seasonal flood plains, planting drought-resistant cassava, and buying food. Equating these costs of adjustment to labor equivalents, such labor is valued at $7 million annually. To this figure should be added the $2.5 million for governmental efforts in meteorological, climatological, and crop-varietal research; weather modification, irrigation, and rural water-supply development; and famine relief, food imports, and provision for migrants. Combined with losses, the average annual social cost of drought in Tanzania is about $18 million, or 1.8 percent of the GNP.

Unfortunately, the short-term prognosis for Tanzania is for increasing social costs. The "Uhuru" decade following independence in 1961 was rather wet. More arid decades have occurred in the past and will recur in the future. The monetary cost, at least, of each incidence of drought is increasing as a result of the growing reliance on marketed grains, emphasis on export crops, popular expectation of aid, and the poor location of commercial grain areas.

Major long-term opportunities to reduce the national cost of drought include: development and adoption of drought-resistant crops; improved drought-related husbandry in socialist farm organization; climatologically sensible regional specialization; more rational collective use of grazing lands; and better policies of storage, pricing imports, and marketing of food grains.

Flood in Sri Lanka

The island of Sri Lanka is the home of twelve million people, a fourth of whom are exposed to recurrent flood hazard both in rural flood plains and city river fronts. Floods are essential to the rice cultivators of the lower flood plains, located in the wet western section of the island; they are a mixed blessing for the upstream farmers; and they represent a threat to the irrigation works of the farmers of the dry eastern section. It is significant that the most highly built-up sections of the capital at Colombo and other major urban centers are located in flood plains.

Up until the nineteenth century, urban flood-plain dwellers shunned the more hazardous flood plains. Farmers adapted to occasional inundations by means of a wide variety of practices, including raised house construction, a considerable number of which were capable of withstanding inundation, and many small but appropriate emergency actions. Such adjustments continue into the present. Added to these are extensive programs of engineering works: levee construction, channel improvement, and dam building were all begun in the nineteenth century.

These practices have been of mixed value, offering protection against the floods they were designed to curb, yet increasing the degree of vulnerability to catastrophes. When the levees are overtopped, they trap the water in the fields, thereby increasing losses; when they break, the losses are excessive. Their protective value has been further complicated by a significant increase in population in the hazardous areas they were designed to protect, a build-up of sediment in channels, and an apparent increase in flood frequency (related to upstream deforestation for plantations and downstream constriction of flood channels).

Assessing the costs of engineering works, household adjustments, flood prevention and warning, crop insurance, and residual losses, the annual toll of flood damage in Sri Lanka is exceedingly high, roughly equal to 2.5 percent of the GNP, or $45 million annually (Hewapathirane, 1975). The prognosis is for continued high losses. While there is a growing realization that the heavy reliance on engineering works is resulting in greater losses (despite the protection afforded to some areas), the emphasis still seems to be on the construction of additional works.

Tropical Cyclone in Bangladesh

In Bangladesh, one of the most densely populated countries in the world, ten to fifteen million people are exposed to recurrent tropical cyclones in the Bay of Bengal. The shore, especially the delta of the Ganges-Brahmaputra, consists of a series of shifting islands (*chars*) worked and reworked by the deposits of silt and sediment of the great rivers. Many of the *chars* are quite fertile. Major efforts at land reclamation have made some habitable by means of cross-dams, which reclaim old river-beds separating the *chars*.

The threat of hunger in this densely populated land has forced farmers to expand outward to marginal shore areas and lands unsettled sixty years ago. Even with crop shares of one-half to one-third paid to absentee landlords, the fertile land and the opportunity to fish have encouraged settlement. This has heightened the vulnerability of millions, including the landless laborers who come to the shore at harvest time.

Such was the setting for the greatest natural tragedy of our century, the cyclone of November 12–13, 1970, in which upward of three hundred thousand persons died, mostly young, old, and migrant laborers without shelter. The storm, although massive, was not truly exceptional; a more severe event had occurred in 1876. But it proved greater than the adaptive measures of the farmers—raised platforms for their homes, tied-down roofs, and shelter belts of trees—could accommodate (Islam, 1970). It also proved stronger than the adjustments recommended by the national government: shore works, cross-dams, tree plantings along embankments, and a warning service. The protective works were breached by water up to eight meters high, the tree plantings were washed away, and the warnings, while timely, were ineffective because the social organization required to relay and respond to them was lacking.

Indeed, one can question how "natural" this natural event was. Protective works ordered in Karachi, designed in Holland, and financed in Washington, D.C., encouraged hungry people to settle in highly hazardous areas. Effective warnings (in a recently changed format) went out to a shut-down radio station, a radioless population, through a corrupt and moribund bureaucracy, to a populace ill prepared by culture and experience to respond. Some of these factors have now been improved, but the basic peril still remains. Other great tragedies are bound to occur.

Earthquake in Nicaragua

Nicaragua, a nation inhabited by two million people, is located along the circum-Pacific ring of fire, the belt of seismic and tectonic activity that parallels the Pacific rim. Its capital city, Managua, has been hit by earthquakes four times during the last century.

The 1931 earthquake struck a city of 45,000 inhabitants, killed 1,000–2,000, left 35,000 homeless, with damages totaling $15 million (1931 values). The 1972 earthquake struck a city of 405,000 residents, killing 4,000–6,000, injuring 20,000, and leaving 70 percent homeless. Damages totaled between $400 million and $600 million.

In the forty-year interim, time had increased the population and property at risk. Some structures (at least six) were built according to the specifications of the California seismic code. A law providing for an improved code for major structures was passed in 1970, but it apparently was never enforced. Upper-income housing was insured because of mortgage-loan requirements, but housing for the poor and the working classes had no such protection. No disaster-preparedness organization was then in existence; indeed, the self-help efforts of a family-oriented culture rescued victims and evacuated the populace.

The prognosis for the future is for greater loss of life and an increase in damages within the lifetimes of the recent victims. This will occur despite progress already made in efforts to rebuild existing structures and decentralize critical facilities. The dense human settlement in the circum-Pacific ring suggests that the locational advantages of settlement outweigh the seismic risk. But for any given location, the burden to society may be excessive. Long after any initial advantage, the city's infrastructure, daily activity, and residents' loyalty create an inertia difficult to change. When the city in question is a primate city of a developing nation, which further exaggerates growth, the disaster potential is enhanced.

To conclude this review, the global toll of natural disaster rises at least as fast as the increase in population and material wealth (probably faster). Each year the population equivalent of a modest-sized city perishes in a disaster. Material losses exceed the per capita development gains of many nations. Among industrial nations, disasters may be less frequent, but they are more catastrophic. They are more costly in terms of lives and relative wealth among developing countries, and increasingly costly in terms of absolute wealth. LDNs appear to suffer less from the impact of intensive hazards of earthquake, cyclone, and flood than developing nations. At the same time, some evidence suggests that LDNs are proportionately more vulnerable to drought and desertification.

These apparent differentials may simply be a function of the least developed–least known syndrome, an artifact of how information is collected and reported upon in an unequal world. But there are theoretical bases for linking development and disaster vulnerability, some of which will be explored next.

Differential Vulnerability to Disaster

Varied explanations exist for the course of disaster (Burton et al., 1978). One in particular relates differential and rising vulnerability to disaster to "marginalization" theory (Baird et al., 1975), which is the hazard derivative of the general theory of underdevelopment (see Szentes, chap. 3).

In a view that I share with I. Burton and G. F. White, differential vulnerability arises from the interactions of nature, society, and technology. This interactive theory attempts to explain the differential vulnerability between rich and poor in the world, the relatively greater vulnerability of the less poor, and the paths of development that the poorest might still seek to avoid.

An Interactive Explanation

Nature is neutral; the extreme events of nature become hazardous only when they intersect the lives and livelihood of people. They become disastrous when the events are very extreme, the population very great, or the livelihood system particularly vulnerable. The intersection of nature and humankind is neither necessarily fortuitous nor foolhardy, for people encounter hazard in the search for the useful. The ideal places to inhabit are the ideal places for landslide, flood, hurricane, earthquake, and drought—places where narrow valleys provide gaps in mountain massives, where hilltops offer views for protection or pleasure, where hill slopes give way to rich valley plains, where mountain and marsh meet the sea, or where grassy plains enable large mammals to thrive.

Coping with Nature

Thus, it is not surprising to find that human beings persist, or even prosper, in areas of considerable and recurrent natural hazard. There are many ways in which humankind copes with the extreme events of nature. Four major modes of response are discernable. The first mode is *absorption*, whereby human beings and societies develop so as to be able to absorb significant extremes of natural events with little or no harmful effects. The mechanisms of absorption are (1) biological, exemplified by adaptation to high altitudes or extreme cold; (2) cultural, exemplified by nomadism as an adaptation to a scarce resource endowment; and (3) incidental, where technical or social practices act to reduce societal vulnerability incidental to some other function. For example, the preference for housing utilizing wood reduces earthquake vulnerability. Because it is deeply ingrained in the structure of everyday life, the measurement of absorption capacity is difficult. Figure 9.3, an interpretive graph of the relative global coping effort, suggests this ambiguity by means of broken bars.

The most common mode of coping is *acceptance*, whereby individuals and societies bear their losses of life and property when they occur or sometimes share them with kith and kin; organized insurance or community, national,

FIGURE 9.3

Modes of Coping

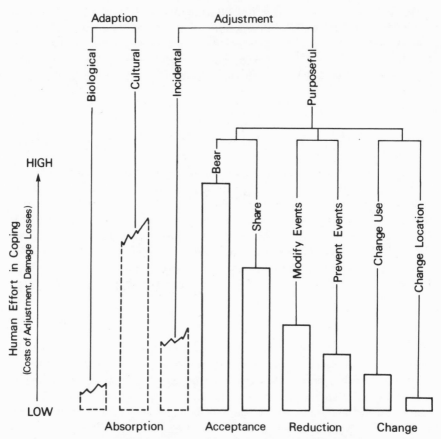

Source: Ian Burton, Robert W. Kates, and Gilbert F. White. The Environment As Hazard. New York: Oxford University Press, 1978, p. 205.

and international relief is usual. Somewhat less common, but also widespread, is *reduction*, where the consequences of extreme natural events are reduced by means of adjustments designed to either modify or prevent the natural event or to diminish the damage potential. Finally, much more rarely utilized is *change*, a radical coping mode that involves fundamental change either in livelihood systems, location, or both.

Generally speaking, more people bear rather than share and accept rather than reduce losses. Of those who seek to reduce losses, the majority try to modify or prevent the natural events from occurring than to make society less vulnerable to consequences. Fewer still change their livelihood technique or land use. Only relatively few move permanently. Specific coping efforts do not differ greatly from this overall pattern. But there is order in such differences, order in the relation between the hazard being dealt with and the technological capacity and social organization of society, and to the change society is undergoing.

Coping as Determined by Hazard

Consider the intrinsic differences among the four major world hazards—flood, cyclone, earthquake and drought—ranked not by their consequences but on a continuum of physical characteristics. At opposite ends of such a continuum are drought and earthquake. Drought is a *pervasive* phenomenon; it occurs frequently, extends over large areas for durations of time measured in months and years, and is relatively low in energy impact per unit of area. Earthquakes are *intensive* phenomena; they are rare, highly localized, with durations measured in seconds yet with energies in multiples of atomic warheads. Between these extremes, floods and tropical cyclones exhibit multiple characteristics. The great deltaic floods rise slowly and cover areas at low velocity; the high mountain floods have a localized impact, exhibit high velocity, and are of short duration. Tropical cyclones also are of two types: those that affect the narrow coastal strip, with high-energy winds and massive rain and storm surge, and those that strike the interior areas, subjecting them to heavy inland flooding from cyclone-induced precipitation.

These differences in natural characteristics of extreme events encourage or constrain certain modes of coping. Pervasive hazards lead to an increase in absorptive capacity. The high frequency of occurrence encourages the development of cultural adaptations. The relatively low energy levels involved enable all societies to develop both technological and behavioral adjustments. By contrast, the characteristics of intensive hazards—their rarity, high energy, short duration, and low predictability—discourage multiple coping strategies and commonly lead either to acceptance by bearing and sharing losses or to limited reduction through the use of high technology.

Coping by Means of Technosocial Organization

Just as nature constrains modes of coping, so do the wealth, technological capacity, and social organization of society. Consider the preferred modes of coping for four archetypal societies: folk societies, industrial societies, mixed societies of many developing countries, and evolving postindustrial societies.

Coping in a folk society is characterized by a high absorptive capacity and a large number of adjustments widely shared among individuals and communities. These often involve modifications in behavior or agricultural practices to harmonize with nature rather than harness it. The adjustments are usually low in per capita cost and may often be supplemented in small increments, although the aggregate expenditure by any one person may represent a substantial share of that person's efforts. To this extent, adjustments are flexible and easily increased or reduced in scale. They are closely related to social customs and are supported by norms of behavior and community sanctions. Total technological and capital requirements are generally low.

While this coping pattern requires cooperative action by community or local groups, it does not depend on outside assistance either in the form of technical knowledge, financial assistance, or legal approval. The pattern may vary drastically over short geographical distances, depending upon local differences in hazard severity or cultural practices. Although it is effective in preventing property losses and loss of life from low-magnitude hazard events, the folk pattern is ineffectual in preventing major disasters. When such events occur, government or social organization may have to intervene if a major disaster or wholesale migration is to be averted.

In the modern industrial state, a different pattern emerges. Acceptance shifts from bearing losses or sharing with kin to sharing with the wider society by means of relief or insurance. The technological capacity to manipulate or manage the environment grows and points to the reduction of hazard by emphasizing the control of nature. These favored adjustments require an interlocking and interdependent social organization. They tend to be uniform in application, inflexible, and difficult to change. The construction of dams, major irrigation projects, seawalls, and the design of monitoring, forecasting, and warning systems utilizing complex equipment are clearly beyond the scope of individual action.

All developing countries consist of major segments of the economy and society that are still folk societies and other segments that are well connected to the commercial world economy. In such mixed societies, a displacement of the more traditional, individual, and community adjustments can be observed. National governments attempt to pick up the slack through limited resources of funds and skilled manpower. The more effectively they are able to fill the gap, the more rapidly the traditional coping modes are likely to atrophy. Moreover, indigenous absorptive capacity is highly vulnerable to the stresses of change so characteristic of a mixed society.

The modes of coping in a postindustrial society are slowly evolving with the evolution of the society itself. There is a marked shift to a broader pattern of coping, a turning away from reliance on the control or modification of nature and toward a lowering of damage potential and concern for the effects of disaster policies on the general populace.

Effect of Technosocial Change

For each of the archetypal technosocial types, nature, technology, and society interact to provide a level of hazard absorption and disaster vulnerability. Nevertheless, an explanation of increasing disaster vulnerability must be related to processes of change.

It is tempting but misleading to view the four types as stages of development. In actuality, such a progression seems to be one of the least likely future global developments. Descriptive stages do not necessarily illuminate a process. However, there seems to be general agreement regarding major historical processes of development.

Common to almost all models of societal change is a focus on unidirectional development, with an explicit or implicit assumption of continued growth. Economies of increasing scale and specialization replace simple structures, and there is an increasingly complex hierarchical integration of function. Growth in economic activity is accompanied by political stability— or attempts to impose it—yet it also seems to involve a decline in the integrative social bonds of family and community life.

Growth, increased scale, greater differentiation, and hierarchical integration appear as common descriptors for the development process. Their impact, however, is in dispute. Specialization may be viewed as leading to increased skills or to the pauperization of the labor force. Hierarchical integration can foster organization, imperialism, or supranational cooperation. New social relationships can find expression in greater personal freedom or alienation.

To describe development in these terms is to make it neither inevitable nor desirable. A growing awareness of the negative implications of growth has encouraged efforts to sever the intimate relationship between growth and development. The potential for destruction of human values or for catastrophic error in large systems spurs interest in less-specialized, decentralized forms. Hierarchical integration is feared because it often leads to the dependency and pauperization of the newly integrated, not to development but to underdevelopment.

Without claiming the desirability of the type of development just described, these structural features of development, despite their deficiencies, do describe historical experience and suggest the dynamic process within which hazard adjustment takes place. As societies move along paths involving enlargement of scale, differentiation of function, and hierarchical integration, their adjustment to hazard changes.

Such changes are shown in fig. 9.4. The number and importance of cultural adaptations and incidental adjustments diminish as folk societies (fig. 9.4A) mix with industrial societies. The absorptive capacity of the society to prevent loss is lessened (fig. 9.4B) as new livelihood systems are introduced. As these come into being, the appropriate skills of hazard coping are gradually acquired. How to cope with extreme events in new settings or new livelihoods is a form of knowledge that is acquired relatively late.

FIGURE 9.4

Modes of Coping by Societal Type

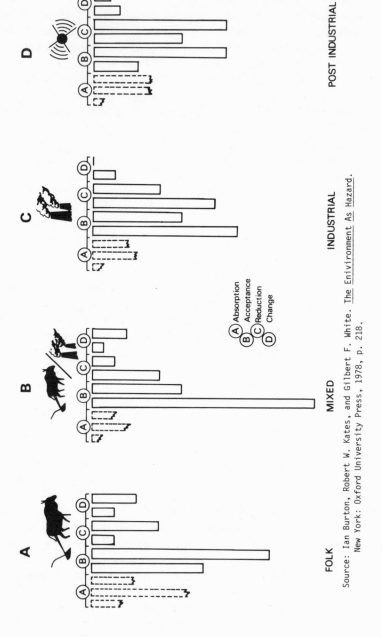

FOLK   MIXED   INDUSTRIAL   POST INDUSTRIAL

(A) Absorption
(B) Acceptance
(C) Reduction
(D) Change

Source: Ian Burton, Robert W. Kates, and Gilbert F. White. The Enivironment As Hazard.
New York: Oxford University Press, 1978, p. 218.

In the process of change, advantages of specialization and enlarged scale lag behind disadvantages. Increased specialization of function diminishes the general pool of coping wisdom; what remains is less applicable. The new specialties needed for hazard coping are developed late because the rarity of extreme events discourages their rapid development in all but the most hazardous sites. While there is opportunity in mixed societies for increased attention to purposeful adjustments, greater technical resources, and specialized manpower and institutions, the ability to organize greater resources may be vitiated by economic failure or political instability. The survival tactics of folk societies may atrophy in the interim.

As development continues and the efficacy of purposeful adjustments is demonstrated, increasing specialization is reflected in the narrowing of adjustments to a few manageable technological alternatives (fig. 9.4C). Irrigation becomes a dominant response to agricultural drought; dams and levees to floods; building construction to hurricanes and earthquakes.

In a static world, these adjustments might lead to a reduction in loss of life and damage. Yet in the dynamics of development, the growth in material wealth capable of destruction may outdistance the pace of adjustment. The increase in scale may favor hazardous coastal and flood-plain locations easily accessible to transportation. Separation of home and work sites for many people will diminish their knowledge of the vulnerability of both sites. Greater specialization and hierarchical integration may increase hazard vulnerability for some hazards and decrease it for others. Time, success with technological solutions in modifying events, and an increase in the institutional capability to reduce loss of life again enlarge the absorptive capacity of society. But this merely serves to reduce the average consequences of hazard while increasing vulnerability to catastrophe.

If the resulting losses to society exceed its tolerance for average or catastrophic disruption, radical changes in use or location will occur: coastal hurricane zones will be evacuated permanently; citrus growers will convert to a less risky crop. As the disruptive impact of extreme events becomes more acute, postindustrial societies employ a broader range of adjustments in their modes of coping (fig. 9.4D) or make basic changes in use and location. In so doing, they seem to rediscover the advantages of diversity and flexibility inherent in folk society.

Differential Vulnerability of the Least Developed

Based on the foregoing theoretical explanation, one can arrive at the following account of differential vulnerability. The least developed are less hazard prone than other developing countries because they have less of a resource base. Being landlocked, many LDNs are remote from the coastal locations of cyclone or earthquake; being arid, they are less prone to large riverine floods. They are, however, more vulnerable to the pervasive hazards of drought and desertification. To cope with these hazards, they possess a greater absorptive capacity.

The mixed societal archetype tends to dominate the economy and social organization of all developing countries. This causes the rapid atrophying of a country's absorptive capacity to cope with hazard and a concomitant increase in both damage and loss of life. Such a path is not inevitable, but developed nations have time to learn from the experience of others and to weigh alternatives for the prevention of disaster.

The Prevention of Disaster

Disaster can be partially absorbed, shared, reduced, or changed in impact, but it cannot be eliminated. Despite the widespread use of disaster prevention as a summary phrase for predisaster activity, disaster really cannot be prevented. Indeed, some preventive measures seem to increase its catastrophic potential.

However, the enormous toll can be substantially reduced and the absorptive capacity of the society can be increased. This has clearly occurred, or is occurring, among industrial nations. Loss of life has been substantially reduced and ways are being found to broaden the base of hazard-adjustment activity sufficiently to reduce the damage potential.

Can this happen in developing countries, particularly among the poorest of the poor? The answer—as with so many questions concerning development—must be a qualified one. Disaster death tolls in developing countries can be dramatically reduced, perhaps by as much as 70 percent, over the next two decades. Losses and costs can also be reduced, thereby yielding annual savings equal to increase of perhaps 1 percent in real GNP. Paradoxically, such gains cannot be achieved by emulating either the development or the disaster-reduction activity of wealthy industrial nations.

Disaster prevention and mitigation has historically lagged behind more common aspects of development. Thus, many industrial nations are peculiarly vulnerable to disaster in ways developing nations can avoid. It is naive to imagine that developing nations, particularly the poorest, will be able to (or will want to) pass through the same stages of the historical process. Increased security against major disasters can and should be a national goal for every nation. It does not require the achievement of a high level of income, education, or industrialization; it does, however, require sensitive inquiry, a special effort, and the development of alternative approaches to hazard reduction and change.

A substantial number of studies, reports, and guides providing insight, expertise, and encouragement in the field of disaster reduction among developing countries are presently available or in press (see chap. 7 of Burton et al., 1978). These materials should be consulted when giving or accepting advice and in the planning and implementation of programs.

Four cardinal principles underlying an alternative program can be succinctly stated and illustrated based on current experience, much of it drawn from among the poorest countries. These principles include: (1) the links between disaster and development; (2) a system for predisaster planning and policy; (3) the study and analysis of the absorptive capacity of a society; and (4) the issue of who pays and who suffers in a disaster.

Links between Disaster and Development

People encounter hazard in the search for useful resources. Development can both increase and decrease catastrophic disaster potential. In turn, disaster can divert needed resources from development or provide new opportunities for development. Development plans, therefore, need to be assessed in terms of their dual impacts; both the opportunity and danger of disaster should be considered.

As development leads to growth, enlargement of scale, specialization, hierarchical integration, and distant dependencies, it enlarges the catastrophic potential of disaster. But some forms of growth, enlargement of scale, and specialization also increase a country's capacity to deal with disaster. Take, for example, the case of the Chinese commune. Major progress in the area of reducing fear of natural hazards has taken place in the People's Republic of China. Serious cases of famine—the usual outcome of a long history of floods and drought—have thus far been successfully averted. Underlying major efforts in coping with drought, floods, and soil erosion are the collective actions of some seventy thousand communes in which over one hundred million families live and work.

The Liu Ling People's Commune, an Enlargement of Scale

Jan Myrdal, in what is now a classic report, illustrated these achievements through the words of the members of the Liu Ling People's Commune, who live among the loess hills, west of the River Nan, due south of Yenan, in northern Shensi. It is a difficult country; the loessial soil is capable of high yield with adequate water, but rainfall is marginal and the cold season is long; drought, frost, hail, and erosion are continuous hazards. Myrdal (1963, p. 443) quotes the young secretary of the commune:

> We have striven to overcome nature's catastrophes and achieve record crops. We have had great results in our efforts to expand the collective economy, and we have carried out comprehensive water-regulation works. The people's commune is now an entrepreneur, carries out afforestation and herds cattle.
>
> We have also carried out big water-regulating works. At the end of 1957, we had only 30 mu of irrigated land. Since then we have built 5 dams, 3 canals and 400 mu of terraced fields, and in 1962 the total irrigated land amounted to 8,320 mu. We have been continuing with this work all the time.

The scale of the commune itself is not large enough for some of the undertakings. Myrdal cites (p. 454) the young secretary's explanation of how labor can be used as a medium of exchange:

Larger undertakings, such as water-regulation works, etc., have to be carried out by several labour brigades collaborating. The work is then managed by a work committee which has its office at the site. The chairman of the committee is always the chairman of the management committee of the commune, while the deputy chairman, who is the one who must always be present at the site, as well as the different labour leaders, are chosen by the labour brigades. Before work begins, the size of each participating brigade's share in the result of the work is fixed. That is, how much of the advantage from the work is for their benefit. In 1958, three labour brigades, Liu Ling Labour Brigade, Kaupo Labour Brigade and Chung chuan Labour Brigade, jointly built the Kaochinko dam. Liu Ling invested 1,900 days' work; Kaupo 1,100; and Chung chuan 890.

As Liu Ling Labour Brigade benefited most by the dam, it transpired at the settling up that Liu Ling Labour Brigade owed the other two labour brigades a total of 494 days' work: 394 to Kaupo Labour Brigade and 100 to Chung chuan Labour Brigade. Liu Ling Labour Brigade repaid this by helping in terracing the fields of the other two labour brigades.

The Chinese word for crisis is composed of the symbols for danger and opportunity. There are questions as to how relevant the remarkable Chinese experience in disaster reduction is for other developing countries, particularly the poorest. The opportunity and danger of crisis are currently at work in the impressive and exceptional disaster-relief efforts by the small Somali nation.

Drought in Somalia, an Ironic Opportunity

Lewis (1975, p. 1) and his colleagues describe the situation as follows:

It is a bitter irony of fate that the worst drought in living memory in Somalia should coincide with the inauguration of the most ambitious development campaign ever conceived for the Somali nomads. Following its successful urban literacy drive and as part of the new Five Year Plan (1974–1978), in August 1974 the government of the Somali Democratic Republic launched a similar, carefully prepared campaign amongst the nomads. Intermediate and secondary schools in the urban centres throughout the country were closed, releasing over 30,000 students and teachers for the campaign. With a budgetary provision of over £10 million, this huge task-force poured into the interior in triumphant truck loads. Organized in companies of eight with a teacher as leader, and assisted by visiting veterinary and medical personnel, these young pioneers of the new Somalia were to teach the nomads the official roman alphabet for Somali, basic civics, hygiene and modern techniques of animal husbandry. Equipped with blankets, a folding blackboard, a water-bottle, and drawing a daily allowance of 2 Somali shillings (approximately 14 new English pence), these privileged urban students were to share the fruits of their learning with their neglected nomadic kinsmen, attaching themselves as guests to nomadic family groups and repaying their hospitality by giving free lessons.

The vicious drought that now grips Somalia, the culmination of four successive years of poor rains, has drastically altered the character of this far-reaching project. What was originally optimistically named the Rural Prosperity Campaign has become a desperate famine relief operation. In over half the land areas of the Republic, the personnel of the campaign are now busy organizing the rapidly expanding relief camps which are being set up in the worst affected regions of Nugal, Sanag (Erigavo), Togdher (Burao) and Bari (Bosasso). Refugees in the camps are already reported to number 200,000 and are expected to reach twice this figure by the end of March 1975. These are reported to consist mainly of women and children—those who in the traditional nomadic economy move with the sheep, goats and cattle, while the grazing camels, or at least those still surviving, are with the menfolk desperately seeking pasture often far from the camps and in regions where they are increasingly dependent on hastily mobilised government transport for supplies of water. If the human death toll appears so far to have been mercifully small (although there is no guarantee that this will continue to be so), large numbers of livestock have already perished and the death rate will inevitably accelerate as arid conditions spread and intensify. Unless the 1975 spring rains, due in April and May, are unusually early and prolonged, there may be by then almost half a million nomads destitute in the camps.

Famine on this scale has drastic consequences for the entire population of Somalia. Unlike so many other countries where nomads form only a small minority, in the Somali Democratic Republic they represent more than three quarters of the estimated national population of 3–4 millions. Livestock and livestock products, moreover, provide not only the backbone of the domestic economy but also the largest single component in Somalia's exports.

Lewis next describes the vigorous way the government moved to set up relief camps and to use the opportunity of having brought together large concentrations of nomadic people:

> Each camp is being run by a committee, chaired by a teacher (from the Rural Development Campaign), with a health official, national security services agent, and three other members elected from among the people in the camp. Radio transmitters are being installed and, in addition to the educational services originally envisaged under the Rural Development Campaign programme, camp activities include work on range-land conservation (bunding), and where appropriate, dam-building and road construction. A brave attempt is thus being made to rescue as much as possible of the Rural Development Campaign and to turn adversity to advantage.

He then details medium- and long-range efforts to provide alternative livelihoods, concluding:

> If, by heroic efforts, wise direction, and good fortune, the agricultural projects mentioned can be accelerated so as to incorporate a significant proportion of those relief camp members who cannot, ultimately, be re-absorbed in the nomadic economy, it may after all be able to seize some long-term national benefit from the present crisis. This opportunity is unlikely to be ignored by a government which on the whole, has a good record for effective and decisive action once the facts are known. As with the prospect of imminent death for the individual, national disasters often help to concentrate the minds of governments.

Disaster Planning and Policy

Every nation should have a disaster policy; these should differ significantly according to hazard, national capability, aspiration, and need. Such a policy should be developed before disaster strikes and should be limited to what can be done reasonably, thoroughly, and well.

To write about disaster policy or predisaster planning implies a need to do something—but it may be equally important *not* to do something. The history of disaster suggests that overreaction often occurs under the pressure of immediate crisis and great human need. Thus, extraordinary commitments to what are essentially rare events may be undertaken, new and unwarranted bureaucracies begun, and resources needed for development diverted to unproductive uses. There is a pressing need to consider, in advance of disaster occurrence, the strengths and limitations of a nation's capacity to respond. Such considerations should not imply a commitment to an expansive and expensive program of hazard reduction; rather, it should place into proper perspective disaster reduction and other developmental and social needs.

For rare-event hazards, a conscious policy of *limited response* might be indicated. For more serious recurrent hazards in countries with extremely limited planning, administrative, and resource capacity, a wise policy might be to concentrate on developing general response capabilities (Lewis, 1975). In some countries, consideration of policies of selected *hazard control*, including the adoption of technologically oriented adjustments for controlling hazards, should be undertaken. In all countries, thought should be given to *damage reduction*, or reducing the hazard potential of the livelihoods and locations of the nation. Finally, *comprehensive multihazard management* should be considered, especially where there are related hazards (e.g., earthquakes and landslides; tropical cyclones and floods). But such comprehensive programs would rarely be justified in the poorest countries.

Whichever policy is selected—limited neglect, disaster relief, damage reduction, comprehensive multihazard management—it is best developed before a disaster. This is advisable, in part, because disaster policies can be more rationally considered before a disaster, but mainly because the major opportunities for disaster reduction occur prior to the disaster. Table 9.4 represents the range of hazard adjustments to tropical cyclones classified by the time of initiation. It is clear that the best opportunity for disaster reduction is prior to the disaster—postdisaster efforts are primarily limited to binding up wounds.

Finally, what cannot be undertaken completely and thoroughly should not be undertaken at all. When a national policy shifts the focus of disaster relief from kin, kith, or clan to government, the old support system atrophies. If new systems cannot be sustained, suffering and loss of life will be increased. A warning network, no matter how sophisticated in terms of scientific and technological capability, must fail if it does not reach the people in need of aid or if they do not respond. A hazard-control technology may exacerbate the damage inflicted if it is only partially applied or not properly integrated with the prevailing social and cultural organization.

TABLE 9.4

ADJUSTMENTS TO THE HAZARD OF TROPICAL CYCLONES

Adjustments	Before Storm	During Storm	After Storm
Modifications of extreme event	Seeding cyclone clouds to lessen intensity of storm		
Modification of damage protection	Protective shore works; levees		
	Afforestation and dune control		
	Warning system signaling approaching events and hazardous areas		
	Evacuation	Evacuation	
	Construction of raised areas as refuges: designation of shelters	Seeking shelter	
		Praying	
	Local regulations governing debris and loose materials		
	Zoning codes		
	Building codes		
	Construction modification		
	Flood- and wind-proofing		
Distribution of losses	Buying insurance		Claims on insurance
	Stockpiling of emergency supplies: water, food, building materials		Emergency relief and construction
			Bearing the loss

SOURCE: White, A. V., 1974.

Indigenous Absorptive Capacity

Every livelihood system, society, and nation has the capacity to absorb hazard, a capacity paradoxically endangered by development and change. A damage-reduction policy should begin by studying the indigenous absorptive capacity of each system or region under threat. It should identify the vulnerability of the existing system, avoid inadvertent or premature destruction of currently practiced adjustments, and provide inspiration for techniques of damage reduction that can be preserved or modernized in newly developing settlements and livelihood systems.

Many of the poorest countries have barely been in existence for a decade; a few are ancient kingdoms. All have been inhabited for a long time; indeed, they are the birthplace of humankind. To survive in a relatively unchanging and harsh environment, these people have evolved, through trial and error, a considerable capacity to absorb extreme events and thereby ensure their survival. A disaster policy should first reflect a clear understanding of these mechanisms of survival. The latter, adaptive in the long run, eventually lead to disaster if the absorptive capacity of a nation is overpowered by an extreme event. If this occurs, the traditional responses may prove counterproductive and dangerous.

Vulnerability of Traditional Nomadic Response in the Sahel

Johnson (1973, p. 11) has described the following sequence of events for the nomadic peoples of the Sahel:

> During average conditions nomads experience drought seasonally when the dry season begins. The pressures represented by desiccating vegetation are experienced by nomads each year. In all cases the response is typical; seasonal water sources, usually surface pools of rainwater, are abandoned and the herds are shifted to the tribe's permanent watering points. As aridity increases, the need to water stock frequently increases pressure on both available water and pasture resources adjacent to wells and upon animals and herders themselves.
>
> The nomadic response to drought occurs when moisture conditions fail to reappear with their expected seasonal regularity. Less reliable water sources are gradually abandoned and concentration on a restricted array of permanent deep-water wells takes place. The result is to concentrate a larger number of animals and herders in increasingly restricted areas within tribal homelands. The situation becomes even more acute when the restricted movement focuses on agricultural areas; where such resources are in the hands of an *in situ* sedentary population, high rents for limited pasture and water are charged. Obligations to assist needy kin add another dimension to the struggle for access to scarce resources and gross overcrowding can take place.
>
> It is important to note that this process replicates the normal patterns and problems of concentration around permanent dry season water facilities . . . although in exacerbated form. As a consequence, the initial response of restricted mobility constitutes a short-term risk minimization policy predicated upon short-term departures from average conditions. The danger inherent in being caught in such a posture, should conditions prove more extreme than expected,

is considerable. Trapped by widespread, prolonged drought, the nomad may be unable to shift to an alternative response and may be condemned to watch first his herd and then his kin die.

Thus, a poor country with a limited capacity to respond to disaster assistance might be well advised to concentrate its efforts on helping its people *only* when their traditional responses become counterproductive. In the Sahelian case, Johnson and Vogel-Roboff (chap. 6) suggest the establishment of a series of emergency escape routes from traditional areas. If deepening drought traps herds in their home bases with adequate water but without pasture, truck-led convoys can lead the herds out of the trap. The trucks carry mobile pumps to be used with a system of drilled, capped wells and fenced forage depots. Similar approaches for government help to supplement, but not replace, indigenous responses can be developed for agricultural droughts, floods, and cyclones.

Ironically, it is much easier to disrupt than improve the absorptive capacity of a traditional settlement or livelihood system. The encouragement of bottle-feeding for infants; the provision of new water without compensatory pasture; the building of low yet inadequate levees; the introduction of cash cropping without alternative food surpluses; the employment of a new classification for cyclone warning without adequate instruction; the shift from wood hut to unreinforced masonry—all provide horror tales of increased disaster vulnerability to drought, flood, cyclone, or earthquake. Some of these changes are simply venal (e.g. enhancing the profits of a multinational food corporation), while others are well intentioned. Results are often difficult to foresee. The same well-intentioned adjustment may lead to very different consequences in what appears to be a similar region. Such is the case in the massive evacuation of the flood plain of the Rufiji River, a project encouraged by the government of Tanzania.

The Potential to Disrupt: Relocation in the Rufiji Flood Plain

In 1968, in response to a devastating flood in the Upper Rufiji Valley, the Tanzanian government undertook to move farmers from the flood plain of the Rufiji to terraces and higher ground. The government's motivation was twofold: humanitarian (to provide a flood-free alternative) and political (to utilize the opportunity to further the organization of *ujamaa*, or communal villages). New roads were built, providing better access to markets and social services. However, the new soil off the flood plain was less productive. Overall, a gain in services appears to have offset losses in soil fertility. The farmers have remained on higher ground (Sandberg, 1973).

In retrospect, however, human ecological study of the indigenous system would have yielded considerable benefits. It would have identified, for example, the crucial role settlement played when adjacent to fields. The farmers' homes provided a living barrier against wild animals, pests, and vermin; the absence of such homes has drastically reduced crop yields. The protection of homes from floodwater damage has been guaranteed in exchange for the increased hazard of pests and vermin.

Even more important, ecological study readily explains the failure of the communal-village policy in the delta region, where fertility and rainfall are high and where protected homesites are available on elevated ridges. The delta inhabitants refused to move because they could see no other viable alternative to cultivating their productive land. Indeed, the deltaic land is probably among the most fertile in the country.

In terms of the interactive model of disaster presented earlier, a well-intentioned misjudgment of nature, technology, and society in the Rufiji delta may be increasing the vulnerability of the delta to disaster. Some degree of misjudgment occurs as a result of a misunderstanding of nature, the failure to differentiate between the intensive upstream floods and the pervasive delta floods. This misjudgment next extends to technological and societal initiatives. According to Sandberg (1974, pp. 54–56):

> Each year the Rufiji River replenishes the fertility of her flood plain and delta, thus making these areas the potentially richest agricultural areas in the Coast Region. In addition the Delta itself does not suffer as much from the erratic floods as do the other parts of the Flood Plain. From Nature's side, the farmer is faced with a relatively predictable environment, both rains and floods being reliable enough to produce a good crop in most years.
>
> The most important resource in the Rufiji Delta is the peasant himself. Those who have spent their whole lives farming in the plains know their environment well and have adapted their farming to this as far as possible. Without such detailed knowledge and experience of micro-variations in the environment, composition of soils and flood-rhythm, farming in the Delta becomes almost impossible. Thus, the continuity of Delta farming should be secured to guarantee the use of this resource for future generations.
>
> The water of the Rufiji River does, however, have other alternative uses. At present there are technical feasibility studies conducted to assess the possibility of constructing a high dam at Stiegler's gorge for generating electricity. It must be noted that the dam as planned would disturb the Rufiji Delta agricultural system. . . . For the Delta, the elimination of floods would render the existing cultivable plains dry and infertile, stop the expansion of farmland and make the now-temporary salinity of large areas a permanent phenomenon.
>
> The solution advocated by the FAO team (1954–55) of irrigating the whole valley, including the dry river banks by the use of furrows from below the dam or from discharge basins on the river levees, is unfeasible.
>
> Current policies on the development of the Delta are neither clear nor based on any serious ecological and agro-economic considerations. Since 1968, there has been a call for people . . . to join specific ujamaa villages outside the Delta. . . . In the 1973 "Operation Pwani" this call was repeated. . . . They did not, however, heed this call. Unless the detailed plans for resettlement after the 1974 flood disaster are changed compared to the 1968 plans, it seems unlikely that the call to move away from their agricultural land [will be heard].
>
> As to the expectation from 1968—that peasants here should give up farming their ancestral land and open new fields close to the new ujamaa villages . . . this

has proved totally unrealistic. Delta peasants know that their land is the most fertile in the district, and their historical experience has been a continuous struggle to protect their land from being taken over by various companies or estates.

The Indigenous System as Inspiration: Alternatives in the Rufiji

Understanding the sources of absorptive capacity in an indigenous system provides guidance not only for a critique of development plans but also for increasing the absorptive capacity of newly developed settlements or livelihood systems. How such guidance, derived from the study of the indigenous system, can be used is further illustrated by the Rufiji case as described (p. 59) by Sandberg:

> In view of the gravity of the situation—both in terms of continued agricultural production, and in terms of the credibility of the policy of ujamaa in this area— immediate steps should be taken to acknowledge the people's right to live and farm in the Delta.
>
> Agricultural production is the backbone of the nation's economy; it is also one of the few areas where collective accumulation of capital is possible. Consequently, everything possible should be done to remove or minimize constraints on farming activity. Examples include: minimizing time wasted by the farmer on walking between home and field, minimizing time wasted on marketing crops and purchasing supplies, and by rationally organizing the process of production (ploughing, weeding, scaring vermin, harvesting, etc.).
>
> As far as possible, an ujamaa village should be located in the middle of the field. This makes every hour spent on agricultural work more effective. (Most workers are women who do not use bicycles.) More important still, it makes the ujamaa village a permanent place to live as opposed to some of the villages located outside the farmed area.
>
> In contrast to the River Valley, the Delta does not suffer from very serious flood damage. Sufficiently large *gongos* (elevated terraces) exist at various places in the Delta to allow villagization of the whole Delta without disrupting the precariously balanced farming system.
>
> In creating these new ujamaa villages in the Delta, only modest government investment is necessary, probably less than the Delta peasants already have paid in taxes and commissions.

In dealing with the proposed large-scale engineering project, Stiegler's Gorge Dam, Sandberg rejects the notion of a vast irrigation project and suggests (p. 56) the following solution instead:

> The solution we have advocated [Sandberg, 1974] as the optimal strategy is, from January to June, to open the dam every fortnight and let out sufficient water to create an average flood. If this can be done according to the moon-phases, the flood should coincide with high tide, thus solving the problems of salination and delta-building. Valley farmers would also be able to improve their agriculture as a result of the higher predictability of floods. Although farmers would have to build small bunds to trap the water in fields when the flood is "turned off," they would still benefit by achieving greater control over their environment without disrupting their traditional farming system. In the technical

plans, no such solution has been provided so far; neither has the subsequent loss of potential energy been calculated. This needs to be done before any policy decisions can be taken on whether to build the dam or not.

Who Pays? Who Suffers?

Disaster, by its very nature and occurrence, is inequitable, but it also magnifies and exaggerates existing inequities within a society. Much of what is considered development also widens the gap in areas of wealth, education, class, and ethnicity. Some reduction of disaster potential is feasible in all societies, but massive, long-term reduction of disaster vulnerability among poor nations requires a type of development that reduces the marginalization of people and groups and limits the exploitation of nature.

It is widely conceded by both critics and defenders of conventional development policies that development exacerbates differences among people and groups. For the "trickle down" or "take off" theorist (Rostow, 1960), it is a necessary process for increasing a nation's resources prior to sharing them. For the concerned "tunnel theorist" (Hirschman, 1973), the enlargement of differences and the failure to "close the gap" is a source of consternation and apprehension. For the Marxist critic, this type of development is an inevitable adjunct to capitalist accumulation and is contemptuously viewed as "the development of underdevelopment" (Frank, 1970).

Unequal Access to Drought Adjustments in Kenya

Wisner (1977) has made an extensive analysis of the marginalization process in relation to increased drought vulnerability. Of particular interest in this context is his exhaustive analysis of the Kenyan farmer's access to the drought adjustments summarized in table 9.5. Seventy-five adjustments are listed, grouped according to nine classes. These adjustments range from just beyond what rich Kenyan farmers already practice (e.g., cloud seeding) to such traditional, widely practiced adjustments as bleeding livestock. For each adjustment Wisner makes a judgment as to its accessibility to each class of farmer. Accessibility varies from 97 percent for the very rich to 54 percent for the very poor. In preparing his analysis, Wisner notes two things:

> First is the greater number and diversity of possible adjustments. Second is the highly unequal access to them. . . . In Kenya the economic, ecological, technological, and social aspects of relative access are not separate spheres, nor is choice purely a subjective matter independent of constraints. Large-scale (farming) and peasant farming are only two separate sectors for the purposes of accounting. In practice they are interdependent and interacting parts of the same political economy, that is, a national (and ultimately international) system for allocating productive resources and surplus. In this system it is clearly the large-scale, rich and very rich farmers who lead. The entire structure of the agricultural economy, including such sub-systems as finance, research, extension, marketing, and patterns of drought adjustment, are tailored to maximize the profits and range of choice of the biggest farmers. Since big farmers and

TABLE 9.5
ACCESS OF KENYAN FARMERS
TO POSSIBLE DROUGHT ADJUSTMENTS

	Accessibility by Class[a]				
Adjustment	*Very Rich*	*Rich*	*Middle*	*Poor*	*Very Poor*
AFFECT OR KNOW THE RAINFALL SOURCE					
Cloud seeding	+?	0	0	0	0
Meteorological forecast	+	+	+?	0	0
Trad. rite/predict	0	+?	+	+	+
Pray	+	+	+	+	+
INCREASE MOISTURE BY:					
Changing Location					
Move stock by truck	+	0	0	0	0
Move stock by rail	+	+	0	0	0
Use fattening yards	+	+	0	0	0
Controlled grazing	+	+	+	0	0
Send stock to kin	+	+	+	+	+
Move with stock	+	+	+	+	+
Plant larger area	+	+	+	0	0
Plant distant field	+	+	+	+	+
Plant scattered plots	+	+	+	+	+
Plant bottom land	+	+	+	+	+?
Shift to new farm	+	+	+	+	+
Sharecropping?					
Improving Soil					
Moisture Storage					
and Distribution					
River-basin transfer	0	0	0	0	0
Sprinkler irrigation	+	0	0	0	0
Pumped irrigation	+	+	+	0	0
Gravity irrigation	+	+	+	+	0
Flood retreat irrigation	+	+	+	+	+
Harvest runoff	+	+	+	+?	+?
Stubble mulch	+	+	+?	0	0
Strip cropping	+	+	0	0	0
Terracing	+	+	+	0	0
Ridging	+	+	+	+	+?
Fallowing	+	+	+	+	+
Intercropping	+	+	+	+	+

(continued)

Table 9.5 continued

Adjustment	Accessibility by Class[a]				
	Very Rich	Rich	Middle	Poor	Very Poor
Scheduling for					
Optimal Soil					
Moisture					
Reseed pasture	+?	0	0	0	0
Plant dry	+	+	+?	0	0
Eliminate phosphate deficiency to ensure good root growth	+	+	+?	+?	+?
Replant if failure	+	+	+	+?	0
Wait for enough rain to plant	+	+	+	+	+?
Plant with first rains	+	+	+	+	+?
Stagger planting	+	+	+	+?	+?
REDUCE MOISTURE NEED BY: Eliminating Moisture Waste					
Selective herbicides against weeds	+?	0	0	0	0
Weed more/early weeding	+	+	+	+?	+?
Prolong fallow if poor rain	+	+	0	0	0
Changing Physiological					
or Technical Requirements					
of Crops					
Plant drought-resistant cash crops	+	+	+	+?	+?
Plant new drought-resistant varieties	+	+	+	+	+?
Plant old drought-resistant varieties	+	+	+	+?	+?
Plant many varieties	+	+	+	+	+
DIVERSIFY					
A share in urban business	+	+	+?	0	0
A share in rural business	+	+	+	+?	0
Nonfarm economic activity	+	+	+	+	+
Find wage work nearby	+	+	+	+	+
Find wage work far away	+	+	+	+	+?
Hunt, fish, or poach	+	+	+	+	+

(continued)

	Accessibility by Class[a]				
Adjustment	*Very Rich*	*Rich*	*Middle*	*Poor*	*Very Poor*
DISTRIBUTE OR SHARE LOSS					
Airlift fodder	+?	0	0	0	0
Crop insurance	+	+	0	0	0
Bank overdraft	+	+?	0	0	0
Loan or help from co-op	+	+	+	+?	0
Other loans	+	+	+?	0	0
Default on loan	+	+	+?	0	0
Move to a settlement scheme	+	+	+?	0	0
Personal tax relief	+	+	+	+?	0
Famine relief	+	+	+	+	+
Ask help (seed, food, labor) from kin	+	+	+	+	+
Ask help from government	+	+	+	+	+
Ask help from church	+	+	+	+	+
Send children to kinsman	+	+	+	+	+
Move to a kinsman's farm	+	+	+	+	+
Move to a famine camp	+	+	+	+	+
Move to an urban slum	+	+	+	+	+
BEAR THE LOSS					
Draw down savings	+	+	+?	0	0
Sell shares/liquefy assets	+	0	0	0	0
Store fodder	+	+?	0	0	0
Buy fodder	+?	0	0	0	0
Buy food	++	+	+	+	+?
Store bumper harvest	+	+	+	+	+?
Sell livestock	+	+	+	+	+
Bleed livestock	+	+	+	+	+
Collect bush foods	+	+	+	+	+
Systematically decrease family food intake	+	+	+	+	+
Eat seed	+	+	+	+	+

[a]Classes of farmers are defined by income. Very rich farmers have an income in excess of £1000 a year. Rich farmers earn between £200 and £1,000 a year. Middle-income farmers earn between £60 and £200 a year. Poor farmers earn an income between £20 and £60 annually. Very poor farmers earn no more than £20 a year. (Ed. note: £1 Kenyan = approx. $3 U.S.)

SOURCE: Benjamin G. Wisner, Jr. 1977. "The Human Ecology of Drought in Eastern Kenya" (Ph.D. diss., Clark University).

small "compete" for the same capital in the form of credit, extension services, veterinary aid, etc., the big farmers' gain is often the small farmers' loss. *The system increases the range of choice of drought adjustment of about 50,000 of the richest farm families at the cost of decreasing the range of choice, that is, adding additional constraints on the action of the rest.*

Wisner demonstrates that factors other than differential access to adjustments enter into the process of marginalization, including industrial development, population change, and urban growth. Clearly, Wisner's work suggests the extraordinary efforts required to ensure that well-intentioned efforts to assist disaster-prone nations do not exacerbate disaster vulnerability.

Marginalization—which results in increased wealth for a small minority, a status-quo situation for the majority, and a major increase in vulnerability for a larger minority—is an important process. But it also needs to be viewed in perspective. Much can be done in any society to reduce the inequity of, and vulnerability to, disaster. U.S. and World Bank initiatives in housing the poor of Managua, while they may be viewed by some as a palliative and self-serving, have actually provided a significant long-term gain in housing for a neglected segment in a highly inequitable society. In the case of Bangladesh, had international efforts in the area of land reclamation been linked to assured evacuation, perhaps as many as one hundred thousand lives could have been saved even without land reform.

However, in the long run—and in the absence of great wealth, which may allow considerable damage reduction even with societal inequalities—alternative approaches to disaster cannot be fully implemented in societies that accept and encourage great differences in the well-being of its people or selected groups. For one effect of disaster is a magnification and exaggeration of the daily inequities of a society. A nation that tolerates, and even encourages, such daily extremes can scarcely be concerned with nature's extreme displays of violence in anything but a hypocritical manner. Witness the tragic failure to report the developing disaster and extend relief in imperial Ethiopia. Conversely, the nation that seriously tries to increase the participation of all its people in a positive development process discovers new resources as a means of reducing the toll of disaster.

FOR FURTHER READING

Baird, A. et al. 1975. "Towards an Explanation of Disaster Proneness." Disaster Research Unit. Occasional Paper, No. 10. University of Bradford.

Bradley, P. et al. 1977. *The Guidimaka Region of Mauritania: A Critical Analysis Leading to a Development Project* London: War on Want.

Burton, I, et al. 1978. *The Environment As Hazard.* New York: Oxford University Press.

Dworkin, J. 1974. "Global Trends in Natural Disasters, 1947–73." Natural Hazard Research Working Paper, no. 26. Boulder: University of Colorado.

Hussein, Abdul Mejid, ed. 1976. *Drought and Famine in Ethiopia.* London: I. A. I.

Johnson, D. L. 1973. "The Response of Pastoral Nomads to Drought in the Absence of Outside Intervention." United Nations Secretariat, Special Sahelian Office, ST/SSO/18.

———, ed. 1977. "The Human Face of Desertification" [special issue] *Economic Geography* 53, no. 4 (Oct. 1977).

Kates, R. W. et al. 1976. *Population, Society, and Desertification.* UNEP/UN. Conference on Desertification, Nairobi.

Lewis, I. M. ed. *Abaar: The Somali Drought.* London: International African Institute.

O'Keefe, P. et al. 1976. "Taking the Naturalness Out of Natural Disasters." *Nature* 260, April 15, pp. 366–367.

——— and K. Westgate. 1977. "Preventive Planning for Disasters: A Long-Term Strategy." *Journal of Long-Range Planning* 10, June: 25–29.

White, G. F., ed. 1974. *Natural Hazards: Local, National, Global.* New York: Oxford University Press.

——— and J. E. Haas. 1975. *Assessment of Research of Natural Hazards.* Cambridge, Mass.: MIT Press.

PART III

ALTERNATIVE APPROACHES TO SOCIAL ORGANIZATION

All who believe in social change, be they reformers or revolutionaries, if they persist, learn a basic lesson: new ways are harder to follow than old ways. It simply takes more effort, more initiative, more care, and more conviction to do things differently. However, if they do not learn to do things differently, the least developed will remain the poorest of the poor.

This section selectively explores the experience of doing things differently. Beginning with the grass-roots level of popular participation and folk knowledge, it next examines the collective self-reliance of integrating developing economies, moves on to a consideration of trade and aid, and ends with a study of the lofty human ideal of solidarity. There is hope in these suggestions, as well as opportunities, but there is also a sobering recounting of past experiences and obstacles.

10. Any discussion of alternative approaches to development, especially for LDNs, would be incomplete without some reference to the Tanzanian experience. Underdeveloped, 70 percent semiarid, Tanzania appears blessed with only two major resources: extensive landholdings and a stable, dedicated political leadership determined to fashion at least one distinctive African path to socialism.

The Tanzanian experience has been under attack recently from both the right and the left. Blue and Weaver (1977) provide a good summary of these issues. Rhetoric aside, most critiques eventually focus on the disparity between aspiration, expectation or promise, and achievement. No less a critic than President Nyerere recently recounted the achievements and failures of the last decade (1977).

The gap existing between promise and achievement in one critical area—the provision of water through popular participation—is M. R. Mujwahuzi's subject. As was noted in chapter 8, there are two important features of an alternative approach to providing access to safe water: conceiving of such access as a human right and self-help in achieving it. In this respect, Tanzania has an ambitious twenty-year goal of providing all its people with access to safe water and a fundamental commitment to a broadened concept of self-help, which Mujwahuzi refers to as popular participation.

Given the need to attain the extraordinary goal of providing water for all—requiring a fourfold increase in the number of people currently being provided for—it is inevitable that this would conflict with other goals (e.g., popular participation). Both Mujwahuzi (1976) and Tshcannerl (1976) have explored the roots of such conflict in the reliance on tried and tested technological fixes amenable to control, initiative, and financing by Western-trained engineers. That such conflict has developed is ironic, for the goal of providing safe water for all will not be realized in Tanzania or in other LDCs if a greater degree of popular participation in all phases of planning, construction, operation, and maintenance is not forthcoming. Chapter 8 explored the need for shifting the locus of responsibility to the people. Chapter 11 will examine the potential for utilizing local knowledge. All three—responsibility, knowledge, and specified technology—are necessary if the promise of popular participation is to be realized.

POPULAR PARTICIPATION: THE TANZANIAN CASE IN WATER SUPPLY

M. R. Mujwahuzi

Tanzania has decided to give top priority to rural development in her development program because, as the argument runs, most of her latent wealth lies in underutilized land and in the energies of rural dwellers. Among the necessary inputs in the development of her rural areas is an improved rural domestic water supply, which is looked upon partly as a factor in the development process and partly as a necessity for the achievement of a better quality of rural life. The goal is for every inhabitant to have access to an adequate supply of water by the year 1991.

A variety of strategies have been utilized in attempting to achieve this goal including: an increase in investment funds for the construction of water schemes; introduction of new and more efficient technology; and the application of an approach of self-reliance involving popular participation in the development of improved rural water supplies. These approaches have operated side by side in different parts of the country, although more emphasis has been placed on conventional engineering methods. In order to gain a better understanding of what has taken place in the area of rural water supply in Tanzania, each approach will be reviewed briefly.

The Conventional Engineering Approach

Active government involvement in the development of a rural water-supply network began in 1946 with the formation of a technical Water Development Department (WDD). The latter's responsibilities included: the provision of rural domestic water for humans and animals; conservation of water to improve river flow and prevent floods; execution of irrigation schemes; hydrological investigations; and long-term planning of major water-development works. During the period 1946–74, WDD constructed 309 earth dams, catchment tanks, and charcos (man-made pools of standing water), 1,025 gravity pipelines and pumped supplies, and 1,161 bore holes, which, taken together, serve an estimated 2,040,000 rural inhabitants.

The rural water program has received assistance in the form of loans, grants, and manpower from foreign countries, especially Sweden. For the period 1964–72, the rural water program received four Swedish loans and grants amounting to U.S.$17.6 million. These funds have been used to cover the cost of surveys and investigations, expansion of existing facilities, training of manpower, and actual construction of water projects. The allocation of these funds among different activities is shown in table 10.1.

In addition to loans and grants extended to Tanzania, Sweden has also been involved in the Staff Assistance Program, aimed at easing the shortage of skilled manpower. For the period 1967–72, Sweden supplied 226 technical personnel drawn from various grades. Recruitment of manpower was, however, not restricted to Sweden. Technical personnel were received from other foreign countries, including Great Britain, Denmark, Bulgaria, Egypt, and India. As of September 1973, 81 out of a total of 120 engineers in WDD were expatriates (Ministry of Water Development and Power, 1973).

In September 1971, the biennial national conference of the Tanganyika African National Union (TANU), the ruling party, issued a directive requiring that every rural inhabitant have access to adequate sources of water by the year 1991. When this directive was issued, it was estimated that only 1,440,000 out of a total of 12,980,000 people then living in the rural areas of Tanzania had access to improved water supplies; only 300,000 additional

TABLE 10-1
SWEDISH CREDITS ALLOCATIONS (U.S. $)

Credit	Time Period	Allocation for Activity Items				Construction of Regular Projects			Construction of Major Projects	
		Loan Provision (millions)	Surveys and Investigations (thousands)	Expansion of Facilities (thousands)	Training (thousands)	Loan Provision (millions)	Number of Projects	Number of People Served	Name of Project	Loan Provision (millions)
I	1964/66	2.00	356	—	—	746	50	40,000	Ismani W/S	460
									East Kilimanjaro Trunk Main	438
II	1966/69	6.00	800	272	—	4,128	213	260,000	Mwamapuli Dam	600
									Drilling Program 32 B/H	200
III	1969/70	3.00	278	438	48	2,056	84	140,000	Drilling Program 30 B/H	180
IV	1970/72	6.60	844	998	22	4,256	168	310,000	Drilling Program 70 B/H	480
TOTAL	1964/72	17.60	2,278	1,708	70	11,186	515	750,000	—	2,358

SOURCE: Ministry of Water Development and Power, internal memorandum, April 1972.

people were annually provided with improved water. It was noted that if the 1991 target date was to be met, the number of people to be supplied with water had to be increased to at least 1,219,000 annually, as shown in the twenty-year rural water-supply schedule presented in table 10.2. The Ministry of Water Development and Power believes that in order to be able to supply improved water to so many people every year, it will have to reorganize and strengthen itself, increase capital outlay in terms of machinery and equipment, and train many more technicians and spread them throughout the country.

Several steps have already been taken. Regarding the question of increased capital outlay and equipment, the Ministry is in the process of buying twelve new (and more powerful) drilling rigs and earth-moving equipment at a cost of U.S. $6.15 million. The goal is for each of the nineteen regions to have at least one drilling rig; under the present situation, the entire country is served by only six rigs. It is estimated that the new rigs will be able to drill anywhere from eight-hundred to nine-hundred bore holes a year. In addition to drilling rigs, the government has established a special fund of U.S. $5.7 million to be used to buy such materials as pipes and fittings, which are needed in the execution of rural water projects. An additional U.S. $428,571 has been set aside for regional use in buying materials and equipment for water development. Five teams equipped with earth-moving machines have been formed. These teams will move around certain parts of the country and construct charcos. Their activities will be concentrated mainly in cattle areas of the Mara, Mwanza, Shinyanga, and Tabora regions. The Masai area will not be covered by these teams since it is already being served under the USAID program. The average rate of construction for each team is estimated at one charco per week. The capacity of each charco is about seven million liters.

To cope with the long-term problem of skilled manpower shortage—and in conformity with the government's goal of self-sufficiency in the area of trained manpower by the year 1980—the Ministry of Water Development and Power, through its training division, has expanded and improved the program at its training school, located at Ubungo, Dar es Salaam. One of the main features of the expanded program is the establishment of a Water Resources Institute to train the subprofessional staff. In dealing with the very serious shortage of local engineers, the Ministry of Water Development and Power has been permitted to select a number of engineering candidates over and above its annual quota of engineering students selected by the Ministry of National Education.

The Popular-Participation Approach

The other approach that Tanzania has attempted to apply in the rural water-supply program is the self-help method. According to the Second Five-Year Development Plan, 1969–74 (United Republic of Tanzania, 1969, I, p. 26), "the development of water resources does, however, require heavy use of

TABLE 10.2
TWENTY-YEAR RURAL WATER-SUPPLY SCHEDULE

Year	Estimated Rural Population	If 300,000 Supplied Annually		If 1,219,000 Supplied Annually	
		People with Water Supply	*People without Water Supply*	*People with Water Supply*	*People without Water Supply*
1971	12,980,000	1,440,000	11,540,000	1,440,000	11,540,000
1972	13,330,000	1,710,000	11,620,000	1,710,000	11,620,000
1973	13,630,000	2,010,000	11,630,000	2,010,000	11,680,000
1974	14,060,000	2,310,000	11,760,000	2,310,000	11,750,000
1975	14,440,000	2,610,000	11,630,000	2,610,000	11,830,000
1976	14,830,000	2,910,000	11,920,000	3,829,000	11,001,000
1977	15,230,000	3,210,000	12,020,000	5,048,000	10,182,000
1978	15,640,000	3,510,000	12,130,000	6,247,000	9,373,000
1979	16,060,000	3,810,000	12,250,000	7,485,000	8,574,000
1980	16,490,000	4,110,000	12,380,000	8,705,000	7,785,000
1981	16,940,000	4,410,000	12,530,000	9,924,000	7,016,000
1982	17,400,000	4,710,000	12,690,000	11,143,000	6,257,000
1983	17,870,000	5,010,000	12,060,000	12,362,000	5,508,000
1984	18,350,000	5,310,000	13,040,000	13,581,000	4,769,000
1985	18,850,000	5,510,000	13,240,000	14,800,000	4,050,000
1986	19,360,000	5,910,000	13,450,000	16,019,000	3,341,000
1987	19,880,000	6,210,000	13,670,000	17,218,000	2,642,000
1988	20,410,000	6,510,000	13,900,000	18,451,000	1,952,000
1989	20,960,000	6,910,000	14,150,000	19,676,000	1,284,000
1990	21,530,000	7,110,000	14,420,000	20,845,000	635,000
1991	22,110,000	7,410,000	14,700,000	22,110,000	-

SOURCE: Ministry of Water Development and Power, *Taarifa ya Maendeleo ya Utekelezayi wa Shughuliza Maji: Progress Report on Water Development Activities.* Dar es Salaam, 1973.

capital resources. The achievement of a full, satisfactory solution to Tanzania's water problem . . . will be achieved by an emphasis on inexpensive schemes, mobilizing self-help efforts of the local people." Thus, Tanzania views popular participation as another essential approach in the development of a satisfactory rural water-supply program. Involvement of the people in the development of water projects has always been encouraged. According to the country's policy, public participation must occupy all aspects of project development, including planning, construction, and maintenance.

Since Tanzania gained independence in 1961, people have participated in the development of many water-supply schemes, both big and small. Wells serving small, local communities have been dug, dams have been built, and pipes have been laid by the people on a self-help basis in many parts of the country.

Although there are numerous instances in which people have participated in the development of their own water supplies, their participation has always fallen short of what it should be, as suggested in both government and party policy concerning public involvement. Generally, where participation has taken place, it has been limited to one aspect of project development. In a majority of cases, public involvement consists of doing such unskilled jobs as digging trenches for the pipelines or collecting building materials. Seldom have people been involved in the actual planning of projects or in running and maintaining them. (The latter observation is based on the results of a study on popular participation in rural water supply which this writer completed in Lushoto, Arumeru, and Masai districts of Tanzania.) The restricted use of public participation raises two very important questions: (1) Why is public participation not used in all aspects of rural water-supply development? (2) What is necessary to increase the role of public participation in rural water supply?

Restricted use of public participation can partly be blamed on the government's approach to the problem of water supply. Basically, the process of water development adopted by WDD lessens the chances of incorporating public participation into the system. The existing working procedures stipulate that water technicians must do all the work, from the planning stage of the project to its subsequent operation and maintenance.

It is not difficult to understand why this should be the case. There are certain advantages in having all the work placed in the hands of technicians who carry out their assignment in the conventional engineering manner rather than by means of a participative approach. For one thing, technicians consider the conventional engineering approach more reliable, and faster to implement because it is supported by experience; moreover, there is a steady stream of research leading to improvements. Conversely, very little is known concerning the participative approach; there is limited research being conducted in this field. Water technicians frequently point out that they would be risking failure were they to rely on public participation. Second, by adopting a conventional approach in water development, it is easier to get help from outside agencies in the areas of funding and technical expertise.

In spite of the fact that the conventional approach to rural water-supply development appears to have many advantages, the 1991 target date cannot be achieved by pursuing this approach because the country does not have the necessary funds or the required manpower. On the other hand, a combination of conventional and participative approaches appears to be a promising alternative for rural water development. If this proves to be the case, in what ways can public participation in water development be effectively employed?

There are many ways in which people can get involved in the planning, construction, and maintenance of their own water projects. For example, public participation in planning can take the form of information generation about the water resource, followed by the public's direct involvement in the decision-making process. Public participation in construction and maintenance is feasible if the technology used in simple, locally based, and produces satisfactory results at a low cost.

Planning and Decision Making

One way to involve people in planning is to have them generate information necessary for planning and allow them to make decisions. Public participation in generating information has the advantage of making people more aware of their water supplies. Moreover, they represent a valuable source of stored information that is usually not available to the engineer.

Rural inhabitants can be approached for information in two ways. One involves the use of a questionnaire, whereby an individual is asked specific questions that he is capable of answering. The other approach would be through group discussions about the water situation in a village or area. Whichever approach is used, the primary aim is to gather information in the following areas: available sources of water in the village and surrounding area; an estimate of the amount of water in these sources; sources of water actually used by villagers; type of water usage; reasons why other sources are not used; problems of water in the village; and what people view as alternative means of solving these problems. The village would be the ideal area of study for such information-gathering procedures since the interviewees or discussants would have firsthand knowledge of the water situation in their immediate surroundings. Furthermore, it is safe to assume that village people would be willing to participate in discussions since they are the immediate beneficiaries of any water improvements that would subsequently occur in the village.

Although both the questionnaire and the group-discussion approaches would generate valuable information concerning the water-resource situation in a particular village, the latter approach should always be used whenever possible. There are two main reasons why the group-discussion approach is preferable. First, given the present national political organization, it is easier to get the village people together for a discussion of matters that affect the community. Second, group discussions generate more reliable information since people tend to correct each other in the course of discussion.

Regarding the process of generating information, the public is in a better position to make decisions on a variety of issues pertaining to the development of improved water supplies. They can, for example, decide on such issues as: suitable sources of work to be used; type of distribution system to be built; and organization of work and materials to be used in the project.

Construction and Maintenance

Public participation in the construction and maintenance of water schemes can be expected to take place when the technology selected (1) is simple enough for local people to easily adopt it; (2) utilizes locally available labor and materials so that there is less reliance on foreign resources; and (3) is low in cost. Although an improved water supply can be achieved by means of many different water-supply systems, not all systems can be developed along the lines of popular participation since the technology used in some systems does not meet the aforementioned criteria. Table 10.3 shows some systems that satisfy these criteria and others that do not. Judging from this table, the following water-supply systems appear to lend themselves more easily to public participation: solar distillation, roof catchment, ground catchment, hand-dug wells, ponds and tanks, and reservoirs.

However, because of spatial variations in Tanzania's water-resource endowment, not every system listed as being suitable for popular participation can be developed throughout the country. Some systems are more suitable in certain areas than others. For example, whereas ground-catchment systems may be developed successfully in almost every part of the country, roof-catchment systems may only be suitable in areas with high rainfall. Thus, the application of public participation in the development of improved water supplies would have to be carried out on a regional basis, depending on the nature of the water-resource base.

Despite government policy statements in favor of popular participation in rural water development, this approach has not been widely used because of the aforementioned reasons. In order to increase the role of public participation, it will be necessary to change the working procedures of the WDD. For example, water technicians working in rural areas should not be limited to certain designs; they should be free to develop other water-supply systems that make use of simple technology and local materials. They can do this in consultation with local inhabitants. The conventional engineering approach should be utilized in areas where the popular-participation approach would not elicit significant results.

TABLE 10.3
PUBLIC-PARTICIPATION POTENTIAL OF VARIOUS
WATER-SUPPLY SYSTEMS

Type of Water-Supply System	Low in Cost?	Simple Technology?	Local Materials Used?	Local Labor Used?
Oceans and Atmosphere:				
Desalination:				
by mechanical plants	no	no	no	no
by solar distillation	yes	yes	yes	yes
Condensation	no	no	no	no
Rainfall:				
Roof catchment	yes	yes	yes	yes
Ground catchment:				
Improving surface	yes	yes	yes	yes
Soil treatment	yes	yes	no	yes
Lining catchment	no	yes	no	yes
Surface-Water Resources:				
Ponds and tanks	yes	yes	yes	yes
Reservoirs	yes	yes	yes	yes
Groundwater Sources:				
Hand-dug wells	yes	yes	yes	yes
Tube wells:				
Bored wells	yes	yes	no	yes
Driven wells	yes	yes	no	yes
Jetted wells	no	no	no	no
Bore holes:				
Percussion	no	no	no	no
Rotary	no	no	no	no

SOURCE: Mark R. Mujwahuzi. 1976. "Self-help in the Development of Improved Rural Water Supply: Tanzania Experience and Potential" (Ph.D. diss., Clark University).

FOR FURTHER READING

Economic Development Bureau. 1977. *Appropriate Technology for Grain Storage*. New Haven: Economic Development Bureau.

Feachem, R. et al., ed. 1977. *Water, Wastes, and Health in Hot Climates*. New York: John Wiley.

International Institute for Environment and Development. 1977. *Clean Water for All*. Washington, D.C.: IIED.

Maystre, Y. et al. 1973.*Technology Assessment and Researh Priorities for Water Supply and Sanitation in Developing Countries (with special reference to rural populations and small communities)*. Ottawa: International Development Research Centre.

National Research Council. 1974. *More Water for Arid Lands*. Washington, D.C.: NAS.

Nyerere, J. K. 1968. *Ujamaa—Essays on Socialism*. Dar es Salaam: Oxford University Press.

Saunders, Robert J. and J. J. Warford. 1976. *Village Water Supply: Economics and Policy in the Developing World*. World Bank Publication. Baltimore: Johns Hopkins Press.

Stein, Jane. 1977. *Water: Life or Death?* Washington, D.C.: International Institute for Environment and Development.

White, G. F. 1974. "Domestic Water: Good or Right?" *Human Rights in Health*. Edited by K. M. Elliot. Ciba Foundation Symposium 23, new series. Amsterdam: Associated Scientific Publishers, pp. 36–54.

—— et al. 1972. *Drawers of Water—Domestic Water Use in East Africa*. Chicago: University of Chicago Press.

11.   As the aboriginal peoples of Australia, Canada, New Zealand, and the United States constantly remind the immigrant majority, neither history, geography, nor science began with the "discovery" of their country by Europeans. Similarly, the project planner or scientific investigator initiating a new project or survey in a LDN does not begin with a blank slate. What is missing in metropolitan libraries or in central government offices is in the daily lives and work of local residents, as well as in the minds, skills and backroom offices of technicians.

The most extraordinary attempt to integrate development knowledge occurred in China, with medicine and earthquake prediction probably being the best-known examples. In both cases, Chinese efforts have stimulated widespread interest in the West. Acupuncture is now generally accessible; major scientific theories of pain must now account for its observed effects in addition to the more traditional responses of drugs. Serious study of animal behavior prior to earthquakes (a major component of ethnoscientific earthquake prediction) is also under way in the United States.

The major achievements of ethnoscience are not in the dramatic fields of surgery or earthquake prediction but in the long-term viability of human occupancy of harsh environments. Success in providing subsistence, however, is denigrated or ignored by those who would prefer to derive large agricultural surpluses from such land or transfer more "modern" agricultural technologies to such peoples. In many instances, "throwing out the baby with the bathwater" has taken on the literal meaning of discarding the indigenous technology with the introduction of irrigation water.

In one well-documented case, Johnson (1977) systematically compares the similarities and differences in two of L. Berry and H. Renwick's three types of scientific knowledge, namely, that of the Otomi Indians residing in the mesquital, north of Mexico City, and that of the *technicos* who staff the agricultural advisory and development service. The net effect of Western technicoscience, as opposed to Otomi ethnoscience, is to diminish knowledge of the regions' resources by perceiving and utilizing fewer categories in their taxonomies and consequently recognizing fewer resources.

It is easier to discuss the integration of these three forms of knowledge than to employ them. Berry and Renwick make a convincing plea for their potential complementarity. The methodology for eliciting local ethnoscientific knowledge, the most poorly understood (by outsiders) of the three forms, is becoming widely available (see field guide developed by Whyte, 1977). What seems to be needed now are well-planned operational experiments that will systematically incorporate local ethnoscientific, regional, technical, and global scientific knowledge into the planning of a wide range of development projects.

ENVIRONMENTAL INFORMATION: INTEGRATING KNOWLEDGE

L. Berry and H. Renwick

LDNs are characterized by their dependence on traditional (or modified traditional) agricultural systems; their future surely includes continued ties with the land. Although large-scale farming and animal husbandry are found in most of these countries, typical land-resource users are currently small scale, including farmers, family herders, and individual charcoal producers. In order to encourage increased production and better distribution of economic wealth at the national level, some planners suggest that greater attention be directed toward improving the well-being of the small farming majority rather than favoring large-scale agricultural interests. However, government services in LDNs are generally poorly organized to deal with the problems, both environmental and social, of the small farmer. The organization of such services is based on inherited colonial forms better suited to large-scale projects, although a number of LDNs have experimented in various ways with new approaches designed to carry out the task.

The divergence between services designed for large-scale agricultural development and those directed toward improving small-holder farming, animal husbandry, and forestry is sharply defined in the data-gathering and information-assessment aspects of planning.

At least two very different kinds of land resource-use knowledge systems can be found operating in the same local area in developing countries. Those small-scale farmers who are long-term residents in the area have made choices about where to locate, what to plant, and how to deal with the element of risk on the basis of traditional knowledge and intimate aquaintance with locally perceived environmental systems. In contrast, privately owned or state-owned large farms have drawn their knowledge from the Western (or global) scientific data base. Soil surveys, water information, and plant and animal knowledge are drawn from this internationally accepted information system.

There has been only a slight overlap and a minimal amount of communication between these two systems. Frequent attempts to introduce foreign technology and knowledge into local systems have not worked well; they have occasionally disrupted both socioeconomic and environmental-use patterns. For example, Blaut (1959), Lance and McKenna (1975), Wallman (1972), Berry and Townshend (1972), Groth (1975), and Peattie (1969) cite vivid examples (drawn from the Caribbean, Tanzania, and Latin America) of the failure of development-planning efforts focusing on the small farmer to recognize or incorporate the latter's knowledge system into the process. Farvar and Milton (1972), Dasmann (1973), as well as others have provided global surveys related to these issues. Scudder (1972), in particular, demonstrates the importance of understanding the local inhabitants' view of their ecosystem. He suggests that even when so-called ecological principles are incorporated into the planning process, they may prove unsatisfactory if the recipients of this planning have a concept of their ecosystem that differs considerably from the concept envisioned by those doing the planning.

Janzen (1973) presents a general overview of the environmental problems associated with transferring temperate-zone agricultural techniques to the tropics. He insists that American agriculture is environmentally unfit for tropical areas and that researchers should develop a more suitable approach.

This chapter focuses on natural-resource information used in the planning process. Common informational inputs and those characteristics applicable to planning are listed in table 11.1. A typology consisting of three different styles and kinds of information is presented; suggestions as to ways in which these might be used are also provided. One should emphasize that any environmentally oriented planning aimed at making life better for the small farmer must, if it is to be successful, view the small farmers' and local authorities' own environmental knowledge and priorities as an integral part of the planning process. In order to encourage this type of integration, a preliminary review is presented of the potential utility to be gained from including both conventional scientific and alternative environmental information sources in planning for the future of agriculture, pastoralism, and forestry in LDNs.

Typology of Environmental-Information Sources

There are, of course, many different ways of classifying information about the environment. This chapter utilizes the following three-part division: (1) Western scientific or global system, (2) ethnoscientific systems and (3) informal technical knowledge systems.

Scientific Information

Scientific information dealing with natural resources is gathered in a variety

TABLE 11.1 *INFORMATION ON NATURAL RESOURCES*

Object of Study	Time Frame of Data	Form of Data Output	Form of Data Base	Areal Cover of Data Base in Any One Subject	Organization Used to Collect Data
Geological mapping	Static	Maps, reports	Photos and ground survey	XXXX	Government
Topo-mapping	Static	Maps	Landsat (satellite and other survey photos)	XXXXX	Government
Terrain	Static	Maps, reports	Photo and ground survey	X	University or Team
Vegetation cover	Changing	Maps, reports, photos	Photo transect Landsat	XX	University or Team
Land use	Changing	Maps, reports	Photos-landsat	XX	University
Soils mapping	Static	Maps, reports	Photos and survey landsat	XX	Government
Soil erosion	Dynamic	Statistics, reports	Isolated studies	X	University
Water movement (hydrology)	Dynamic	Statistics, Reports	Recordings, estimates	XXX	Government
Other process geomorphology	Dynamic	Statistics, reports	Isolated studies	X	University
Climatic system	Dynamic	Maps, reports	Recordings, remote sensing Data surrogate	XX	Government
Ecosystem analysis	Static Changing	Maps, system diagrams	Photos, landsat, remote sensing, isolated studies, detailed ground surveys	X	University
Total regional system	Static	Maps, imagery	Economic, landsat mapping, and other statistical indicators	X	University or Team

LEGEND: Five-Point Scale: XXXXX National coverage; XXXX Extensive coverage; XXX Regional coverage; XX Found only in some areas; X Very local.

of ways, ranging from the lone researcher pursuing an idiosyncratic theme to highly bureaucratized government agencies systematically investigating large areas. Three main types of data-gathering systems exist:

Research Investigations. Conducted by a university, individual, or agency; typically focused on a particular research theme or hypothesis.

Project Investigations. Conducted by a group or agency; typically focused on a particular project, usually in a restricted location, and oriented in time and place to project needs.

Systematic Surveys. Conducted by a government agency or ministry; typically focused on gathering recurrent data on a regular basis.

Each of these methods has its own specialization: the research investigation has its theme or hypothesis; the project has its areal and project goals; and the systematic survey has its disciplinary specialization. Each of these methods easily permits one to focus on an issue of a sector yet results in minimum integration with other endeavors. Products of each kind of study differ, and retrieval of each presents special kinds of problems.

The kinds of natural-resource scientific information collected in one form or another in LDNs are set forth in table 11.1. The table characterizes both the type of information sought and the kind of agency involved in collecting and using it. In Tanzania, for example, geological and topographical mapping is carried out by specialized government departments; hydrological and climate data are collected and sometimes synthesized by other government departments; and studies of vegetation are periodically but unevenly undertaken by yet another government department. Data regarding terrain, use, soil erosion, and ecosystems are not regularly collected by government agencies, but have been part of university and visiting researcher studies. The amount of information collected is thus highly uneven for each of these areas. The only place the various topics have been integrated is in the context of specialized river-basin studies, such as the Rufiji Basin Study of the FAO or in some regional compilations that served as pilot approaches to regional planning.

Most other LDNs have a system of data collection similar in general outline to that described for Tanzania. In these countries, government agencies carry out geological mapping, topographical mapping, and soil and hydrological surveys. The coverage is usually most complete for topography and least complete for soil regardless of the level of detail. Other forms of data collection are usually not a continuing-survey function of a government agency, but they may be undertaken on an intermittent basis by ministries for special purposes; usually they are carried out under the auspices of universities or visiting technical teams.

The result of all this is that when natural-resource data input is needed for planning decisions, it is likely that:

1. Some data at the national level of generalization exist.

2. Time sequences of dynamic data are relatively short.

3. Many ecological aspects of national resources have not been studied.

4. Levels of detail of data will vary from topic to topic within the same area and from area to area.

5. Published data are widely scattered in different journals and papers, frequently not easily available in the country of study.

6. Disciplinary specialization will obscure the presence of data in other fields of study.

In many planning situations there is need for synthesis of data, the focusing of data onto particular geographical areas, the supplementation of data with specific areal studies, and access to new forms of information.

Ethnoscientific Information

Throughout U.S. history, farmers and agricultural scientists have learned much from one another. The abstractions and theories conceived in college laboratories have been consistently "brought down to earth" by farmers' critical responses. The wealth of pragmatic, day-to-day, and long-term information that the farmer gathers about soil, weather, and crop characteristics on his own land and in his own region has served as the necessary feedback that has made U.S. agricultural practice so successful in its own environmental and cultural context. Without this communication, the system might quickly slip out of balance, as has been pointed out by Carter (1977) with respect to soil erosion.

Past successes in this communication process may be due, in large part, to the fact that the American farmer and scientist see the world in a similar way. Coming from the same broad cultural background, they are able to communicate ideas and solutions to problems fairly easily. This dialogue approach in agricultural research and planning should be equally informative in the development context abroad. Generally speaking, however, solutions to agricultural problems among LDNs have not resulted from such a dialogue. When Western global scientific knowledge comes into contact with that of the small farmer in non-Western cultures, barriers of language and goals stand in the way of communication. The farmer has historically had good reasons— environmental, political, economic— for distrusting what the nonlocal scientist or government worker tells him (Blaut, 1959; Lance and McKenna, 1975). Communication and exchange of information ends at a very early stage in the crossculture context.

Beyond these barriers, in the hearts and minds of local agriculturalists lies a great deal of hardheaded information about local conditions and techniques. Westerners refer to this type of knowledge as the "ethnoscience" of any given group or culture. Ethnoscientific information becomes a part of the knowledge of a culture group over a long period of time through a largely deliberate process of trial and error. It is the collected understanding and conceptualization of how the world works and how to deal with that world successfully—or at least how to minimize misfortune in it. Ethnoscience is as pragmatic and rational an explanation of perceived global phenomena as that of the global scientists, yet it makes use of terms and explanatory devices that Westerners often consider superstitious or naive. Thus, the "ethno-" tacked onto "science" for this type of explanation is often used in a slightly derogatory manner; nonglobal sciences are viewed as containing much extraneous material that is nonscientific (i.e., nonfunctional) in relation to operations of the "real" world as defined by the West. However, recent reorientations of global science in the direction of a holistic or "ecologic" approach to scientific study and planning may narrow the different approaches to environmental-resource use.

These other cultures frequently do not see themselves as separate from their soil; they do not view their position as one of human beings in a world of inanimate objects and inferior organisms, as do Westerners. They see themselves as actively interacting with their world and performing favors for it in return for food and good health.

This is not to suggest that local systems are perfect either as production or as ecological systems. Rather, the point to be emphasized is that at the local level present farming systems are the environmentally and socially integrated products of long-term interaction and feedback between the people and their resource base.

One hypothesis has shown that supposedly conservative societies do adapt readily to change, modifying the farming system to deal with different numbers of people or fluctuating monetary conditions. Boserup (1965) cites examples from West Africa where increased land use for higher production correlates with increased population density. Berry (1976) cites other examples.

However, this is not always the case. Berry (1976) and Eckholm (1977) have both shown how, under certain circumstances, local farming systems do not respond to changes in population size quickly enough. Under these conditions local ethnoscientific knowledge cannot cope with the new situation (Knight and Newman, 1976). Environmental and perhaps even social deterioration consequently occurs.

The successful small-farms approach has been partially incorporated into recent thinking concerning ecological approaches to development, though some ecodevelopers feel that local knowledge is inferior to the objective ecosystems viewpoint of the expert (Scudder, 1972). The opportunity is there for the small farmer's human-oriented ecosystem knowledge to be integrated with the material-ecological-system approach of some scientists. This marriage of conservationist and preservationist viewpoints could lead to more realistic planning. A recently proposed development project in Kordofan, Sudan, represents a first step toward such an approach (Kornfeld, 1977).

An understanding of local-system interaction is important for any kind of development planning. In addition, a proper understanding of the structure of the local system, devised in response to its own traditional rationale, may be a vital factor in resolving problems of susceptibility or resistance to change.

A study of Tanzania that revealed the existence of over 120 different farming systems highlights the need to use the local farmers' knowledge of these systems as an important factor in economic and social planning (Conyers, 1973). There is no other effective way to build on these systems for development.

Informal Technical Knowledge

This type of knowledge is less easily defined than either scientific or ethno-scientific knowledge. In the present context it describes the knowledge of a region acquired by many experts and local technical workers who have had experience in that area. In some cases it is the well-informed amateur who knows most about an area, while in others it is the professional in one field who has, through a particular areal interest, widened his or her scope or knowledge. The district agricultural officer, the area water engineer, the political agent, or the long-term resident can all fill this role. Their knowledge is often not written down; like much ethnoscientific information, it is carried around in the head. When it is written down, it is usually in the form of one or two copies of an "internal memorandum" available only in a local office.

In several respects, informal technical knowledge serves as a bridge between ethnoscientific and scientific knowledge. First, informal technical knowledge links the two other fields in kind of information; like scientific information, it is founded on a formally educated base. Like ethnoscientific information, it is related to personal knowledge of the area involved. Also, the vocabulary is cognizant both of the scientific and local world. Perhaps most importantly, the scale of understanding acts as a bridge. The ethnoscientific world of information is usually related to a particular local scale; informal technical knowledge enlarges on that scale and links it with national and international scientific scales.

At its best, informal technical knowledge provides a powerful overview of an area and its problems, coupled with an understanding of people and institutions at the local and regional level. At its worst, of course, it can provide an idiosyncratic, personally biased view of a region and its situation. It often promotes Western scientific goals at the expense of local needs (Johnson, 1977). If the right question is asked of a number of people, in most cases such knowledge can be a vital component of environmental information.

Current Applications of the Three Components of Environmental Information

It is clear that three diverse and very rich data sources of environmental information do exist. The difficulty is, first, to make available the various types of data and, second, to use them effectively. The demands of time, budget, and clear-cut, quick results all too often supplant the real parameters of development thinking, namely, the needs of the field situation. A large-scale problem elicits a large-scale response, with little consideration of small-scale, localized implications. Conversely, a small project is given very local attention, with little thought given to the long-range effects or to wider implications of the solution in other spheres of life or among other localities. Available information is badly abused when one category is used to the exclusion of the other two. Conventional planning does not, at present, operate in terms of data mixes from varying sources.

Dealing with Resource Information at Different Scales: Some Examples

The problems and dilemmas of dealing with resource information at different scales may be better understood by looking at one or two illustrative cases. The literature in this area is filled with case studies of development projects where the *local* level of interaction between people and the environment has not been properly understood; the development effort has proved, at best, only a partial success. Even in well-intentioned indigenous plans for change, problems can occur (see Kates, chap. 9). A few years ago, major flooding of the Rufiji River in Tanzania created an emergency situation for local inhabitants living on abandoned levees of the river, rising in narrow ridges just above the flood plain. The people were "rescued" from the flood danger and a permanent resettlement plan was quickly put into effect to relocate the villagers away from the hazard zone on a wide, old terrace of the river. However, the flood plain location, hazardous though it was at times, had been chosen as the best suited site to connect easily with the rice fields on the flood plain. Moreover, crops were generally satisfactory. The terrace site proved to be too far away to permit a ready movement to and from work in the paddy. The terrace was relatively unfertile, as a result of which production and the economy stagnated (Sandberg, 1973).

Similar mismatches of information sets can occur at the regional level. In a water-supply improvement program, important benefits can be gained from a mingling of various types of data. An analysis of regional geological structure lines and groundwater hydrology, by employing available geological maps and remotely sensed imagery, can provide a general framework for a decision about where water is likely to be found; the latter may vary in precision from the delimitation of general areas for drilling to the location, within one hundred yards, of the drill site. Local technical knowledge can then supply the necessary experience, for the area as a whole, of well drilling in the different sites, eliminating some localities and emphasizing others. When this process is complete, local knowledge may be critical in determining the best place to drill in terms of land tenure, access to the water point, and microphysical conditions. Unfortunately, it is more common to find technical knowledge gained from remote sensing and groundwater studies serving as the sole information source in the location of wells and bore holes.

National programs of resource use and information collectors can also be considered in this context. A sampling of a nation's rainfall is normally obtained by means of a network of rain gauges. At best, the gauges represent a fraction of the total environment. Moreover, the raw data derived from them have some significant limitations. The usefulness of this information can be considerably increased both by rainfall reports supplied by technical officers (who have an overview of the pattern and general amount of rainfall in a district) and, if necessary, by detailed, often local, and usually verbal accounts of the pattern of moisture supply to a farm or a village. The three sets, taken together, are all essential components of the national rainfall resource inventory. Too often only the information the gauges collect is taken into consideration.

Toward a Division of Labor in Natural-Resource Information:
An Example

All three information types cannot always be put to equally good use in every development situation. To a large extent, each situation should be considered unique, requiring its own particular mix of different types of information. To this end, it would be helpful to develop a general framework for understanding the degree of usefulness of different information mixes in different situations.

The key notion here is that of *scale*: the size of project, in terms of the number of people and size of the area involved and the scale at which different types of environment knowledge are accurate.

Scales of organization of societies and environment are arranged in separate hierarchies. For example, the climatologist uses generalized global models as a basis for analysis; it is frequently difficult to relate this to smaller environmental scales. Similarly, local people may possess detailed knowledge of areally limited environments yet have difficulty in generalizing this knowledge. Figure 11.1 suggests that there may be nested regularities of organization useful in linking scales of information. Although it may have some more general validity, the concept is considered here mainly in the context of the Sudan-Sahel zone (West Africa).

Field experience and comparative-literature surveys suggest that the different units have empirical validity. Resource units of 15 km² in a nomadic community generally represent the basic dry-season residence focus and subsistence territory of an extended family and its animals. Clan organizations, representing the smallest nomadic political unit of two hundred to five hundred individuals, claim preemptive rights to dry-season well and pasture sites of approximately 150 km². Subsistence-oriented peasant villages of a similar size in the southern and better-watered fringes of the Sahel most frequently derive their primary sustenance from territories of comparable scale. Higher-level political and cultural organizations in both nomadic and sedentary societies maintain usufruct rights to progressively larger regional units, although the effectiveness of such usage frequently fluctuates with the political fortunes of the tribal and ethnic structures and their leaders. Varying degrees of integration of these units at differing stages in regional ecology and seasonality create a kaleidoscopic yet rational pattern of resource assessment, manipulation, and exploitation.

FIGURE 11.1

Human Use Areal Scale (km^2)

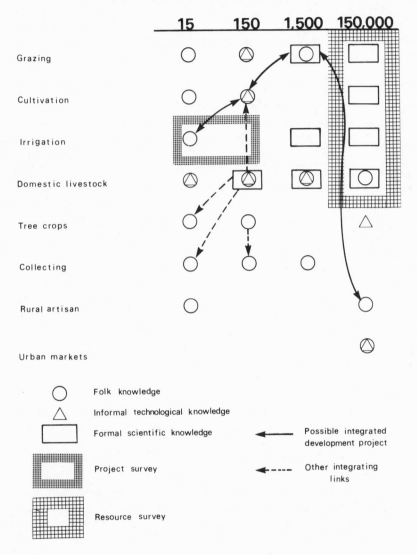

Grazing

Cultivation

Irrigation

Domestic livestock

Tree crops

Collecting

Rural artisan

Urban markets

○ Folk knowledge

△ Informal technological knowledge

▭ Formal scientific knowledge

▦ Project survey

▩ Resource survey

◀─── Possible integrated development project

◀- - - - Other integrating links

Small social groups function as resource users in microenvironments and are linked, in nested fashion, to other groups and environmental complexes at progressively higher levels of integration. Formal knowledge about these relationships is greatest at the extreme ends of this continuum and weakest at the intermediate levels of 150 to 500 km^2 or two hundred to five hundred people. It is at these intermediate scales of organization, where complementarities among micro units are discernable, that data gathering for development purposes needs to be concentrated. Effective new strategies for development require the integration of the major variables affecting the development process.

Plotting available knowledge in its formal, informal, and folk states for each livelihood activity reveals interesting relationships. Formal scientific knowledge is concentrated at the broad provincial scale and seldom penetrates to lower levels of regional organization. Folk knowledge is greatest at the most intimate scale; informal technical knowledge tends to fill the gap between scientific and folk information. It is important to stress the fact that this analysis does not suggest the relative strength of each type of knowledge at each scale. For example, it is clear that while folk knowledge may be comprehensive and exhaustive in its understanding of local water sources, it may possess significantly less information about such activities as tree cropping or the marketing opportunities of urban areas. The dominant kinds of activities listed in figure 11.1 might be both part of the current resource-use system and part of a development perspective in the area.

Folk knowledge will obviously be greatest for long-established activities at familiar scales. But there may well be possibilities of diversification of local economies that have not traditionally proved viable because of, say, prices and markets. Lack of local knowledge of these possibilities may be the case for all levels. Even a simple data matrix of this type might disclose what type of information is missing from the system.

But the figure reflects more than that. It illustrates the hypothesis that if there are unused resources and unnoticed opportunities in Sudan-Sahelian environments, many of them might be realized through a much closer integration of different scales of activity.

For example, an irrigation prospect occurs at a local level (15 km^2). How can this opprtunity be used to serve resource systems at 150 and 1,500 km^2? There is a rural artisan capacity in one localized area. Can this be developed to serve a wider market? Can "collecting" be developed as an economic activity to improve the well-being of pastoral or settled people without disturbing their current work patterns?

Development does not merely require the resource survey (vertical) at large scales (fig. 11.1) or the project survey (horizontal) at local scales; it also requires a pattern of environmental data that feed into a complementary resource system at a mixture of scales; in other words, it requires environmental data for integrated regional development.

Project surveys tend to deal only with one system; they invariably operate at small scales; and they seldom identify complementarities among resource-use activities. A small change in perspective emphasizing intermediate organizational scales would enable the project scheme to avoid the restrictions imposed by vertical or horizontal analysis and to stress a "diagonal" orientation incorporating a number of activities at differing scales, nested within one larger region. The simple initial example of this type of integration (indicated in figure 11.1) can be made more complex by developing and stressing subsidiary links (broken lines) with other complementary, if less immediate or obvious, livelihood activities.

Comparative Advantages of the Three Types of Knowledge at Different Scales

All information has a cost. Clearly the costs and benefits of each approach will differ for different types of projects. Although it is extremely difficult to quantify the trade-offs precisely, this section will attempt such an analysis in general terms. Figure 11.2 provides a summary of the argument.

First, let us examine the roles of the three different types of information within the small-scale context of building a dam for a village community. In order to build this dam using global science and technology, costs are involved for time, travel, salaries, materials, transport, consultation, and training. Local people may easily be shut out of the process except for provision of unskilled labor. What are the benefits? There may be a flow of benefits from the dam itself and its water, but strictly in terms of dam construction it is evident that the foreign-supply company gets business and a nonlocal person gains valuable research experience.

Let us now look at the situation from another angle and ask what the costs and benefits would be if local information and skills were used. The costs would involve: a small government or other agency loan or grant; time diverted from other tasks; political disagreement; and use of local materials and labor. Benefits result from the fact that local residents would be applying their understanding and management abilities in carrying out the project; simultaneous with this, communication between the local level and other parts of the country would be strengthened.

At this small scale, therefore, it is apparent that, in terms of quantifiable and nonquantifiable costs and benefits, using local knowledge and skills is much less expensive than using Western knowledge and skills.

For the purpose of examining costs and benefits of different information sources utilized for an intermediate-scale project, one can look at a region (one or more districts) within a nation in the context of an issue such as regional pest control. The costs, using Western science and technology, would involve: time, travel, salaries, consultant fees, the cost of research methods, and application of solutions. Various benefits would accrue from

FIGURE 11.2

Comparative Strengths of Different Knowledge Types

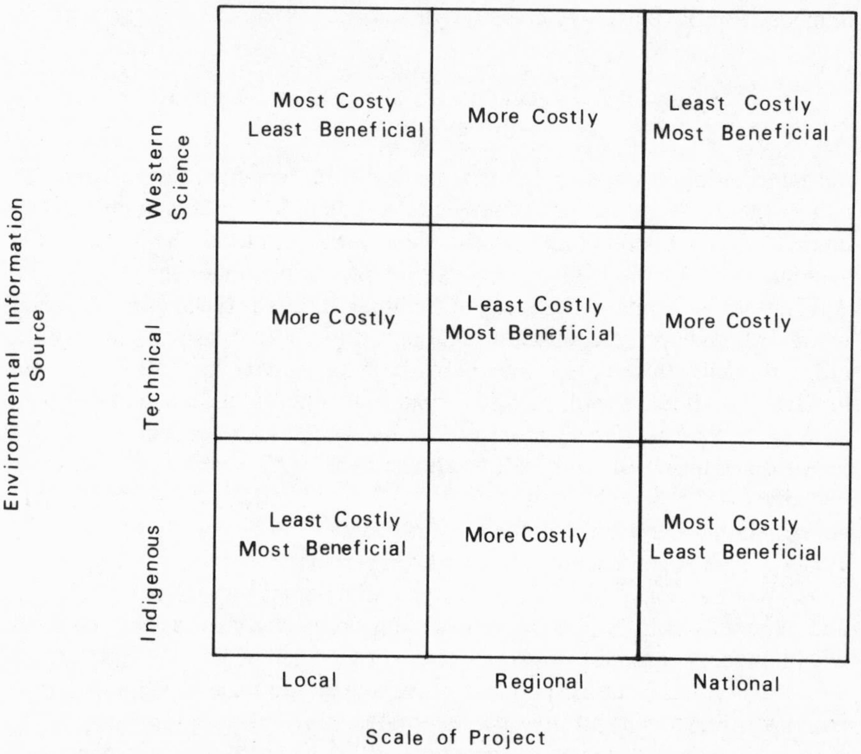

	Local	Regional	National
Western Science	Most Costly Least Beneficial	More Costly	Least Costly Most Beneficial
Technical	More Costly	Least Costly Most Beneficial	More Costly
Indigenous	Least Costly Most Beneficial	More Costly	Most Costly Least Beneficial

Environmental Information Source

Scale of Project

the anticipated success of the project and the downstream effects resulting from a focusing of constraints imposed by the pest. In addition, benefits would accrue to the foreign agrochemical companies involved.

Using local skills and knowledge, costs would involve: time diverted from other tasks, elementary and advanced training required, the possibility of extreme disinterest and resentment on the part of locals who are pressured into participating, lack of a regional framework necessary for pest control, and lack of appropriate levels of technology to complete the project. The benefits accruing would include the following: the locals learn, at great expense, occasionally useful skills; local materials are used; and at least temporary links are set up among local and other settings.

It is safe to say that both these information sources, at the regional level, are rather expensive, though the local approach is slightly less so than the Western approach. It is at this scale that one should point to the usefulness of the *technical* environmental information and skills source: extension workers and locals who have an understanding of an area at a more general, and yet more integrative, level than would either expatriates or locals.

Thus, the costs of a regional pest-control plan using extension and technical workers with regional knowledge include: time diverted from other tasks, supplemental training, the need for extension workers to enlist local helpers, and regional links to obtain appropriate materials and labor. The benefits include: a strengthening of regional links, the technical and extension workers' store of knowledge is brought into the system, the solution is communicated to local residents, and regional and local technology is used. Of the three environmental information and skills sources, one can conclude that the technical source is the least costly and most beneficial at this scale.

As a final example, one might next consider the theoretical costs and benefits of the three different information sources at the national scale. The project is to set in motion a nationwide survey of some particular resource or environmental process in order to build a uniform, reliable data base upon which the central government can rely and to which it can refer in coordinating planning efforts.

What are the theoretical costs and benefits in using local information and skills to gather this data? The costs involve: training large numbers of people to interpret maps and operate machinery, diverting time from other tasks, providing salaries for trainers, dealing with idiosyncratic data collection, transport and material costs, both original and in terms of maintenance, and probable dislike and distrust by locals regarding the purpose of the task and resentment of intrusions by outsiders. The benefits accruing include: people involved learn a skill (of very limited use), foreign supply and manufacturing companies get business.

The costs of using technical (i.e., regional) knowledge and skills involve the following additional expenses: specialized training, time diverted from other tasks, salaries of trainers, and original and maintenance costs. The benefits accruing include: people involved learn a skill of limited use, and foreign companies get business. Thus, use of technical information and skills is somewhat less costly than is use of local information and skills for this particular task and scale.

It is at this scale and for this purpose that Western science and technology is perhaps the least costly source. The costs include: training one to two persons (with previous Western scientific knowledge) to interpret satellite imagery as well as other survey sources and to use tools; expense of satellite imagery to government or institution from the United States or other country; recording and long-term interpretation. The benefits accruing include: a nationwide, uniform data base possessing long-term reliability, one comparable with other data bases collected by means of similar techniques.

To summarize, local knowledge, skills, and control are least costly and most beneficial for all involved at the local scale. At the intermediate (regional) scale, technical knowledge is most suitable. For nationwide surveys and monitoring of environmental information, Western science and technology have the most to offer at the lowest cost. This general statement is intended as a flexible framework, not a rigid formula, aimed at illustrating how various environmental information and skills sources can be successfully integrated into development planning.

Integrating Scales and Knowledge into Planning: Monitoring Desertification

A recent paper (Berry and Ford, 1977) set forth a series of recommendations for monitoring desertification. Although desertification is not viewed as a global problem, it is viewed as a problem having a complex variety of regional and local manifestations. The technique of monitoring desertification thus becomes one of linking data gathering at various scales into one information system. The system recommended in the above paper included the monitoring of five variables at the global scale and others at regional and local scales. It is possible to use a variety of techniques at the global scale—some of them quite sophisticated—to monitor albedo, dust storms, rainfall, soil erosion, sedimentation, and salinization. Landsat imagery and digital tapes are a vital component, but ground measurements and conventional air photography are recommended as component parts of the system. The approach appropriate for these variables is basically a Western-scientific one using international, regional, and national data-collection systems.

At the regional (international) level, the monitoring project (Berry and Ford, 1977) has proposed that monitoring should focus on regional indications of productivity to include measurement of such variables as standing biomass, climate, nutrition, and salinization.

The approach at this level would involve much the same mix of Western technology, remotely sensed imagery, and scientific data-collection systems. However, a variety of techniques have been suggested for productivity and nutrition, including simple local measures of child nutrition and the use of schools in this program.

Productivity, human well-being, and human perception of desertification are best studied at national and local levels. A variety of approaches appear to be appropriate, including some that deal directly with local system resource knowledge. For example, demonstration-type fenced plots can be used to increase local farmers' current knowledge of how land can be made to recover its productivity. Data collection on nutrition and productivity can alert local people to the issues involved and encourage the integration of their knowledge set with that derived from external sources. The monitoring project thus provides an example of the integrated approach that has been suggested.

The basic hypothesis of this chapter has been that a variable mix of three different kinds of environmental information is needed in order to improve development planning. A suitable combination of the global scientific approach, the insights of ethnoscience, and technical knowledge can provide the optimum type and quality of environmental information. Of course, varying proportions of formal and informal knowledge are appropriate for individual planning situations and scales. Ethnoscientific data may be most effective at local scales in rural situations, technical know-how may prove best at intermediate scales, and scientific information may be the right choice at broader or more generalized levels of inquiry.

The incorporation of various kinds of resource knowledge into development planning and development action can further goals of development not only among LDNs but in the development of rural and urban areas generally. The present challenge is to develop institutional structures and overcome the sense of inertia growing out of established procedures.

FOR FURTHER READING

Berry L. and J. Townshend. 1972. "Soil Conservation Policies in the Semi-arid Regions of Tanzania: An Historical Perspective." *Geografiska Annaler* (series A) 53, nos. 3–4: 241–253.

—— and R. Ford. 1977. *Recommendations for a System to Monitor Critical Indicators in Areas Prone to Desertification.* Worcester, Mass.: Clark University.

Blaut, J. M. et al. 1959. "A Study of Cultural Determinants of Soil Erosion and Conservation in the Blue Mountains of Jamaica." *Journal of Economic and Social Studies* 8: 403–420.

——. 1977. "Theses on the Peasantry." *Antipode.* Vol. 9, No. 3.

Boserup, E. 1965. *The Conditions of Agricultural Growth*. Chicago: Aldine.

Chang, Jen-Hu. 1977. "Tropical Agriculture: Crop Diversity and Crop Yields." *Economic Geography* 53, no. 3: 241–254.

Dasmann, R. F. et al. 1973. *Ecological Principles for Economic Development*. London: John Wiley.

Eckholm, E. 1977. *Losing Ground: Environmental Stress and World Food Prospects*. New York: Norton.

Farvar, M. T. and J. P. Milton. 1972. *The Careless Technology*. New York: Natural History Press.

Gladwin, F. 1970. *East Is a Big Bird*. Cambridge, Mass.: Harvard University Press.

Janzen, D. 1973. "Tropical Agroecosystems." *Science* 182 (Dec. 21): 1212–1219.

Lance, L. M. and E. E. McKenna. 1975. "Analysis of Cases Pertaining to the Impact of Western Technology on the Non-Western World." *Human Organization* 34, no. 1 (Spring): 87–94.

National Research Council. 1974. *More Water for Arid Lands*. Washington, D.C.: NAS.

———. 1975. *Underexploited Tropical Plants with Promising Economic Value*. Washington, D.C.: NAS.

O'Keefe, E. and M. Howes. 1978. "The Uses of Indigenous Technical Knowledge in Development: An Annotated Bibliography." Background paper for Indigenous Technical Knowledge workshop held at the Institute of Development Studies (IDS), Sussex, April 1978.

Peattie, Lisa R. 1969. *Views from the Barrio*. Cambridge, Mass.: MIT Press.

Wallman, S. 1972. "Conceptual Barriers to Cross Cultural Communication." *Cultural Adaptation Within Modern Africa*. Edited by S. H. Irvine and J. T. Sanders. New York: CEA Teachers College Press.

Whyte, Ann V. 1977. *Guidelines for Field Studies in Environmental Perception*. MAB Technical Notes, 5. Paris: UNESCO.

12. In the last few years, two African nations, Ethiopia and Zaire, have fought secessionist movements to prevent further Balkanization that would, as A. Seidman writes, further reduce their industrial development potential. But doing so in one case required the acceptance of old colonial masters and, in the other, massive Cuban and Soviet aid and intervention. At the same time, press reports describe a new statement of intent for economic cooperation to be undertaken by several countries of eastern and southern Africa meeting in Zambia.

Thus, the reality of internal conflict and external control still weakens the obvious and necessary potential for economic integration, one that would pool production amd markets among developing countries to provide the minimum capacity necessary for genuine regional collective self-reliance and development.

Judging from the historical cases presented by Seidman, as well as from her analysis of problems encountered on two occasions where there was a possibility for regional integration, it is obvious that *both* regional economic inequality and global ties mitigate against successful economic integration of the free or common-market variety. Such arrangements simply lead to further regional disparity by replacing metropolitan overseas control of the economy with capture of the weaker parties' market by the stronger regional partner—itself often linked to overseas corporate control.

Thus, unique and specific economic arrangements are required to make such integration work and to avoid a further increase in regional disparity. Such economic arrangements demand a special political vision that can transcend the day-to-day difficulties of realigning economies, with the accompanying short-term gains and losses, to permit a fundamental restructuring and reorienting of the small but important industrial sector. Such a political vision occasionally asserts itself among LDNs, but its simultaneous, sustained appearance in bordering countries has not yet occurred.

REGIONAL INTEGRATION: SOME POSSIBILITIES IN EAST AND CENTRAL AFRICA

A. Seidman

Almost fifty nations have attained independence in Africa in little more than a decade. The national boundaries they inherited were carved out three-quarters of a century ago without regard to geographical resources, economic viability, or ethnic groupings. The resulting national units are so small that in the majority of cases their populations are smaller than those of a good-size European city. Small populations, combined with extremely low per capita incomes, has left these nations with markets too small to establish optimum-size factories in any but a handful of light industries. Their divided resources are incapable of supporting the range of basic industries required to contribute significantly to a sustained pattern of nationally balanced, integrated development. Since most of them lack the capital to build manufacturing industries, they must depend heavily on outside financing for whatever small factories they do try to establish. (For an extensive discussion of the problems of Balkanization, see Green and Seidman, 1968.)

An examination of the typical manufacturing sectors that have emerged since independence—even in the somewhat larger countries—shows that they have increasingly imported parts and materials needed to produce items demanded by higher-income groups, using greater amounts of capital-intensive machinery and equipment. This pattern of industrialization is, if anything, increasing rather than reducing the dependence of new African nations on external supplies. They must expand their traditional exports to finance growing imports, which now include initial capital machinery and equipment and the continuing importation of intermediate parts and materials to facilitate local last-stage processing and/or assembly of goods formerly imported in a finished state. This trend seems to persist regardless of whether the new factories are built entirely by private enterprises—in most cases, affiliates of multinational firms, sometimes with a few prominent Africans on the board of directors or as shareholders—or by state corporations in some form of partnership with foreign firms (Seidman, 1974b).

Part of the explanation for this pattern of manufacturing growth lies in the adoption by new African governments of import-substitution policies in the context of only marginally changed inherited institutional structures. This approach leaves decisions concerning investment in new manufacturing capacity in the hands of multinational firms. The latter seek to maximize their profits in a distorted market in which less than 10 percent of the population controls perhaps 50 or 60 percent of the nation's purchasing power. The vast majority of most African urban populations spend over half of their cash incomes to buy: food, mostly in the form of starchy staples; scanty clothing, often secondhand; a few plates, pots, locally produced wooden chairs; and, if they're a little better off, a bicycle or a transistor radio. Most rural families grow their own food, construct housing, and fashion utensils, spending their limited cash incomes on a narrow range of simple manufactured items like cloth, kerosene, matches, and salt (Seidman, 1962, 1973). Even if an African government seeks to alter its institutional structure, in most cases the small size of the national market severely limits the possibility of building a broader range of industries.

On the other hand, efforts to attain regional integration within the framework of inherited institutions have offered little in the way of more balanced, integrated regional economic development; in some cases they have actually aggravated the lopsided, externally dependent character of regional growth.

The twofold aim of this chapter is to consider: (1) the limitations of common-market integration as a strategy for balanced regional development, drawing on the experiences of the East African Common Market, the Federation of Rhodesia and Nyasaland, and the Southern African Common

Market; and (2) the necessary ingredients of an alternative approach to regional integration, with two illustrations drawn from central and eastern Africa.

The Inadequacy of Common-Market Integration

It is commonly agreed that economic integration is essential to speed rapid industrial growth in Africa. Even the multinationals, especially in trade and manufacturing, are today pressing for common markets to broaden their marketing possibilities for the last-stage assembly and processing plants being established in the larger African economies. It is interesting to note that whereas manufacturing firms are interested in broadening markets through common-market integration, mining companies generally do not support integration. Copper-mining companies, for example, were taxed more heavily by the Federation of Rhodesia and Nyasaland than they had been previously. They apparently believe that it is to their advantage to keep Zambia, Zaire, and Botswana separate so that they will not formulate joint demands to control remaining concessions as well as refining and fabricating industries. However, agencies like USAID, the World Bank, and others—which are constitutionally required to foster private firms' (almost all multinationals) investment and sales efforts—are today in the forefront of efforts to encourage economic integration among the Balkanized African states.

But the African experience, like that of Latin America (Marano, 1964; Hirschman, 1968), has already underscored the fact that economic integration per se is not a viable solution to alleviate underdevelopment and the poverty of the African masses. The *form*, the *way* in which integration is achieved, and the *institutional framework* within which it operates are all crucial factors contributing significantly to African efforts to attain development and a greater degree of economic independence.

Economic integration is not new in Africa. To mention only the case of the former British colonies, measures have been taken during the past several decades to unite the following groups of nations into single common-market areas: the East African Common Market; the Federation of Rhodesia and Nyasaland; and the Southern African Common Market area, including Botswana, Lesotho, and Swaziland. The approach was similar in each case: a common market was created, surrounded by a common tariff wall, with more or less central planning of economic infrastructure for the enclosed region. All of the above methods were designed to lead private firms to invest in manufacturing industries in order to meet the needs of the newly created and protected broader market.

Not surprisingly, in each case the results were similar: large multi-nationals—often the same ones in all the regions (National Christian Council of Kenya, 1968)—established affiliated manufacturing branches and/or subsidiaries in the more developed areas of the newly created common markets: Nairobi and Mombasa in Kenya; Salisbury and Bulawayo in Southern

Rhodesia; and Durban and Johannesburg in South Africa. Local-settler interests, which dominated the government and domestic economies of these areas, were often invited to participate in the projects as individuals or by way of supplying machinery and capital. By importing and assembling (or last-stage processing) the parts and materials provided by their overseas concerns, the multinationals thus assured themselves of a well-established foothold in the larger protected regional markets. In all cases, they relied heavily on government support, tax incentives, and cheap African labor to ensure profit margins that usually exceeded those they could expect at home. For example, U.S. firms investing in manufacturing in Africa—four out of five of them in South Africa—have reported average rates of profit of 19.11 percent, a percentage higher than those they obtained in other areas of the world (Adler, 1967). The resulting augmentation of outflows of investable surpluses from the region (in the form of profits, interest, and high salaries of foreign managers of these projects) was accepted by the participating governments as the necessary price of these investments.

The host economies in all three regions, particularly in the towns cited above, became the most industrialized in sub-Saharan Africa. The masses of Africans living in the regions, however, did not benefit much from resulting economic growth. On the contrary, it became increasingly evident that the prosperity of the newly emergent regional "centers" was being achieved at the expense of continuing and further underdevelopment of the "peripheries" (Keatley, 1963; Seidman, 1972). Today these peripheries are often totally independent yet still remain LDNs.

Alternative Approaches to Integration in Southern and Central Africa

An analysis of past efforts to achieve economic integration in Africa suggests that the crux of the matter lies in the pattern of institutional arrangements governing the regional-cooperation agreements. It appears that common-market agreements, even when backed by joint infrastructural development, are unlikely to contribute significantly to the attainment of major gains promised by proponents of economic integration so long as they leave key industrial investment decisions to existing distorted market forces. This suggests that fundamental changes must be made in inherited institutional structures if the potential gains of integration are to be achieved.

In the first place, there must be political-economic agreement among regional partners on the industrial-allocation pattern to be achieved over a period of, say, twenty years, to ensure that all major investable surpluses produced in the region, as well as any obtained on favorable terms from outside, are directed to its fulfillment. Once this regional pattern of industrial development is agreed upon, the necessary institutional changes must be made to ensure its fulfillment.

The possibility of improving resource use through this alternative approach to economic integration may be illustrated by two examples drawn from east and central Africa, each involving a LDN with stronger partners. Given the resource potentials of one region the potential economic benefits to be gained are great. But the problem of creating appropriate sets of institutions appears difficult, if not impossible, to surmount at the present time. In the second case, although existing resource development is not as great, first steps to institutionalize regional cooperation have already been undertaken. Their success may contribute to a wider awareness of the advantages of integration.

Botswana, Zaire, and Zambia

The first case involves the construction of a heavy industrial sector, combined with a hydroelectric grid, based on the copper wealth of Zambia, Zaire, and Botswana (Seidman, 1976). The primary source of wealth of all three countries today is the output of mines on the copper belt, which radiates in an arc northward from Botswana through Zambia and Zaire and then curves westward into Angola. Copper has been the main export of Zambia and Zaire for half a century. In Zambia's case, copper constitutes over 90 percent of its exports. Botswana has only begun to produce copper, as well as nickel, in the last decade at its Selebi-Pikwe mines.

The mines of all three countries were developed by big international mining firms: Zambia—the Anglo-American company (South Africa), American Metal Climax (U.S.); Zaire—Union Minière de Haute Katanga (Belgium); Botswana—an Anglo-American/American Metal Climax consortium. For the most part, the companies have shipped copper out of these countries in semiprocessed forms. In Zambia, more extensive refining capacity was established, perhaps because Anglo-American viewed its mines (located in what was formerly the British colony of North Rhodesia) as part of its southern African domain. Yet even Zambia sells almost all its copper in bulk form, though refined, to be fabricated into final products in the factories of Europe and, more recently, Japan. All three countries must still buy almost every item that incorporates copper in a finished form from Europe, America, or Japan. This is still true even though the governments of Zambia and Zaire intervened in the late 1960s to acquire 51 and 100 percent, respectively, of the ownership of their mines. (The government of Zaire has since sold new concessions to Anglo-American and Japanese interests, retaining only a minority share.) The companies still manage the mines and handle overseas sales.

Domestic regional production of the inputs required for the copper industry could contribute to the building of basic regional industry in several respects. First, copper smelting and refining require large amounts of hydroelectric power. Zambia has already developed an extensive hydroelectric capacity to lessen its dependence on power produced by the Kariba project (built by the colonial authorities on the Rhodesian side of the border during the days of the Federation of Rhodesia and Nyasaland). Today, Zaire is constructing the first phase of the Inga project, linking it with the copper belt in Lubumbashi by over one thousand miles of high-tension cable. Over a period of time, the Inga project could be expanded to provide more hydroelectric power than is presently produced in all of western Europe. By linking up Zambia and Zaire's expanding hydroelectric power-production capacity, the foundation for a transcontinental power grid would be laid, which could facilitate the expansion of industrial capacity throughout central Africa. This grid might be extended to Botswana to reduce that nation's current dependence on South African electricity supplies.

Second, the mines require other inputs that could increasingly be provided by the resources resulting from the expansion of a regional industrial base. These inputs include construction material, explosives, and a range of tools and equipment—from picks and shovels to a vast array of complex machinery, including steam shovels and giant trucks used in open-pit mining.

Zambia has expanded its explosives production and has begun to utilize some of the by-products in fertilizer production. It has built up a fairly extensive small-scale industrial sector capable of repairing the complex machinery and equipment required for the mines; and it even manufactures some of the simpler equipment by utilizing imported parts and materials. Zaire is also moving in this direction. Botswana, which is least developed, is forced to rely almost entirely on the industrial capacity of South Africa for these inputs—a significant reflection of its external dependence on its white minority-ruled neighbor.

If Zambia, Botswana, and Zaire could jointly expand the production of these essential inputs, their combined market would make possible the establishment of basic engineering and chemical industries large enough to take advantage of the available economies of scale. They could gradually begin to produce a full array of machinery and equipment required to work the mines; they could use local resources and thereby provide increased employment opportunities for large numbers of workers currently unemployed in the three countries. Over a period of from ten to fifteen years, these industries might become major buyers of the output of an integrated iron and steel complex located within the region.

At the other end of the copper-production sequence, the three countries could more effectively expand their refining and copper-manufacturing processes in the context of a coordinated regional plan. Zaire, most of whose copper is now refined in Europe and Japan, is reportedly planning to expand its refinery capacity to process all of its crude copper output by 1980. Mutual benefit might result from a joint planning effort with Zambia, whose existing refineries are located about fifty miles from Lubumbashi, the capital of Zaire's mining sector. Botswana, on the other hand, is required by the companies who manage its mines to ship crude copper to an American Metal Climax–owned refinery in the United States before it is reshipped to Metallgesellschaft in West Germany for final processing. Inclusion of Botswana's output in regional refining plants would also contribute to building up the regional industrial base.

The combined output of the three countries might warrant the major capital expenditure on development of the continuous smelting-refining process, which is presently rendering existing refining technology obsolete. Installation of this new technology in the region would help to reduce the continuing dependence of these countries on the technology-marketing-processing networks dominated by multinational mining corporations. It has been suggested that control of technology may be one crucial means by which the multinationals will retain their domination of the world copper industry despite the efforts of producers to obtain ownership and control of the copper mines themselves (Mezger, 1976).

The initiation of joint planning to expand regional copper-based industrial growth could best take place within the context of cooperation for development of a more extended regional industrial complex. Fabricated copper is primarily sold to factories that process copper into a range of products to meet industrial and durable consumer-goods requirements. The copper-exporting countries would confront almost insurmountable obstacles were they to sell copper at more advanced stages of manufacture in the markets of industrialized countries of Europe and the United States, markets that are strongly protected by tariffs and the interests of multinational firms. Increased copper fabrication in the copper-producing countries requires the expansion of markets in developing countries themselves. This, in turn, necessitates extensive new industrial growth geared to the economic and social transformation of the entire region.

Copper wire and cable, for example, constitute a considerable market for copper output, but the expansion of the market for these items is dependent on the development of regional industries requiring wire and cable. It might be noted, in passing, that more than one thousand miles of high-tension wire connecting Zaire's Inga project with the mines in the Lubumbashi region are to be fabricated from aluminum instead of copper. The French contracting firm that built the project insisted that aluminum has certain advantages over copper, this despite the high costs involved in importing the cable and the failed opportunity of expanding Zaire's own cable-producing capacity to provide this large regional requirement.

Only the planned coordination of the regional wire and cable industry, in the context of an overall regional industrial strategy, would make it feasible to risk the large amounts of capital required to take advantage of this and other market possibilities. Given the fact that no such planned coordination now exists, there has actually been a reduction in preexisting linkages between the copper sectors of Zambia and Zaire. Zambia has expanded its own sales of wire and cable through Zamefa, a government-owned firm managed by Phelps Dodge, a U.S. firm. Zamefa sells its own imported products to supplement the limited range of items produced in a very small, new Zambian plant. As a result, Zambia has stopped importing wire and cable from Zaire, imports that had previously constituted an important market permitting the establishment of a small Zairois wire and cable factory.

The short-term obstacles to regional integration of the three copper-producing countries are great. The existing infrastructure of each country was built by the respective colonial powers to orient their economies away from each other and toward the factories of Europe and, increasingly, the United States and Japan. To this day, there is no railroad, or even a tarmac road, linking Botswana and Zambia. Botswana was initially perceived by the colonial powers as a labor reserve for South Africa's mines and plantations. Today, copper and nickel are being produced under the management and control of South African and U.S. consortiums. The participating firms insist on supplying the necessary inputs and determining the recipients of the output of the mines in the light of their own South African and global considerations. Their insistence is backed up by the fact that all the institutions governing finance and trade in Botswana are linked to those in South Africa. Botswana has only recently reached the stage where it can now implement the establishment of its own currency, controlled by its own central bank.

The gulf existing between Zambia and Zaire is likewise far greater than the fifty miles along the border that divides the copper belt running through the two countries. The barrier created by the adoption of English and French, respectively, as the official languages of Zambia and Zaire is not a primary obstacle; Zambian and Zairois citizens on both sides of the border speak Bemba. Moreover, many are related through extended family ties. More serious is the fact that the multinational mining companies on both sides of the border are orienting the development of their mining operations away from each other and toward providing the raw materials for the industrial complexes with which they have connections overseas. They also produce the mining inputs, technologies, and finance in ways calculated to maximize their own global control and profit. Even Anglo-American, which today has interests on both sides of the border, appears to be making no effort to plan the joint coordination of its Zambian and Zairois concerns. The two governments appear to be making plans for industrial development in a completely uncoordinated, competitive, and even conflicting manner. While there is extensive government intervention in the mining industry on both sides of the border, no effort has been made to jointly plan the development of the industry.

The short-term prospect for increased coordination of the copper-mining industries among the three countries appears gloomy. Despite this fact, long-term planning should nevertheless be undertaken. It is certainly logical for government personnel and policy-oriented research institutions in all three countries to begin to explore the technical possibilities for closer industrial coordination, as well as the kinds of institutional changes that may be required to implement it.

Mozambique, Tanzania, and Zambia

An illustration of a more immediate possibility of regional economic integration is provided by Tanzania (one of the original least developed countries),

Mozambique, and perhaps Zambia. Unlike the case involving copper, the potential here does not lie primarily in further development of resources that are already being exploited. Rather, it lies in the fact that Tanzania and Mozambique, although relatively underdeveloped, encompass vast land areas with extensive resources for potential development, contain outlets to the sea, and have significant human populations. These are all features that Zambia needs if it is to build an advanced, integrated industrial base—despite the fact that it has the highest per capita income (derived from its mines) in sub-Saharan Africa. Zambia, together with Tanzania and Mozambique (under its new government), might be able to reach an agreement concerning the pattern of industrial development needed to transform the region, in the next twenty years, into a self-reliant, integrated area capable of providing productive employment opportunities and raising the standard of living of the the entire regional population. Together, the three nations have the resources and the markets needed for basic industries. With careful financial planning in the context of an effective-income policy, they could muster sufficient capital to invest in a considerably expanded set of basic industries. United, they could bargain far more effectively to obtain favorable terms for technical assistance and funds from a variety of foreign sources, including multinational corporations as well as socialist countries.

Tanzania, for example, might want to build an integrated iron and steel industry based on its deposits located near the new Tazara railway; this industry could utilize nearby coal deposits. Initially, it might use Zambia's coal resources, since the latter's hydroelectric capacity and oil resources are now replacing coal as a source of energy for the mining industry. Mozambique might develop a range of engineering industries by using the power generated by the Cabora Basa dam project, which could be linked with Zambia's hydroelectric grid and extended to expand Tanzania's present limited capacity. These kinds of developments might be supplemented by projects based on Mozambique's little-known mineral deposits and agricultural resources. In this context, Zambia might well begin to produce copper-intermediate inputs, essential for finding an expanding market in new industries established by its neighbors.

Important steps have already been taken to facilitate the expansion of cooperation among these three countries. Tanzania and Zambia jointly obtained U.S. assistance to build a tarmac road alongside the "hell-run"; this road provided Zambia with its first outlet to the sea through friendly territory after Rhodesia illegally declared its independence. They jointly planned the Tazama pipeline, constructed by the Italian firm ENI, whose purpose was to ship crude oil to Zambia's new oil refinery. They are jointly managing and financing the railroad, completed by the Chinese in 1975, thus providing Zambia with a means of transporting its heavy copper cargoes to ocean ports.

Both Tanzania and Zambia were staunch supporters of Frelimo during the decade of guerilla warfare to liberate Mozambique from the Portuguese. It is to be hoped that they will extend this cooperation to the joint planning of a long-term industrial strategy for the region. Tanzania and the newly independent government of Mozambique have already announced specific measures to coordinate their industrial development particularly with respect to the establishment of key basic industries. They have agreed to hold regular meetings attended by the responsible ministers in order to consider how this may be achieved.

While decisions are being made to invest in growth pole industries—carefully planned to link up with the expansion of a range of agricultural and industrial projects to augment output and employment in each participating country—each government will need to make critical institutional changes to ensure the plan's success (Green and Seidman, 1968). This is not meant to suggest that continental unity is essential to attain the benefits of economic integration, but similar institutional changes appear necessary in the regional context. First, each country must guarantee that it will purchase an adequate share of the output of new key industries established by its neighbors to make these projects viable. Each country will have to agree to ban imports of competing products from outside the region. It will probably be necessary to make institutional changes in order to exert a sufficient degree of control over the importing sector to enforce these agreements. A 51 percent government ownership of importing houses that leaves management of the latter to foreign partners is probably not adequate. Available evidence indicates that foreign managers in such partnerships perpetuate past patterns of importation of goods (if they have been profitable to them) without regard for national development needs; the Zambian case provides a prime example (Seidman, 1974b). It will probably be necessary for participating member governments to institutionalize more direct control of all imports.

Tanzania, Zambia, and Mozambique all appear to have initiated some institutional changes in the areas of export-import and internal wholesale trade, both of which are required to support the planned implementation of a joint, long-term industrial strategy. Tanzania and Zambia have established some degree of control of imports through the use of state trading forms. While difficulties have been encountered in the process of reshaping these institutions to support national development programs, procedures are being worked out that may, over time, ensure that goods imported support and supplement, rather than compete with, the output of regionally planned industries. Mozambique's new government is apparently in the process of attaining greater control in this critical field, but it will undoubtedly take time to develop the necessary new institutions and procedures (Saul, 1975).

Several features of the process of implementing an agreed-upon regional plan for allocating new industries require a fundamental restructuring of inherited sets of financial institutions to permit effective general financial planning. The prices of the outputs of new industries would need to be relatively stable if each participating nation is to purchase fixed quantities. The introduction of unexpected price changes would undermine efforts to develop long-term national plans. Attainment of the required price stability would, however, require a sufficient degree of direct control over national monetary supplies and financial institutions to ensure that essential credit could be allocated to the planned sectors without spurring inflation. A private, foreign-dominated banking system in any of the member countries would probably continue to direct credit to the profitable import-export and internal-trade sectors instead of expanding the new industrial and agricultural projects. (For information relating to the role of banks in typical African economies, see Newlyn and Rowan, 1954, and Seidman, 1974b. For the Zambian case, see Harvey, 1971; Bank of Zambia, 1972; and Seidman, 1974a.)

The problem of establishing appropriate prices for the agreed-upon exchange of output of new industries is rendered more complex in the case of Tanzania and Zambia. Zambia's cost-price structure is roughly one-third higher than that of Tanzania as a result of a set of complicated historical causes. This is true, in particular, for goods purchased by lower-income groups, although Tanzania's high taxes on luxury items, purchased by higher-income groups, render prices of such items comparable to prices in Zambia (Tenu and Seidman, 1973). It has been suggested (Goodman, 1971) that Zambia would have to devalue its currency if it wished to enter the East African Common Market in order to enable its goods to compete with those of its East African neighbors. But devaluation in Zambia would further distort its already lopsided economy. Zambia is already selling as much copper as it can produce at prevailing world copper prices. Devaluation, which would necessitate a reduction in local production costs, would do little to expand world sales. Instead, it would primarily contribute to increased profits of the copper companies, half of which would be shipped out to foreign partners. Zambia is also heavily dependent on imports, whose prices in *kwacha* would be increased as a result of devaluation, thus contributing to further domestic inflation and reducing the living standards of the urban population.

The argument in favor of devaluation rests on the assumption that the purpose of creating a common market is to facilitate competition, including unimpeded monetary movement, so that the most efficient firms may survive. In the case of basic industries in Africa, however, each industrial complex would require the entire regional market to become economically viable. None of these basic industries are likely to be established unless there is a political-economic agreement, backed by essential institutional changes, to guarantee that benefits are distributed so that the population of all the participating nations profit from the increased productive employment opportunities stimulated by the pole-of-growth impact. In other words, planning, not competition, is essential in order to achieve the agreed-upon allocation of resources and investable surpluses over a given period of time.

In the Zambian-Tanzanian case, only a small fraction of each country's output is initially likely to be sold from one country to the other since each country presently exports items which the other consumes in insignificant amounts. The real gains in the division of labor and the expansion of trade will only take place gradually as new basic industrial complexes are planned and built. Hence, instead of introducing a massive devaluation that would affect all of Zambia's external trade relations, it would be far more fruitful to maintain tight exchange controls to ensure that each country buys from the other the specific, agreed-upon output of the new industries at fixed prices. Initially, these prices would be higher in Zambia and lower in Tanzania, reflecting the underlying structural cost-price differentials. The extra profits generated by the sale of low-cost Tanzanian produce in Zambia could be used to reduce the cost of Zambian items sold in Tanzania. The need to maintain tight exchange control and regulate prices is an additional reason for the exercise of strong control of monetary and financial institutions by participating governments. As trade among participating nations increases, these controls could gradually be utilized to reduce differences in cost-price structures of the two countries.

Attainment of the kind of control necessary to implement this kind of financial planning implies that each member state must exercise control over its national banking system. Tanzania has nationalized its banks and has developed a range of techniques to achieve the degree of financial planning needed to implement an effective-income policy and to allocate essential surpluses to planned projects. Mozambique's new government has taken similar steps to attain far-reaching reform of its financial institutions. The major banks in Zambia, however, remain in foreign hands even though they are locally incorporated. Barclays, Standards, and National Grindleys—the three big banks that previously conducted almost all of Tanzania's banking business—still dominate Zambia's financial scene. The government owns one small bank and has shares in another. Zambia will undoubtedly need to reexamine the way its financial institutions function if it wishes to participate seriously in plans for regional industrial growth.

Over a period of time, it will be necessary to work toward common incomes and tax policies in order to direct all available investable surpluses to proposed new industrial and agricultural projects throughout the region. The persistence of distorted income patterns and significant differences in tax policies would hinder the eventual integration and development of industrial growth, as well as coordinated pricing and monetary policies. Attention must be directed to coordinating monetary policy, incomes and tax planning in the context of a long-range financial plan paralleling the long-term strategy for physical industrial development. This will require the close cooperation of governmental agencies involved with finance ·and financial institutions providing credit and setting prices for industrial and agricultural production.

There is undoubtedly a political precondition for the attainment of those institutional changes required to give the participating member governments suficient control of what President Nyerere has termed "the commanding heights" in order to implement a long-term regional industrial development strategy. The participating state governments must be guided by the concerns and requirements of average citizens rather than by the interests of a corps of elites who are bound by social status, education, and/or ideology to upholding the status quo. The political apparatus must be structured so as to ensure that working people, peasants, wage earners, and growing numbers of urban unemployed are increasingly able to participate in the critical decision-making process responsible for the shaping of the regional development program (Saul, 1973). There is evidence that the political leaders of Tanzania and Mozambique recognize the importance of this prerequisite (TANU Guidelines, 1971). Whether the same holds true for Zambia's leaders remains to be seen.

The postindependence experience of Balkanized African states suggests that the existing set of inherited institutional structures, operating in the context of small populations and limited markets, tends to aggravate externally dependent resource and ownership patterns. Such economic growth as does occur primarily benefits a narrow economic circle of elites closely linked to the giant multinational firms that dominate the national export enclaves.

It is generally agreed that a partial solution to this problem would be to broaden the resource bases, markets, and available sources of capital by means of economic integration. Past African experience indicates that common-market integration may foster replication and further aggravate distorted inherited paterns within and among participating nations, often to the sole detriment of LDNs among the partners.

What is required is a degree of political-economic agreement necessary to formulate a regional industrial-allocation policy, accompanied by major changes in key institutions governing basic industries, export-import and internal wholesale trade, and finance. This should permit the participating member nations to make the best use of their combined resources, markets, and available investable surpluses in order to create pole-of-growth industries and set off chains of development throughout the entire region. United, they will be in a better position to bargain effectively with external sources of technical assistance and finance in order to better implement proposed regional plans. This approach is far more likely to contribute significantly to the rapid spread of productive employment opportunities and a higher standard of living for the masses of Africans in the region than common-market integration.

The potential technological advantages resulting from the coordination of the copper-based industries of Zambia, Zaire, and Botswana are clearly significant; from a short-term perspective, obvious difficulties will more than likely hinder their full realization. More hopeful is the possibility of coordinating the long-term industrial strategies of Tanzania, Mozambique, and perhaps even Zambia. These countries have a combined land area roughly the size of western Europe and a combined population of over twenty-five million. Their governments have already made some of the necessary institutional changes to facilitate regional coordination and have taken significant steps toward cooperation in other areas. Their success may set off a dynamic for growth that will gradually lay the foundations for the planned coordination of physical resources and institutional change capable of transforming the entire central and southern African region.

FOR FURTHER READING

Cliffe, L. and J. Saul, eds. 1972. *Socialism in Tanzania*. Nairobi: East Africa Publishing House.

Frank, A. G. 1970. "The Development of Underdevelopment." *Imperialism and Underdevelopment*. Edited by Robert I. Rhodes. New York: Monthly Review Press, pp. 4–17.

Ghai, D. P., ed. 1973. *Economic Independence in Africa*. Nairobi: East Africa Literature Bureau.

Green, R. H. and A. Seidman. 1968. *Unity or Poverty? The Economics of Pan Africanism*. Harmondsworth: Penguin African Library.

Keatley, P. 1963. *The Politics of Partnership: The Federation of Rhodesia and Nyasaland*. Harmondsworth: Penguin African Library.

Lewis, W. A. 1966. *Developing Planning—Lessons of Experience*. New York: Harper & Row.

Leys, Colin. 1975. *Underdevelopment in Kenya: The Political Economy of Neo-Colonialism*. Berkeley: University of California Press.

Myrdal, Gunnar. 1957. *Economic Theory and Underdeveloped Regions*. London: Duckworth.

Seidman, A. 1972. *Comparative Development Strategies in East Africa*. Nairobi: East Africa Publishing House.

———. 1974. *Planning for Development in Sub-Saharan Africa*. New York: Praeger.

———, ed. 1976. *Natural Resources and National Welfare: The Case of Copper*. New York: Praeger.

——— and N. Seidman. 1977. *South Africa and U.S. Multinational Corporations*. Westport, Conn.: Lawrence Hill.

Szentes, Tamas. 1971/1973. *The Political Economy of Underdevelopment*. Budapest: Akademiai Kiado.

13. The conventional development wisdom of the fifties and the sixties was "trickle-down" wisdom. In all areas, including development aid, the good things of life would pass down the hierarchy of national capacity to grow and develop until they reached the nations most in need. The possibility that such a process may never reach the beneficiary lowest on the ladder, or the fact that it may even increase the distance between lowest and highest, is now widely recognized. What is not clear is what can be done to rectify this situation. For that, conventional wisdom was clearly the most comfortable wisdom, and the alternatives, as G. K. Helleiner carefully points out, are either ineffectual in meeting the needs of the poorest or cannot easily be effectuated, given the melange of interests and motivations of both rich and moderately affluent nations.

According to Helleiner, a wide range of alternatives has been proposed for more selective aid both to the poorest peoples and the poorest nations, including special trade considerations, new monetary and financial arrangements, increased and more flexible aid, efforts aimed at selected strata of the population or specific nations, and assistance from wealthier developing nations.

One massive experiment launched in the aftermath of the Sahelian drought should be of particular interest to LDNs and those who assist them. During the drought of 1968–1974, Chad, Mali, Mauritania, Niger, Senegal, and Upper Volta banded together to form the Permanent Interstate Committee for Control of Drought. Following the drought, the committee (now including Gambia and the Cape Verde islands) entered into a formal arrangement with potential donor nations, who also organized themselves as the Club des Amis du Sahel, for the purpose of long-range assistance to the Sahelian nations. Funding for the program, a suggested $7.5 billion over a period of twenty years, represents a 500 percent increase over previous commitments. Even more important is the nature of the development aid. The latter will serve as a test of whether such massive support will increase self-sufficiency and regional self-reliance or simply increase the burden of dependence.

INTERNATIONAL TRADE AND AID: BENEFITS OF A NEW INTERNATIONAL ECONOMIC ORDER

G. K. Helleiner

What are the specific interests of the poorest countries in discussions of a new international economic order (IEO)? Based upon the composition of their exports (as described in chap. 2) and their extreme dependence upon development assistance, it should be evident that *particular* commodity trade agreements or initiatives and increased or reallocated aid flows are the areas of greatest hope for the immediate future.

Commodity Trade Agreements and Least Development

International agreements supporting certain commodity prices and the stabilization of earnings from such prices seem more likely in the present international climate than at any other time in the past thirty years (i.e., since Lord Keynes argued vigorously for them in connection with wartime plans for the postwar order). Fear of supply restrictions and the demonstrated power of the OPEC countries have effectively modified the positions of the governments of some consuming nations; the latter had formerly opposed market organization despite the fact that such arrangements had long been common within their own borders (and within the multinational firms). The Lomé Convention's STABEX scheme for guaranteeing export earnings from selected commodities and countries, while still subject to some grave limitations, is probably a harbinger of better and more comprehensive schemes to come. UNCTAD invested considerable energies in the elaboration of such commodity schemes—buffer stocks and funds, financing arrangements—and focused upon them at its 1976 conference. At the Conference on International Economic Cooperation in Paris, OPEC countries successfully insisted that commodities be discussed in conjunction with oil. While the government of the United States remains divided between the State and Treasury departments, it, too, has now backed off from its former hard-line opposition to discussions on commodities. With the exception of the United States and West Germany, most OECD nations now seem ready to work out some sort of accommodating arrangement with the Third World in the commodity arena, although progress remains painfully slow.

For individual poor countries, the major question remains: For which commodities are there to be arrangements? The STABEX list of commodities (now totaling 36, including subproducts) includes some that are of great interest to poor countries (e.g., coffee, cotton, and some major oilseeds are on the list) as well as some that are less interesting. The list of products in UNCTAD's integrated program for commodities (ten "core" and eight "other" products) is similarly varied. The share of the gains to be realized by the poorest countries from such agreements may not be too large. That is part of their problem. LDCs derive their only bargaining strength for their relatively weak commodities from their association with countries selling "stronger" commodities, not the least of which is, of course, petroleum. The intercountry distribution of gains from commodity agreements may therefore always look skewed toward the developing countries, which are already relatively well off. One must obviously always be careful that resource-poor countries are not left with absolutely worsened terms of trade in consequence of such agreements; the oil experience demonstrates that awful possibility. The fact remains, however, that of all the "IEO" topics, these agreements offer the greatest prospects of absolute gains for the poorest countries. (Needless to say, the gains may not actually reach the poorest people in the poorest countries.)

There is an explicit built-in bias toward assistance for the poorest thirty-four countries (out of a total of forty-six) in the Lomé Convention's STABEX agreement. They qualify for assistance more easily; moreover, whereas the stabilizing payments made to them are in the form of grants, in other cases they are made as loans. Moreover, since nineteen of the twenty-nine LDCs are signatories to that convention, it can, quite apart from its special provisions, be viewed as generally beneficial to some of the poorest countries. This instance of superpreferential *trade* treatment for the poorest countries is virtually unique in major international economic agreements. It might serve as a precedent for additional special preferences. The European Economic Community (EEC) and Norway, for example, have already taken steps to liberalize the terms of the general preferential tariff for the benefit of LDCs.

When the special drawing right does become the basis for the new international monetary system and plans for new issues thereof are again drawn up, discussion of the means for their allocation among member countries of the International Monetary Fund (IMF) will be resurrected. The poorest countries have a strong claim to receive increased allocations and preferential interest rates to be paid on their use: In the long run, this automatic means of development financing may be of great significance for LDCs even though it may not be put into operation for the next few years. For the present, the greatest hope in the monetary sphere (a fairly slim one) is that increased OPEC earnings might be recycled in the direction of the poorest countries through a multilaterally financed interest subsidy and/or guarantee scheme (i.e., a vastly expanded World Bank "Third window" or some alternative institutional arrangement).

Many of the proposals on the international agenda, on the other hand, are of relatively limited significance for the poorest countries. The extension of the generalized system of (tariff) preferences (GSP) to semimanufactured and manufactured products or, more generally, to improved market access for these products, are not of prime concern to these countries since they are in a relatively weak position to benefit from them. (In the slightly longer run, the eligibility of the more successful less developed countries for the GSP may lapse, leaving the LDCs as prime beneficiaries.) More important to the latter would probably be a general lowering of effective protection on early-stage raw material (especially agricultural) processing activities in the developed countries; this might come about from a sectoral approach to tariff bargaining in current or future General Agreement on Trade and Tariffs (GATT) negotiations. LDCs might also be major beneficiaries of extensions of value-added tariffs (e.g., the type found in items 806.30 and 807.00 of the U.S. tariff) since their low incomes make them progressively more competitive locations for the labor-intensive exporting activities that these tariff systems encourage. (There may be other problems associated with the development of this kind of export in LDCs. See Helleiner, 1976.)

Debt-default or debt-relief arrangements are not especially important to most of the poorest countries, with the exception of those located in southern Asia. The biggest debtors have been countries, mainly in Latin America, that have already attained reasonable income levels. Defaults by these countries, however, might further prejudice the chances for "latecomer" borrowers to find lenders at reasonable rates. LDCs may therefore have a considerable indirect stake in the resolution of conflicts over debt. On the other hand, LDCs are already such bad risks (at least in the short run) that the marginal impact of default by others upon their borrowing prospects would probably be small. Moreover, recurrent debt crises among better-off countries and the fear of the effects of default upon the stability of the world financial system might generate an increased realization, on the part of donors, that in the future LDCs must receive assistance in the form of grants rather than loans and/or that this should result in the write-off of some of the debts they have thus far accumulated. Canada, the Netherlands, Sweden, and Switzerland have already written off debts owed to them by LDCs.

Development Assistance and LDCs

Any discussion of the international dimensions of the problems of the poorest countries must eventually return to the question of external aid. Conventional development assistance has been especially difficult for LDCs to "absorb." Specifically, its project orientation and its tying to overseas suppliers, among other factors, has reduced not only its value but also its volume. The poorest countries are those least likely to be able to prepare detailed projects for assessment by potential donors. Even when they do so, they are the least likely to be able to demonstrate a high benefit/cost ratio, as it is conventionally calculated, since it is in the very nature of their problem that rates of return for conventional investments are low. The additional requirement that the funds made available should not only generate a positive rate of return but should also be spent in the supplying country virtually rules out the most promising areas for improvement. In all of these transactions, the local cost component is bound to be high. Use of local materials and labor-intensive programs designed to meet mass needs cannot be financed by conventional aid programs. What is worse, the anxiety of aid donors to demonstrate that they are active in the poor countries in question, coupled with their own bureaucratic requirements, is likely to channel local resources into the preparation of the wrong types of projects merely because they can be aid-financed. The U.S. experience in this respect has been carefully analyzed by Tendler (1975). The scarcest resource in countries of this type is frequently planning expertise; its channeling into inappropriate projects can involve severe opportunity costs.

Nor can these problems be overcome simply by providing more technical assistance. LDCs still receive a slightly greater proportion of official development assistance in the form of technical assistance than do other less-developed countries: 26 percent as opposed to 25 percent in 1974; these percentages were 41 percent and 9 percent, respectively, from 1965 to 1968 (UNCTAD, 1976b, supplement 1, table 11). According to Allen (1970), "technical assistance has been . . . probably the least efficient segment of all foreign aid." There is every reason to believe that LDCs (and regions) have been especially poorly served by such aid (Helleiner, 1976). Poorer countries and regions are less attractive assignments for technical assistance personnel; they therefore tend to attract either young and inexperienced staff or rejects from more desirable posts. At the same time, they have the poorest capacity to assess the value of any form of assistance they are offered or the usefulness of the advice that accompanies it. Contrary to common assumptions, technical assistance is not cost-free to the recipient. Even more important than the obvious direct local costs of housing, transportation, office space, furniture, and secretarial services (some of which may be offset by tourist earnings) is the opportunity cost of the few truly skilled and invariably overworked local personnel. There are also the self-evident disadvantages of having crucial decision-making posts held by foreigners who subsequently leave the country, thus carrying their experience and "memory" with them.

It should be evident that the real value of technical assistance cannot be measured, even in an approximate manner, by aid-donor expenditures. In the poorest countries these budget items are especially likely to overstate the value of such assistance quite apart from its unquantifiable (but probably negative) effects upon dependence, self-respect, and aspirations. Since technical assistance essentially consists of expatriate salaries, its unit cost must increase at roughly the same rate as professional salaries in developed countries. Thus, a poor, gradually developing country will have to devote an increasingly greater proportion of its income to this form of import unless it consciously embarks upon a program of substitution by local employees.

The new "poverty" orientation of the World Bank and many bilateral aid donors, while admirable, does not begin to solve the difficulties of aid use by the poorest countries. If a greater share of aid allocations is directed to the poorest countries while the usual rules for the development and assessment of projects and their procurement remain unchanged, little that is useful can result.

While it may not be possible to immediately ease the numerous external domestic constraints upon more effective use of available resources, there is no reason to delay in altering the practices of aid donors that inhibit such use. Procedures that may make some sense for less disadvantaged countries have typically been transferred, without modification, to the poorest countries. Thus, the responsibility for meeting local recurrent costs has been imposed in circumstances where, in effect, to do so disqualifies the potential recipient for assistance since there are no additional local revenues to be had.

Detailed administrative requirements for project preparation and monitoring have been imposed upon planning and management systems scarcely able to keep abreast of their own simplified planning arrangements. Local counterparts and/or support staff have been required for technical-assistance agreements in such numbers that, were they actually produced, they would totally denude the ranks of high-level manpower available for other domestic activities. The project approach previously discussed has been adhered to even in circumstances where it is quite evident that the real requirement is for the degree of flexibility found in program assistance. As has been demonstrated, there is an equal degree of rigidity with respect to local cost financing and procurement tying. The benefit/cost criteria for the acceptability of projects has been rigidly transferred to the radically different context of LDCs, where bankability is, by definition, an unlikely prospect. There is also a good deal of lofty talk among donors of LDCs' "limited absorptive capacity for development assistance"!

Some bilateral-aid donors have recognized the special needs of LDCs for assistance in relevant training, institution-building, infrastructure, resource surveys, and advisory technical skills. But these efforts are geared to long-range results. Not nearly enough effort has been expended on "activities that might make a significant contribution to current welfare levels and at the same time reinforce the basis for longer run social and economic objectives" (UNCTAD, 1975b, p. 7). A suggestive list of such activities is presented in the same UNCTAD study:

1. Providing the means for improving current consumption, medical, and health standards.

2. Supporting local, small-scale labor-intensive rural public works projects (e.g., potable water supplies, soil conservation, drainage works, multipurpose community centers, access roads) employing both food-for-work schemes and paid labor.

3. Providing financial and commodity support for the purpose of expanding and initiating voluntary agency activities at the community level (e.g., primarily small-scale, local self-help projects).

4. Speeding up the initiation of project-feasibility studies in priority-development sectors, as well as reviewing completed project proposals with a view to expediting donor financing decisions.

5. Examining the feasibility of providing additional physical inputs into the agricultural sector as a means of increasing productivity, particularly of foodstuffs.

6. Providing selected types of new or expanded education (particularly non-formal functional and vocationally oriented training opportunities) for both adults and young people.

7. Encouraging simple, small-scale agro-industrial activities based upon locally produced agricultural products.

Clearly, all of these activities—and many other equally suitable ones that could be added to the above list—require considerable delegation of decision-making authority to the local level and a very high proportion (often 100 percent) of both local and recurrent costs.

Conventional aid practices deflect attention from such activities through their emphasis upon size, foreign-exchange costs, and bankability. The poorest countries could be greatly assisted through changes in aid practices geared toward long-term commitments, grants and softer loan terms, untying, local and recurrent cost financing, program assistance, eased administrative and reporting requirements, and so forth.

In some instances the rules have already been bent or changed. The most obvious shift has been toward softer loan terms. The creation of the International Development Association (IDA), the soft-loan arm of the World Bank, constituted an early acknowledgment of the special needs of the poorest countries. More recently, the Development Assistance Committee (DAC) of the OECD has formulated an explicit guideline stating that the average grant element of bilateral donor commitments to LDCs as a group should be at least 90 percent (or 86 percent to each country over a three-year period, which has not yet elapsed). Japan and the United States are among the donor countries that have not yet complied with this target (UNCTAD, 1976a, annex tables 1 thru 5). At the same time, there has been considerable expansion in multilateral (IDA) soft loans to the poorest countries.

Procurement restrictions and project approaches, however, have proven to be more difficult to alter. Sweden has been exemplary with respect to procurement. Its assistance can usually be employed for local costs or purchases from any foreign country, as required, although, not surprisingly, Sweden tends to favor projects for which the foreign country has products to offer and where moral suasion has been used regarding procurement. Other countries have liberalized portions of their aid budgets. The United States now permits the financing of more local costs than was formerly the case. Twenty percent of Canadian bilateral aid can now be employed for local costs. Most donors now permit procurement in other less-developed countries in "tied" aid contracts. Even the World Bank has gradually been moving in the direction of more program loans and loans that permit the financing of local costs.

An effort is now being made to employ different, poverty-oriented criteria, either through formal procedures or qualitative judgments, in project evaluations. There has been a consequent shift in the composition of new aid-financed projects in the past few years. However, it is not as large as one might think after reading the development literature.

The selection of different projects provides no guarantee that the outcome will be more beneficial to the poorest of the poor. Even with the most careful planning, the complex constellation of local social and political forces may frustrate the newly stated objectives of the donors. Grants and loans to raise smallholder incomes may boost the incomes of local landowners, traders, and moneylenders. Low-cost housing schemes may assist the relatives and friends of the most politically powerful individuals. Any external attempt to control or significantly influence the eventual outcome would involve such major (and unpredictable) interventions as to be politically impossible, even if one thought that, on balance, such donor interventions were likely to move events in a favorable direction, which is itself a very doubtful proposition.

One must remember that the "fundability" of local resources greatly reduces the opportunity of aid donors to influence domestic income distribution in the Third World even if they want to do so. If support is offered for rural dispensaries, this may, to a significant extent, merely free budgetary resources that would otherwise have gone into urban hospitals, steel plants, or military hardware. If there is little political will on the part of the aid recipient to improve the lot of the poorest, there is little a foreign donor can do about it. All manner of ostensibly equitable aid schemes can be "captured" and end up supplying benefits to those who are better off. As has already been noted, donor efforts to ensure that the outcome occurs as planned is quite properly viewed as intolerable interference in a recipient's domestic political affairs. There seems to be no other option, then, but to resort to the principle of selectivity—helping those countries that are genuinely trying to alleviate domestic poverty. But then the problem of donor motivation for selectivity rears its head. Who is still so naive as to believe that poverty alleviation per se is a major criterion in the intercountry allocations of major powers?

The question of whether or how to exercise intercountry selectivity in one's aid or other international arrangements so as to ensure that the poorest people are truly assisted is a vexing one. After all, is it not the exercise of country selectivity by developed countries that has led to the unsatisfactory distribution of such benefits as the system now provides? Many observers understandably despair at trying to alter the criteria employed by the most powerful states, advocating instead a shift to a more automatic system of country distribution such as would be inherent in an expanded Special Drawing Currency (SDC)-based monetary system, thus minimizing the opportunity for donor discretion. If this idea seems, for the present, to be hopelessly unrealistic, then attempts to influence intercountry donor allocations may be helpful, at least marginally as second-best strategies, in shifting some resources to the poor. Specifically, these efforts may reap some returns in small donor countries with no great power aspirations. For the latter, it may be possible to redirect substantial aid toward those governments that are seriously addressing the problem of poverty, although such redirection may do little more than rectify the imbalances in allocations generated by the larger powers' decisions.

One way to circumvent some of these problems is to utilize the device of identifying countries that are *internationally* recognized as "deserving" of assistance. These countries would be entitled to assistance not because of their political complexion or the likelihood that their governments will try to help the poor but as a result of their overall level of poverty—as one of the "least developed." Even then, political considerations could not be completely excluded from the process of identifying those countries to be so favored. The large south Asian countries, for example, were excluded from such a list. (Bangladesh, however, was eventually added.) A similar advantage results from the identification by the United Nations of the thirty-two "most seriously affected" (MSA) poor countries in the post-1973 period. By identifying such countries, the governments of developed countries were relieved of some of the need for exercising selectivity; similarly, recipient governments were relieved of some of the odium associated with being beneficiaries. On balance, the creation of such lists represents a small step in the direction of a more equitable and automatic global-distribution system. It legitimizes the need for special international efforts to assist the poorest nations without increasing the room for inappropriately motivated bilateral donor discretion. The ultimate power to redirect assistance to these countries, however, continues to rest where it has always rested—with donor governments. Despite declarations of intent, the practical consequences for several important bilateral aid programs have remained fairly small. For example, in 1976 LDCs still accounted for only 16.7 percent of total OECD development assistance, as compared with 16.6 percent in 1973; this proportion typically rises in years of climatic disasters (OECD, 1977). As far as multilateral assistance is concerned, there have been some important concrete changes. The IDA now directs 22 percent of its loans to those countries identified as "least developed," whereas this percentage used to be only 5 percent. The UNDP has also committed itself to raising the LDCs' share of its expenditures from 19 to 26 percent over the next five years.

In 1974, as has been demonstrated, the net per capita aid flow to the twenty-nine "least developed" countries was, in real terms, only slightly higher than it had been from 1965 to 1968. However, most of these countries also realized improvements in the grant element in these grants and loans during this period. The average grant element in OECD and multilateral commitments to developing countries with per capita incomes under two hundred dollars rose from 77 to 80 percent between 1967/69 and 1973/74, while the same element in their commitments to countries with per capita incomes over three hundred dollars fell from 56 to 47 percent over the same period. Thus, the *relative* position of these countries in terms of aid allocations improved because of their increased receipts and their improved terms.

When one includes other very poor countries that were not included in the UN definition of "least developed" (notably India and Indonesia) within the category of "poorest," this conclusion still stands. The share of official development-assistance commitments, in terms of grant equivalents, accounted for by countries with per capita incomes under two hundred dollars rose from 44 to 46 percent between 1967/69 and 1974.

While the per capita grant element of development assistance to the UN-defined "least developed" countries was, by 1974, higher than the average for all other developing countries, the same could not be said of aid to the poorest (i.e., those countries with per capita incomes under $200). Per capita grant equivalents received by this poorest group of countries was still less than one-third of that of the $200–$300 income range, about the same as the $300–$500 group, and less than the $501–$800 group. Even excluding India, Indonesia, and Nigeria, the under $200 per capita income group received, on average, about half what the $200–$300 per capita income group received in 1974. While the shares of the poorest have been rising, it still cannot be said that the international development assistance system is primarily aimed at alleviating poverty at the bottom end of the spectrum. (A portion of the foregoing section is based upon the findings of Edelman and Chenery, 1977, pp. 34–38.)

The attacks upon official development assistance from both left and right are unlikely to alter the demands, on the part of representatives of the poorest countries and regions, for more aid. Nor is there likely to be any abatement in pressure exerted by socially concerned groups and individuals in developed countries for its extension and improvement. What the ultimate effects of such aid (or, for that matter, the effects of other trade or financial measures established in their favor) within the Third World might be, particularly measures affecting the welfare of the poorest people, very much depends upon the nature of the recipient government—its objectives, its planning systems, and so forth.

If possible, aid flows should always be placed within a total planning effort by the recipient government in such a fashion that they do not distort basic priorities or make the effort too vulnerable to outside influences. The recipient country has, and must employ, the power to reject aid projects that do not fit into its own planning priorities. It is not, in this writer's judgment, proper for external actors to push or "lever" their own priorities onto independent governments, a move that is neither politically wise nor expedient. However difficult it may be, one must hope that local priorities will be sensibly set and restrict advice to that which can be offered at arm's length and unconditionally.

In aid agencies of developed countries one thus has little recourse but to seek to ease the most obvious constraints upon the use of foreign assistance by increasing its automaticity, removing procurement restrictions, raising grant proportions, and softening the terms of remaining loans. In the third-best world, where this degree of easing seems unlikely and where selectivity is daily being employed, one ought presumably to do what is increasingly being done: develop new assessment criteria, resist the orthodox ones, and alter the distribution pattern among countries.

Collective Self-Reliance and the Least Developed

To this end, it has implicitly been assumed that a new IEO providing significant gains for the poorest countries would have to be the product of a planetary bargain to which the developed countries are parties. In order to realize some gains for LDCs, it may not be necessary for developed countries to be involved. What are the prospects for Third World solidarity in support of its weakest members?

On a priori grounds, the outlook is not very encouraging. If governments of powerful Third World states have shown scant interest in the less fortunate members of their *own* societies—this is unfortunately frequently the case—one can hardly expect them (except upon the basis of some self-interested political calculation) to exhibit greater interest for less fortunate *foreign* countries. (The introduction of the new internationally respected concept of LDCs was itself, in part, the product of a bargain by means of which the African countries were induced to support the generalized system of preferences from which they were themselves unlikely to derive much gain.) If such solidarity materializes within the Third World, it is more likely to be found among its ruling groups than in connection with attempts to overcome bottom-end poverty. One is even tempted to hypothesize that the interests of the poorest might be better protected by democratically elected governments in rich countries, bargaining out a new world order that takes equity into account, than by many of the more powerful Third World political regimes.

Still, there are several glimmers of hope—more than existed a few years ago—including:

1. Substantial aid commitments by OPEC countries to less fortunate poor countries, admittedly on a fairly selective basis and *without* the requested preferential oil prices for the poorest.
2. Insistence, on the part of OPEC countries, that other raw materials in addition to oil be discussed in the Paris North-South meetings.
3. Maintenance of a solid front by forty-six African, Carribbean, and Pacific states, against all odds, in negotiations leading to the Lomé Convention, part of which offered special concessions to the poorest signatories.
4. Increased interest in, and strength of, regionally and functionally organized Third World international bodies—development banks, common markets, producers' organizations—and a new emphasis at UNCTAD in "collective self-reliance," all of which include some LDCs as members (UNCTAD, 1976b).

Clearly, LDCs often stand to gain by entering into alliances with other, more powerful developing countries. But just as evident is the fact that they may frequently be enjoined to participate in collective efforts that are not in their best interests. For example, commodity-supply restrictions are usually not in the interests of those countries which still account for small shares of the relevant world market. Nor are there obvious gains to be won by an industrially backward country in joining a common market with more advanced countries as members (see chap. 12). Again, the adoption of common regulations for foreign enterprises, in connection with joint bargaining efforts with more advanced countries, may imply the relinquishing of special concessions that alone might induce firms to pay attention to the weakest countries. In all these circumstances, cooperation on the part of LDCs must be predicated upon a degree of assurance that they will not be required to bear an extra cost and, more positively, that they will derive an equitable share of resulting gains.

In the absence of any improved global bargains that might provide significant gains for both Third and Fourth Worlds, *individual* LDCs would have to act independently to protect and improve their future welfare.*

---

*See chap. 2 for an outline of some of the elements of a more self-reliant national strategy vis-à-vis the world economy.

FOR FURTHER READING

Amin, Samir. 1977. "Self-reliance and the New International Economic Order." *Monthly Review* 29, no. 3: 1–21.

Bhagwati, Jagdish N. 1977. *The New International Economic Order: The North-South Debate*. Cambridge, Mass.: MIT Press.

Fishlow, A. et al. 1978. *Rich and Poor Nations in the World Economy*. New York: McGraw Hill.

Helleiner, G. K., ed. 1976. *A World Divided: The Less Developed Countries in the International Economy*. Cambridge: Cambridge University Press.

Organization for Economic Co-operation and Development. 1977. *Development Co-operation: Efforts and Policies of the Members of the Development Assistance Committee, 1977 Review*. Paris: OECD.

Overseas Development Council. 1977. *The United States and World Development, Agenda 1977*. Washington: ODC.

Sampson, Anthony. 1975. *The Seven Sisters: The Great Oil Companies and the World They Made*. New York: Viking.

Sauvant, K. P. and H. Hasenpflug, eds. 1977. *The New International Economic Order*. Frankfurt: Campus.

Shaw, T. M. and K. Heard, eds. 1976. *Cooperation and Conflict in Southern Africa: Papers on a Regional Sub-System*. Washington: University Publications of America.

Tanzania Delegation to the Nonaligned Nations Summit Conference. 1973. "Cooperation Against Poverty." *The Political Economy of Development and Underdevelopment*. Edited by C. K. Wilber. New York: Random House, pp. 373–389.

Tendler, Judith. 1975. *Inside Foreign Aid*. Baltimore: Johns Hopkins Press.

UNCTAD, 1976c. *Economic Cooperation among Developing Countries*. Item 14—Supporting Paper. TD/192/Supp. 1. Nairobi: United Nations.

14. In a 1978 article published in the *New York Times* (April 4, 1978, p. 33) Peter Bourne, a spokesperson for the Carter administration, wrote:

> We have to rededicate ourselves to alleviating the terrible human suffering that still afflicts millions of people in the world, and to have the American people understand that this is what foreign aid ought to be all about. . . . Our export sales ($40 billion this year) to the developing world surpass those to Europe and Japan, supplying millions of jobs for Americans. One out of every eight manufacturing jobs and one out of every three acres of farmland produce for export. The developing world is not only the market for our products, it provides us with the raw materials essential to maintain our industrial economy.

This dualistic position of serving others and serving one's self is, despite the protestation of the author, the characteristic pose of most rich countries toward the poorest countries; it is a way of justifying, in the same breath, the practical benefits to themselves of foreign aid and the humanitarian responsibility to tender it.

At times either motive is emphasized, but the confusing dichotomy is always placed before the public, whose support is needed. It is not surprising, therefore, that public support flags on the question of development aid, that almost all wealthy countries lag behind in their joint commitments, and remain far behind their aid potential. Moreover, there are few ideal programs for other countries to emulate, although Canada and the Scandinavian countries appear to be struggling toward such a position.

What may be missing is neither money nor conviction but an ideal, a principle to rally around and to use as a guide, given the inequality of world relationships. For Denis Goulet, such a principle is solidarity. It is not clear, despite its seeming sophisticaton, how far Goulet's solidarity principle has traveled from our own naive post–World War II hopes of "one world." It recognizes inequality, dissensions, and conflict in a manner totally different from the fresh, liberal vision emanating from the victors of World War II. But in its appeal to the universals of mankind, the common planetary ties, it echoes Adlai Stevenson's early plea for a fragile spaceship earth.

The fact that thoughtful and compassionate scholars such as Goulet return to the older, unfashionable moral ideals of responsibility and solidarity, albeit in a more knowledgeable way, testifies to a persistent and important need. In the final analysis, the contemplation of least development is the contemplation of human need and the assertion of human need is an assertion of common humanity.

THE MORAL BASIS OF WORLD SOLIDARITY

D. Goulet

At international assemblies nowadays, talk of interdependence is rife. Spokesmen for rich countries, stung by fuel price increases and new Third World demands, plead for an interdependent approach to world problems. Meanwhile, Third World leaders urge greater solidarity among themselves to counter the rich world's superior bargaining strength. As endless claims and counterclaims vie for legitimacy, thematic conflicts center on ground rules for a new IEO. U.S. officials solemnly declare their support for a new world order yet continue to reject *the* new order championed by Third World coalitions in the United Nations.

A new international order—legal, political, economic, and symbolic—is no doubt in the process of gestation. Jockeying for position are several aspirants to play the role of steward of the transition. Candidates include an enlarged club of great powers, an alliance of multinational interests (corporate, bureaucratic, scholarly, financial), and those whom Richard Falk calls "global populists"—opponents of political, technocratic, or bureaucratic elitism. At stake is the power to shape the future order.

The aim of this chapter, however, is neither to survey diverse models of world order nor to evaluate competing strategies of the transition. (On these topics, see Mendlovitz, 1975, and Falk, 1975). Rather, it seeks to clarify the basis of a new moral order in which genuine development for all can become possible. The type of moral order needed is outlined and a brief inquiry is made into the nature and foundations of solidarity.

What Kind of Moral Order?

What kind of moral order should be created? The only valid answer is: an order of genuine development for all. Much of what has been called "development" benefits only small, privileged groups. Moreover, as Erich

Fromm has pointed out (1966, p. lx), alienation amidst wasteful affluence is no less dehumanizing than is alienation amidst misery. True development embraces not only specific benefits but their modes of access and distribution as well. How benefits are obtained and whom they reach are vital questions. Hence, an essential link exists between human solidarity and the possibility of development for all. It is futile to speak of "partners in development" (Pearson, 1969) unless the quality of that partnership is defined (Mazrui, 1975).

One cannot shake off the troubling image of that ambiguous symbiosis that binds masters and slaves: interdependent partners in a single enterprise—the plantation. Patrons and clients likewise continue to "need each other," as do sadists and masochists. Interdependence alone is not enough; reciprocity, or mutuality, must lie at the heart of the relationship. The Third World will no longer settle for mere lip service to reciprocity: it now calls for new rules in the areas of economics, ocean legislation, financial voting rights, and resource bargaining. Development strategy remains a choice arena where the good intentions of the rich are put to the test. If their prescriptions center on palliatives, they will be judged insincere in their profession of partnership, for authentic development has now come to mean genuine benefits for all.

Development for All

Prestigious international officials like Robert McNamara (World Bank) and Kurt Waldheim (United Nations) now acknowledge that neither foreign aid nor development planning has reduced poverty or unemployment in poor countries. "Economic miracles" in Brazil, Korea, or Saudi Arabia do not necessarily mean more essential goods for the masses. For the world at large, as for national societies, a developmental order is one in which needed benefits are made accessible to all in ways that respect their dignity. Every human group needs to be treated by others with respect regardless of its utility or attractiveness. Esteem and recognition are as essential to life as is bread.

Lord Keynes once remarked that "economic development is but the possibility of development." Or, as L. J. Labret put it, all societies must "*have* enough in order to *be* fully human" (Labret, 1961). Although the elimination of misery is technically feasible, large numbers of humans still lack essential goods: this is the monstrous aberration of underdevelopment. Yet one must not suppose that only materialistic models of development are valid. Indeed, material progress itself cannot be isolated from deeper levels of meaning and symbolism. Although it is no guarantee of happiness, material development is avidly sought by many because it promises to abolish misery, endemic disease, and the special hopelessness that marks stifled opportunity.

The alienated or guilt-ridden rich in industrial societies can indulge in the luxury of despising material pursuits only because they no longer fear starvation or feel defenseless in the face of floods or droughts. Integral development may well imply transcendence (Goulet, 1966, 1974a), but one must continue to insist on the prior urgency of guaranteeing basic sufficiency for all. Underdevelopment is a combination of absolute deprivation and relative indignities flowing from systems of status attribution that insult the human spirit. Gandhi himself, no devotee of material success, declared misery to be a certain kind of hell. Yet underdevelopment is not some lack or lag to be remedied by judicious investments or "enlightened" fiscal policies. This patronizing view implicitly endorses prevailing ground rules governing the circulation of goods, capital, personnel, power, and knowledge itself. Throughout the Third World revolutionary alternatives spring up that reject dependency, class privilege, technocratic elitism, and the primacy of personal gain as the motor of developmental effort. One image stresses material acquisition, the other popular control over processes of change. Both are fraught with the potential for conflict. Hence, one is led to ask whether conflict will undermine the necessary quest for solidarity. Can conflict be avoided only by sacrificing forms of solidarity rooted in developmental justice?

A Dangerous Tension: Peace versus Justice

Notwithstanding ritualistic bows to dissident views, most Western experts on international relations contend that superpowers have a primary responsibility to contain nuclear armaments and nuclear war. They invoke variants of the balance-of-power theory or spheres-of-influence imagery and draw invisible lines on one side of which lies intolerable provocation and on the other manageable conflict.

Such thinking, at least in the United States, legitimizes a policy that opposes even limited wars of national liberation when these are thought to upset a precarious balance of power or violate spheres of influence. However, inasmuch as wars of national liberation frequently aim at revolutionizing internal social structures as well, this posture serves to veto liberation models of development and to buttress domestic repressive policies.

Most leaders in underdeveloped countries, on the other hand, are not persuaded that superpowers have received a historical mandate to monopolize world-conflict management so as to prevent nuclear annihilation. The notion that each superpower has legitimate spheres of influence strikes them as a feebly disguised rationale for their continued domination of world geopolitical arenas.

If the American and Soviet publics have been socialized into equating "peace" with the successful avoidance of nuclear warfare and with keeping the lid on potentially explosive revolutionary wars, a deeply troubling question arises. Is this kind of peace compatible with the demands of justice? A basic dilemma exists here, for if peace means stabilizing the present tenuous world order, and if that order is, in development terms, structurally unjust, then a radical contradiction exists between justice and peace.

Those committed to justice within their own societies and in the world at large conclude that success calls for struggle against the stewards of the present order and their vested interests. Those very interests, by their power to define issues in the world forum, have already equated peace with a system of abiding structural injustice that is inimical to any but domesticated forms of development. The tragedy is that such ersatz development rules out genuine solidarity founded on reciprocity.

Must those who yearn for peace, then, despair of winning the battle for justice? Or should carte blanche be given to revolutionaries throughout the globe in recognition of the justice of their cause and the enormity of the oppressive structures they would overthrow? And what of the ever-present danger that uncontrolled violence might annihilate the human species or destroy the essential institutional fabric from which a new world order might be constructed once the old disorder was destroyed?

The quest for peace—if it is to be a just peace—will involve much violence and conflict. In an article entitled "The Threat from the Third World," Fred Bergsten argues that the increased leverage poor countries now have in bargaining with the United States is a threat to which the latter might respond in myriad ways (1973). Bergsten's imagery, however, is upside down: in truth, the threat posed by the United States to vital Third World interests is far greater than the dangers to the United States arising from economic leverage enjoyed by oil-producing or copper-exporting countries. If rich countries truly mean to be stewards of peace, they must link the defense of peace to the creation of greater equity in international exchanges. They would do well to heed Myrdal, who writes that the theory of international trade itself had as its purpose the *"explaining away of the international equality problems"* [emphasis added] (1970, p. 277).

A New Global Bargain

One hears much of late of a new planetary bargain between rich and poor (e.g., McHale and McHale, 1975). The idea is to win agreement on a new social contract that would bind all global actors to protect the vital resource interests of rich and poor societies, even in times of crisis or shortage. There is doubtless great merit in rallying all energies to ensure optimum development in a way that would benefit everyone. The elimination of absolute misery also implies the abolition of waste and superfluity. The enterprise is technically feasible, but major obstacles to success lie in the realms of will, spirit, and moral values. One dare not be too sanguine, for, as the Egyptian social philosopher Mirrit Boutros Ghali has written (1972, p. 59): "We are putting our pride in technical achievements, probably because they are less arduous than social betterment, less hard than spiritual improvement, and because they entail no heart-searching, no laborious choices, as do social ends based on human values." Optimum development of natural and human resources also signifies a relative equalization of wealth. On this score, one marvels at the durability of the bankrupt theory of "trickle down," according to which poverty will be wiped out if those already rich are given proper incentives for increasing production. A major portion of the increase, so the theory runs, will go toward eliminating poverty. In response to pleas for redistribution as a better equalizer, trickle-downers reply: "You can't redistribute poverty." But if one lesson can be learned from China, a large and poor society that has abolished mass misery, it is that overall incentive systems are the key to success (Lin, 1975). More important than redistributing wealth is redistributing effective access to resources. The locus of access is crucial: the poor must gain access to resources "upstream," that is, early in the sequence of decisions regarding their use, not merely "downstream" as some corrective afterthought to a vitiated system. Any new global bargain must therefore avoid merely dividing the world into donors and recipients of charity. A new understanding of structural justice should state, as its initial postulate, that the rights of human societies and their members are founded on the requirements of integral development for all. Effective solidarity should become the operative value. This means institutionalizing the principle that the world's wealth belongs to all its inhabitants on the basis of priority needs and not on the basis of geographical location or the different technological abilities to extract or exploit resources that some groups enjoy.

Political obstacles to the creation of such institutions are monumental. The intellectual difficulty of getting the principle accepted is equally great. The very thought of it is upsetting: all peoples are the owners of the earth and its wealth. The geographical location of resources or the instrumental ability to process them constitute no prior claim upon them. Within this vision of solidarity one perceives how puerile are the theses of "triage" or "lifeboat ethics." Advocates assume that the possession of wealth, power, or (to use their favorite euphemism) "viability" is a sign of superior wisdom or prior rights. The language of triage and lifeboat ethics, however, is but a shallow rationalization permitting the "viable" rich to exclude the "nonviable" poor from vital resources. The virtuosic language of the formulas fools no one but their creators (Howe and Sewell, 1975).

Paternalism, no matter how well it is disguised, can never serve as the foundation of global solidarity. In the absence of genuine solidarity, all human societies will lose their own self-respect; they will display and refine their own worst qualities as they lunge at each other's throats. If power competition becomes the rule, there will be no prospects for the survival of the human race (Heilbroner, 1974).

A new moral order of development for all—one that accepts the need for limited creative conflict to build a just peace and strikes a resource bargain founded on priority needs of the human race—adheres to such primary values as minimum violence in human relations, equity in economic exchanges, justice in sociopolitical relations, and ecological integrity. These goals, however, have been harnessed to two quite different scenarios, the first implying the maintenance of "dependent development" and the second opening up contrary possibilities. Meadows' *Limits to Growth* (1972) and Forrester's *World Dynamics* (1971) postulate future ecological, political, or demographical catastrophes. Counterpart research by Third World scholars retorts that the future catastrophe postulated by the M.I.T. model—hunger, illiteracy, a miserable standard of life—is already the lot of most people living in developing countries.

The lesson is obvious: it is futile to plead for one dimension of development—ecological sanity, say, or peaceful transition to a new world order—without simultaneously championing equity in international exchanges, cultural respect for the powerless, and effective access to vital resources.

Building Solidarity: Foundations and Obstacles

Solidarity is a sham if only lip service is paid to it. It is genuine only when it becomes an effective norm of institutional behavior. Along the way it must do battle against particularisms of all types, the competitive quest for differential profit or power, and the fear of others, which poisons the collective psyche of most human societies. In recent years, Third World nations have begun to close ranks and practice forms of solidarity in economic and political arenas that are dictated by their common vulnerability to social forces over which they have little control. Thus, Andean Pact countries have pooled their bargaining strength to negotiate investment and technology contracts with multinational corporations. Oil producers in the Third World have banded together (OPEC) to change the ground rules of vital commodity exchanges.

Most global discussions, however, look beyond Third World collaboration; they center on worldwide solidarity between rich and poor nations. What can be the basis for such solidarity? It is generally argued that the rich have some degree of responsibility toward the poor. Too often these appeals are cast in misleading terms that equate responsibility with guilt. Nevertheless, as the French social philosopher Pierre Antoine has pointed out, responsibility and guilt are not synonymous. On the contrary, they obey opposite dynamics. Responsibility looks to the present and the future and presupposes freedom— the possibility of responding to an exigency perceived and accepted as worthy. We are all responsible for creating conditions that humanize life. Guilt, on the contrary, is the negative burden of past fault or injustice; it is passive and recriminating, not active and creative. In an illuminating essay on collective responsibility Antoine (1959) explains that:

> . . . individuals, groups and nations which, even by ethical means, have secured for themselves an advantageous, strong and prosperous position in the world, and by so doing have impeded (even if it is only indirectly because goods available on this planet are limited) the economic development or the social promotion of other individuals or other peoples, are responsible to the latter for the deprivation and they ought to remedy it, by making use of the very possibilities which their better position confers on them . . . *an obligation rooted in justice can exist as a consequence of our acts even when no fault of injustice has been committed* [my emphasis].

Thus, the responsibility of rich classes and nations to create justice need not rest on scapegoat theories of history that brand them guilty of present inequalities. Guilt there surely has been—in the form of imperialism, exploitation, and oppression. Nevertheless, even where there is no guilt there is responsibility.

Responsibility, however, is no warrant for more powerful partners to assimilate others in a reductionist spirit. Accordingly, cultural diversity must be deliberately fostered in the face of standardizing influences inherent in social changes channeled by technology and "modernization." The deliberate effort to promote sound cultural diversity may well prove a touchstone of true solidarity. Doubtless, untrammeled diversity may lead to fragmentation. What is needed, therefore, is neither reductionist homogenization nor irresponsible, uncoordinated diversity.

Foundations

What, ultimately, are the foundations of solidarity as a worldwide goal? There is talk, expressed in alarmist tones, in favor of solidarity on the grounds of planetary survival. But survival alone cannot be the main pillar of collective effort: all societies need, as a priority, a stake in enterprises above and beyond survival (Ways, 1959). Joint stewardship of the planet is necessary because the human race, given its diverse cultural and political forms, has a collective historical destiny to actualize and express its potentialities. More concrete bases also exist for global solidarity, including the unification wrought by technology, the common occupation of a single planet, and the unity of human destiny.

Technology.   Modern modes of communication have made isolation impossible. Over forty years ago Lewis Mumford noted that "the joint stock of knowledge and technical skill transcends the boundaries of individual or national egos; and to forget that fact is not merely to enthrone superstition but to undermine the essential planetary basis of technology itself" (Mumford, 1934). To which French economist François Perroux added that "technical conditions for the establishment of a planetary economy now exist" (Perroux, 1958). Not only have technological production and consumption of its products unified the globe; our dreams and lifestyles have also been influenced by the standardizing impact of technology. Homogenization of behavior is well under way.

More important than identical patterns of consumption or behavior, however, are the general images gaining ascendancy throughout the world. Everywhere one finds the same confidence in man's ability to master nature, a sense of the importance of earthly existence, and the notion that all human beings should be judged according to their performance. Beyond technology's unifying effect, however, lie deeper bases for human solidarity.

Occupation of One Planet.   A second foundation is the occupation by all peoples of a planet governed throughout its extension by identical laws and subject to the same indeterminisms. Notwithstanding variations in climate, relief, and geography, the planet has a specific identity distinct from all other cosmic bodies. Even when they do not interact directly with each other, people are indirectly related by virtue of their common links to a single planetary ecosystem. Prospects opened up by space exploration in no way modify this organic bond tying humans to one planet. If ever permanent emigration to other planets were to occur, human solidarity would simply acquire an expanded basis, namely, the unity of a cosmic planetary system instead of a single planet.

Unity of Human Destiny. Philosophical doctrines and popular wisdom have proliferated in various human cultures. Though they differ widely as to the precise meaning of the term *human* all agree that, beyond differences of race, nationality, culture, and social organization, a common humanness can be found. This natural sameness of humans constitutes an ontological basis for solidarity. There is a properly human destiny for all persons. Whether they be farmers, fishermen, artists, machinists, or healers, all must fulfill themselves in a human mode. What is more, all philosophies and religions postulate a common fate. Hence, the universality of human destiny is no sectarian fancy, but the common patrimony of human thought. This is not, however, to say that existential solidarity can be readily translated into cooperative behavior. On the contrary, humans consistently act as though they were not bound together in webs of solidarity. In effect, the establishment of world solidarity is beset by enormous obstacles.

Obstacles

Partial claims are habitually put forth as supreme rather than as subordinate to some larger good. Behind the verbal facade of cooperation, nations and classes dominate their peers. Lip service is paid to the "global community," but development problems are still defined, by and large, through the prisms of parochial mercantile, strategic, and ideological interests. Solidarity will not be achieved by waiting for some hidden hand to arbitrate competing interests; the major obstacles preventing its appearance must be combated.

Unequal Development. Since nations are at various stages of development, identical norms cannot be applied. For example, countries once colonized or economically dominated need to assert their nationalism vigorously in order to achieve what Myrdal has called "emotional integration" around development goals. On the other hand, developed nations may have to limit their claims to sovereignty if harmful structural effects arising from their disproportionate power are to be neutralized. It is the same with tariffs: nonindustrial countries will demand high tariffs to nurture their fragile, incipient industry, whereas industrialized countries should, on the grounds of equity, lower their tariffs to facilitate entry of Third World goods to buyers' markets. Unless all countries make solidarity an effective rule of conduct, such requirements will appear to them as a double standard, both irrational and unjust.

Conflict and Sham Consensus. A further obstacle to genuine solidarity is traceable to shallow thinking about the role of conflict in eliminating sham consensus. Because domination by the strong relies, in great part, on the apathy of the weak, conflict breeds solidarity among the latter. This is why sociologist Irving Horowitz does not hesitate to write that "dissensus, while dysfunctional with respect to the ruling powers, is quite functional for the newly emergent nations" (Horowitz, 1966). Consensus in and of itself is no absolute value; one must look at its quality and source. Consensus rooted in elitist manipulation of the masses is a sham, as is interdependence founded on threats by the strong against those who "rock the boat" of social equilibrium. In developed countries, in particular, there exists a widespread form of allergic fear of conflict or confrontation. Yet social conflict often helps build solidarity by expressing needs that must be satisfied. Even in revolutionary Marxism, class warfare is viewed as an instrument of heightened solidarity within the proletariat and the society as a whole after the revolution has ended. The same "instrumental" relationship between conflict and solidarity is present in other ideological doctrines. Whether it is viewed as disruptive or constructive, conflict is always interpreted as a stepping-stone to some terminal condition of solidarity or peace. In a word, the dynamism of conflict can become an illuminating principle of institution building and of development itself.

Additional Obstacles.   One has only to contrast the perceptions of Arab and Israeli or of blacks and whites in South Africa to understand how potent an obstacle to solidarity is fear. Eugene Rostow, under secretary of state under former President Lyndon B. Johnson, has described the role played by fear in high policymaking circles. In the course of an interview (Whitworth, 1970) on the value assumptions that led U.S. decision makers into the Vietnam War, Rostow plaintively asked:

> Can't we free ourselves of the fear of hegemony, the fear of being dominated, which has led men to war so often in the past? What does the fear of dominance do to people? Perhaps psychiatrists can answer that question. I can't. All I know is that that kind of fear is a reality in human affairs.
>
> I don't think we are a new breed of men, immune to the diseases and fears of history. And I remain of the view that foreign policy should not allow such fears to develop, that the best—the only—cure for such fears is to prevent the convulsions in the distribution of power which have always been their cause.

Fear aside, there is a further obstacle to genuine solidarity: the lure of material riches. It is not an accident that solidarity thrives in adversity and not during conditions of abundance. No situation is so unfavorable as one of glaring contrasts between the wasteful affluence of the few coexisting along-side the stark misery of the many. The resignation of the poor, however, has now been shattered; they are still poor, but images of abundance have begun to people their dreams. Not surprisingly, they are inclined to interpret overtures made by the rich to solve problems on the basis of interdependence as "tricks" for legitimizing present inequities. The rich, in turn, instinctively fear that demands by the poor for structural reform are threats to what they regard as their legitimate and hard-won affluence. But solidarity cannot be built on incentives like material acquisition and competitive striving. On the contrary, the conviction that austerity (Goulet, 1971) is a permanent feature of authentic humanism is necessary if rich and poor are to be weaned from the seductions of mass consumption, either presently enjoyed or avidly sought. Moral incentives and solidarity have no place except where austerity— understood to mean sufficiency for all—and not affluence or mass consumption is the first priority of any developmental effort.

Two simplistic formulations must be avoided. The first is naively optimistic by assuming that a just order of mutual interdependence can be built in ways that will benefit everyone and cause loss to none. The second misleading view holds that each concession made to oppressed groups will harm the vital interests of the privileged clases. Although these vital interests themselves must be redefined, the legacy of structural injustice is so great that no new "social compact" founded on reciprocal solidarity can be obtained without entailing losses to privileged groups. The lack of realism concerning the probable social costs of change and the bearers of these costs is an obstacle to the establishment of solidarity. (For an excellent discussion of social costs in national-development efforts, see Berger [1974].)

Putting Solidarity into Practice

No task is more difficult than to incorporate noble ideals in institutional practices. How, for instance, can public bureaucracies relate to populations they allegedly serve in ways that are not damaging to their values? (Goulet, 1974). How must developed countries express solidarity with the Third World in terms of concrete policy?

One recent illustration of such an effort is described in a document drafted by the Canadian University Service Overseas (CUSO), entitled "The Third Imperative for Canadian Immigration Policy: Interdependence with the Third World" (CUSO, 1975). CUSO urged that Canadian immigration policy be changed so as to demonstrate effective interdependence with the Third World. The document stated that Canada must formulate its immigration policy in ways that help Third World countries limit the "brain drain" of their professionals to industrialized countries. It also insisted on the responsibility of rich countries to adopt a refugee policy that is both humane and flexible. It is possible that CUSO's recommendations will never be adopted. They nonetheless represent a praiseworthy attempt to translate solidarity into concrete actions.

The authors of the document rejected the notion that Canada was free to design an immigration policy responsive solely to its own employment needs or economic interests. A direct link was drawn between Canada's programs to place technically qualified Canadians overseas and the need felt by Third World countries to make the best use of their limited supply of skilled nationals. Any immigration policy, therefore, that entices Third World professionals to settle in Canada sabotages poorer countries, which have a limited number of highly trained personnel, and contradicts the declared goals of fostering Third World self-reliance. CUSO urged a revision of the "point system" now used by Canadian immigration officials for judging the relative acceptability of immigrants and concluded that it was unfair to "skim off" desirable foreigners whose education may have cost their own country dearly in order to staff Canadian jobs. A new weighting system granting prior rights to needier countries was recommended. At the same time, of course, care was taken to protect the freedom of individuals to work where they choose.

There is no need to analyze more closely the document in question. It is mentioned merely to illustrate the principle that solidarity must be translated into institutional practices, policies, and decisional criteria.

To conclude, not any kind of solidarity will do. As Samir Amin has written (n.d.): "One could conceive of a genuine international transfer of resources from the rich to the poor once it is universally accepted that the existing division of labour can be scrapped and a more equitable one take its place." Solidarity, therefore, will be gained only after much struggle and after basic structures governing international and transregional exchanges have been drastically modified. Solidarity is at the same time desirable, necessary, and difficult.

FOR FURTHER READING

Amin, Samir. 1973. *Neo-Colonialism in West Africa*. Harmondsworth: Penguin.

———. 1976. *Unequal Development*, New York: Monthly Review Press.

———. 1977. "Self-reliance and the New International Economic Order." *Monthly Review* 29, no. 3: 1–21.

Berger, Peter L. 1974. *Pyramids of Sacrifice*. New York: Basic Books.

Bergsten, C. Fred. 1973. "The Threat from the Third World." *Foreign Policy*, no. 11 (Summer): 102–124.

Brookfield, H. 1975. *Interdependent Development*. Pittsburgh, Pa.: University of Pittsburgh Press.

Cole, J. 1976. *The Poor of the Earth*. London: Macmillan.

Erb, Guy F. and Valeriana Kallab, eds. 1975. *Beyond Dependency: The Developing World Speaks Out*. Washington, D.C.: Overseas Development Council.

Falk, Richard A. 1975. *A Study of Future Worlds*. New York: Free Press.

Ghali, Mirrit B. 1972. *Tradition for the Future*. Oxford: Alden Press.

Goulet, Denis. 1971. *The Cruel Choice*. New York: Atheneum.

————. 1974a. "Development and the International Economic Order." *International Development Review* 16, no. 2: 10–16.

————. 1974b. *The New Moral Order*. Maryknoll, N.Y.: Orbis Books.

————. 1976. "World Interdependence: Verbal Smokescreen or New Ethic?" Development Paper, no. 21. Washington, D.C.: Overseas Development Council.

Haq, Mahbub ul. 1976. *The Poverty Curtain: Choices for the Third World*. New York: Columbia University Press.

Heilbroner, Robert L. 1974. *An Inquiry into the Human Prospect*. New York: Norton.

Herrera, Amilcar O. et. al. 1976. *Catastrophe or New Society? A Latin American World Model*. Ottawa: International Development Research Centre.

Horowitz, Irving. 1966. *Three Worlds of Development*. London: Oxford University Press.

Howe, James W. and John W. Sewell. 1975. "Let's Sink the Lifeboat Ethics." *Worldview* 18, no. 10 (October): 13–18.

Jolly, Richard. 1978. *Disarmament and World Development*. Elmsford, N.Y.: Pergamon Press.

Lin, Paul. 1975. "Development Guided by Values: Comments on China's Road and Its Implications." *International Development Review* 17, no. 1.

Mazrui, Ali A. 1975. "The New Interdependence: From Hierarchy to Symmetry." *The U.S. and World Development: Agenda for Action, 1975*. Washington, D.C.: Praeger/Overseas Development Council.

Meadows, D. H. et. al. 1972. *The Limits to Growth*. A Report for the Club of Rome's Project on the Predicament of Mankind. New York: Universe Books.

Mendlovitz, Saul H. 1975. *On the Creation of a Just World Order*. New York: Free Press.

Myrdal, Gunnar. 1970. *The Challenge of World Poverty*. New York: Pantheon.

Pirages, Dennis ed. 1977. *The Sustainable Society*. New York: Praeger.

Schumacher, E. F. 1973. *Small Is Beautiful*. New York: Harper & Row, Harper Torchbook.

Streeten, Paul. 1977. "The Distinctive Features of a Basic Needs Approach to Development." *International Development Review* 19, no. 3: 8–16.

Tanzanian Delegation to Nonaligned Nations Summit Conference. 1971. "Cooperation Against Poverty." *The Political Economy of Development and Underdevelopment.* Edited by C. K. Wilber. New York: Random House, 373–89.

Tinbergen, Jan, ed. 1976. *Reshaping the International Order: A Report to the Club of Rome.* New York: Dutton.

Ward, Barbara and Rene Dubos. 1972. *Only One Earth: The Care and Maintenance of A Small Planet.* New York: Norton.

PART IV

OVERVIEW

15. LEAST DEVELOPED NATIONS

L. Berry and R. W. Kates

Measured against the basic needs of the world's population, the current economic order is insane. In the aggregate, all the basic needs are met; but in terms of distribution and consumption there coexist the obese and the hungry, the three-bathroom home and the open sewer, the unemployed graduate and the illiterate. A small symbol of that insanity was the hoped-for benefit accruing to countries designated "least developed."

At a seminar held in East Africa in 1969, exploring "appropriate" criteria for least development, participants were assured that, by all the criteria that could be devised, Tanzania would surely qualify. It is ironic, of course, that this was considered good news at the time, for it was hoped that by highlighting the special conditions that apparently exist in countries like Tanzania, a rationale would be provided for special aid and trade initiatives.

Events rapidly overtook the situation. Worldwide changes in the pricing of commodities, particularly oil, resulted in a very different national economic situation for a number of developing nations not included in the original least developed group. Concern over the problems of the least developed, exacerbated by the Sahelian drought, merged with problems of those countries most affected by the oil price increase and subsequent inflation.

As a result, there was a rapid, nonuniform increase in the number of countries eligible for special treatment. Despite this fact, the original group remains a core designation for a number of purposes. The focus on the least developed and most affected countries has, by some measures, been effective at least in the short run. Many donor nations give these countries priority in aid allocations and bestow a higher proportion of outright grants in their assistance to countries in these groups (see chap. 13).

Poorest People or Poorest Nations?

Whatever the criteria—least developed or most affected—the nation-state still serves as the basic unit of designation. However, an alternative focus on the poorest people, wherever they may be, has been legislated by the U.S. Congress and selected by the World Bank. Of course, the two are not mutually exclusive. In our detailed analysis of the least developed, we explained the differences between the plight of poorest nations and poorest peoples. Our conclusions relate to nation-states and the peculiar inconsistencies that result when jurisdiction over portions of the earth's surface is divided among 160–200 units of enormously varying size.

The complicated process of forming nation-states has resulted in some strange contrasts: the huge states of Brazil, China, the United States, and the USSR; tiny nations such as the Maldives, Gambia, Benin, and Guyana. In comparing nation-states, one is comparing very different units. The smaller nations tend to have a greater uniformity of natural, cultural, and economic conditions; the larger nations usually combine these conditions in a greater variety. But most statistics and analyses are structured in such a manner that they emphasize the national unit and facilitate comparisons among nations. Indeed, regardless of their size, nations are the basic economic and decision-making unit in the modern world.

The debate over poorest nation versus poorest people is played out in this context and involves important issues. It is surely a *world* problem that poverty is so widespread. But when poverty is found in pockets within large and comparatively wealthy nations, it becomes primarily a *national* problem to refocus attention and redistribute wealth. The international community has important responsibilities toward the poorest people, but the problems of the world's poorest nations can only be addressed in the context of the international community.

Among the world's poorest and most affected nations, there is little surplus wealth to be redistributed, few centers of economic growth from which to initiate changes in the national well-being, scant resources to meet the hardships of drought, famine, and disaster. During favorable periods, extended assistance is useful to generate new growth; in times of need, aid has been a necessity to maintain health and life. The least developed and the most affected have necessarily become the concern of the world community.

The Causes of Least Development

It is easier to place nations on scales of development than to explain the causes of their predicament. Competing theories that attempt to "explain" the poverty of nations tend to emphasize one of three causes: the inherent characteristics of the nations involved; the processes of underdevelopment; or the artifacts of the scales of measurement employed. Thus, less-developed countries are precisely that because they are young, unfortunate, or inept; or because they have been underdeveloped in order to develop other countries; or because the choice of measurement scales do not favor their characteristics. A rich and disputatious literature advocates all these views. It is not the purpose of this chapter to review the latter, but to ask how well they explain the phenomenon of least development.

In addition to these major general theories of development, a special theory of least development involving random "leastness" asserts that, "after all, someone must be last." In the context of a theory of stages of economic growth (Rostow, 1960), the least developed would include those nations that, by some accident of history, culture, and location, got a late start. They would therefore be the random residuals at the very base of the economic ladder.

A study of the characteristics and location of the least developed suggests that there is more to be said on this matter. A map designating the least developed (see chap. 5, map 5.1) does not appear to show a random selection of poorer nations. On closer examination, most of the least developed appear to be in Africa; the majority are located in arid or semiarid environments; and many seem physically or economically isolated to an extraordinary degree. Study of the environmental, political, cultural, and geographic aspects of the least developed raises numerous questions about the group. Randomness, however, appears to be the least likely explanation for their existence.

Setting aside the theory of randomness as an adequate explanation for least development, none of the major theoretical orientations uniquely account for the phenomenon. Almost all the least developed are, in terms of location and economic linkages, peripheral to the world cores of power and wealth. Most have environments marked by shorter growing seasons resulting from aridity or cold, and by the absence of known mineral resources. Although many are young nations concentrated in Africa, a few number among the continent's oldest. Most rely on a few agricultural export crops. The least developed encompass a wide variety of political, economic, and cultural systems. They surely have characteristics that set them apart from rich nations, but these traits are shared by other poor nations.

Nor can the processes of underdevelopment have worked exclusively to their disadvantage. Mercantilism and capitalism in Europe, and later in North America, led to major reorientations of trading links. Places once central to the caravan trade subsequently found themselves at a great distance from even the regional links of the new centers of wealth. Independent nomadic peoples bore the brunt of conflict with colonial invaders. As a result of these and other activities, the growth of the least developed was halted during the colonial era. Underdevelopment surely occurred. More recently, a case can be made for the least developed suffering relative neglect, rather than exploitation, of colonial powers and world investors. The generally weak integration of many of these countries into the world system may have buffered them against the more rapacious processes of "global accumulation."

The conventional indicators of economic and social well-being are, by definition, biased against the least developed. Richness of extended family life, wealth of traditional culture, depth of religious feeling, and effective participation in village activity are all well-developed values among LDNs. They may inversely relate to GNP, literacy, or the manufacturing work force. LDNs appear to share some of these more favorable cultural characteristics.

The present writers prefer to adopt a cautious stance as to cause. Explanations of least development that rely on intrinsic characteristics come perilously close to "blaming the victim," a familiar justification for maintenance of the status quo. A similar situation exists for those explanations that "exalt the victim" by idealizing the social milieu of the folk society. Such explanations may serve to discourage criticism of local ineptitude or indigenous exploitation and thus prevent the development of self-reliance.

While it is preferable to eschew single-cause explanations of least development, the latter is not simply a random condition existing among the world's poor nations, nor is it a pragmatic but arbitrary classification. Some nations may soon lose their place among the least developed, possibly contingent on the vagaries of mineral exploitation. Others will be included in the formal classification for purposes of geographic representation (Latin America, Oceania) or excluded because of size (Bangladesh). But for most countries it would seem that peripheral location within regions and environmental marginality combine to exacerbate the inequalities of the current economic order.

Peripheral Regional Location

The least developed share with the less developed a location that is peripheral to the core of world wealth and power; moreover, many of the former share, within their own regions, a location peripheral to their wealthier and more powerful less-developed neighbors. Thus, in a regional setting the coastal areas of West Africa, especially Nigeria and the Ivory Coast, may be considered cores surrounded by the peripheral states in the Sahel.

West Africa.   In precolonial times, the inland states of West Africa were the seat of great kingdoms founded on the principles of nomadic flexibility and power. The coast was a somewhat isolated region plagued by disease. The arid and semiarid areas were the heart of the major lines of communication and trade, the centers of knowledge and learning.

With the European penetration inland from the coast, which led to the establishment of seaports, trading routes, and the growth of the slave trade, the entire region underwent a radical change. Later, colonial development, which was centered on the ports and the boundary road and rail network linking them, confirmed this pattern of economic supremacy. As a result, Senegal, the Ivory Coast, Nigeria, and Ghana are among the more prosperous developing countries, while Mali, Chad, Niger, and Benin are among the poorest of the least developed.

East Africa.   In East Africa, a more complex historical and physical setting serves as a backdrop to a different set of relationships. For a variety of colonial historical, geographic, and climatic reasons, Kenya became the early focus of white settlers' farming and business activities and investments. Although this interest developed gradually, the post-World War I accession of Tanzania to British control emphasized the role of Mombassa and Nairobi. The pattern of communications and trade was focused more clearly on Kenya. Despite the efforts to concentrate East African community activities at Arusha, in northern Tanzania, and the various agreements to "allocate" industrial investment among the three East African states, Kenya has continued to be the center of modern industrial, agricultural and tourist activity. Political factors may have aggravated present dichotomies, but the total effect has been to produce very different patterns of development within each of the three countries. Per capita income is higher in Kenya than in Tanzania or Uganda (though income distribution is more equitable in Tanzania).

More significant, it appears from a variety of indicators that core growth in one country has accompanied a slower growth and trade-dependent situation in others. Tanzania has independent outlets and a political will that may enable it to overcome the ties of long-established patterns of growth, but this is proving to be a long and difficult task.

In a second-tier arrangement in eastern Africa, Tanzania, Kenya, and Uganda collectively comprise growth areas in relation to the very poor and crowded states of Rwanda and Burundi. Formerly linked on the west through the Belgian colonial network, these two isolated countries have struggled to establish eastern links; they now rely on these routes for imports and exports. The great distances, high cost, and uncertain nature of the links have greatly handicapped these resource-poor countries in their attempt to develop economically.

Ethiopia and Somalia do not seem to fit the regional-peripheral model quite so neatly. Ethiopia is one of the larger (in terms of population) LDCs. It may be that a combination of strong historical factors (including a strong feudal system and later colonial subjugation), internal communication difficulties, health and disease problems, and relative isolation has prevented this country from following a path of stronger economic growth and internal integration. Somalia, a once isolated desert country, has now assumed some strategic importance, but it does not seem to have been greatly influenced by its relations with local (regional) neighbors. It is ironic that these two exceptions to the model came perilously close to open warfare.

Southern Africa. The three least developed states of southern Africa clearly illustrate the regional marginalization process. Lesotho and Swaziland, the two smaller states (i.e., inland area), became residual to the territory of the Republic of South Africa. Marginal hilly lands of relatively low agricultural value, they have become densely populated, independent territories dependent on South Africa for trade and income from migrant labor. Botswana is much larger in land area but equally small in population (650,000). It has also developed a strong dependence on South Africa for trade and income. Opportunities for growth are more hopeful in at least two of the states, namely, Botswana and Swaziland, since the discovery of mineral resources may serve as the economic catalyst to create a new pattern of future development. However, existing communications and trade ties with South Africa may be tightened as a result of new investments for mining development and thereby exacerbate the dependence of these states.

Himalayan Mountain States. The Himalayan countries present some striking analogies with the Sahel. Like the latter, they lack outlets to the sea, are isolated from the world trading network by physical barriers, and have larger, more prosperous neighbors. India, though a poor country, has much greater aggregate resources; Russia and China, to the north, present a similar contrast. The Himalayan states have remained relatively isolated until recently; even now they have tenuous links with the world economic system. Two states were incorporated into their powerful neighbor, leaving Nepal, Bhutan, and Afganistan, areas possessing comparatively rich cultural heritages yet isolated by harsh physical surroundings. Their links with the rest of the world have mainly depended on their larger neighbors; this state of affairs may continue in the future.

Environmental Marginality

Many developing countries, and a number of developed nations, may be characterized as having harsh environments, but the least developed display three distinctive patterns. For most, physical isolation is a common characteristic. In sixteen countries, arid or semiarid environments, with little internal diversity, add to the effect of isolation. For a number of others, the high relief of mountains or dissected plateaus are distinctive features. For a few, a humid, tropical environment in a small national area, high population density, and/or an insular or mountainous location combine to provide yet a third group of marginal environments.

While particular environmental features are by no means unique to LDNs, in only a few cases are the environmental constraints to agriculture and communication alleviated by the presence of actively developed mineral resources or other significant economic growth points. Where these are present in significant quantities, as in Botswana, exploitation is still in an early phase.

Strategies for Coping with Least Development

There is no easy or quick solution to the problems of the least developed. The development of new resources and changes in development strategy or political relationships may modify the economic status of a few LDNs. The discovery of oil reserves has, for example, dramatically changed the economic and political position of Libya in the last twenty years. Mineral development in Botswana may be the stimulus for rapid change. But in all probability the present group of LDNs will be recognizable, using current limited criteria, in twenty or thirty years' time.

Being "least" in a world of "most" places a special burden on those who formulate development strategies. In the second and third sections of this work we discuss three suggested sets of strategies: (1) those that are designed to promote an economic catch-up, focusing on economic growth at higher rates; (2) those that encourage regional integration by linking richer regions and states with one or more LDCs to enhance the possibility of steady economic growth; and (3) those that attempt to isolate LDCs from the full impact of the world economy and thereby preserve the essence of the local cultural and economic systems. Discussion of these strategies has proliferated in recent literature (O'Keefe and Wisner, 1977; Seidman, 1974b). A review of the attitudes and concepts put forward by the various contributors to the book provides a somewhat different set of viewpoints. In general, our coauthors both deny the possibility of catch-up in the prevailing economic order and eschew the centrality of economic growth implicit in such a strategy. They replace this with a call for both a new economic order and an emphasis on noneconomic forms of development. But they also draw on aspects of the prevailing strategies: seeking harmonious linkages rather than catch-up with richer nations; emphasizing self-reliance but not autocracy; and searching for nonexploitative regional linkages.

New Economic Order. New sets of relationships between "first" and "third" worlds are implicit in almost all the preceding chapters: they are presented in sharp contrast in Szentes' plea for a totally new economic structure (chap. 3) and in Goulet's cry for a new ethic to guide future world relationships (chap. 14). Both contributors address the whole of the developing world and suggest that for the least developed the issues are even more serious. Helleiner perceptively (albeit cynically) suggests, in a personal communication, that it is possible to institute new economic relationships with LDNs while doing little to change the global picture. The shift in world resources would be relatively modest and could ease the consciences of the rich.

Emphasis on Noneconomic Forms of Development. A major theme in many of the foregoing chapters is the emphasis on development sectors that are generally considered as resulting in rapid economic growth yet also address other aspects of national and personal well-being. In their discussion of health care and nutrition (chap. 7) Haraldson and Sukkar emphasize the importance of programs that impact directly on rural populations and the poorer sectors of the population. These authors point out that the traditional Western approach involving curative medicine does not work for most of the least developed and consequently necessitates that utilization of a wide-spread preventative approach in health care. Their views on nutrition suggest a similar approach. Mujwahuzi (chap. 10), Kates (chap. 9), and many other contributors emphasize the social infrastructure as a means of alleviating the slow progress toward economic growth that characterizes the least developed.

Harmonious Linkages. There are advantages in harmoniously linking Western knowledge and attitudes with the internal understanding of local conditions in developing countries. Is there a way in which less-dominating intellectual relationships can evolve? This is a central theme of Johnson and Vogel-Roboff (chap. 6), who attempt to define ways in which the modernization of pastoral nomadism can take place without a destruction of this important and productive way of life. They are relatively optimistic that this can occur. Berry and Renwick (chap. 11) approach the information problem directly and make a case for the integration of three sets of knowledge: international scientific information; technical, holistic understanding of the conditions and problems of particular areas; and indigenous wisdom about local resources and their proper use. They show that the relative, sometimes total, neglect of all but the scientific source of knowledge is an important reason why development programs do not attain their projected goals. Ways are suggested in which different types of integration of knowledge might lead to new styles of development.

Lastly, Mujwahuzi (chap. 10) shows that in the improvement of rural water supply, there is a need to incorporate local decision making in the overall process and to integrate "internal" and "external" know-how in a participatory manner. These and other chapters suggest that when the developed interact with the least developed, differences in conditions are so great that care must be taken to integrate concepts from both systems in order to create effective programs.

Self-Reliance. Conversely, several chapters imply that a partial removal from the international market scene would be advisable for the least developed insofar as every attempt should be made to be as self-sufficient as possible. Helleiner (chap. 2) espouses this view as part of his general approach to the international trading problems of the least developed. For some countries, such as Tanzania, this degree of self-sufficiency is already a major component of national policy. Helleiner sees little hope of economic catch-up in the short run and advocates the adoption of defensive strategies.

Kates (chap. 9), in his analysis of the impact of natural disasters on LDCs, advocates self-reliance as an important component of prevention and recovery measures. He points out the built-in nature of any adjustment mechanisms. However, the strategies he suggests for coping with major natural hazards involve a large measure of international assistance and involvement. None of the contributors have advocated a Burmese-style withdrawal strategy (chap. 4), nor do they encourage any attempt to seek total autocracy.

Regional linkage and integration.   Only one chapter deals explicitly with combinations to increase the scale of market and resources and to take advantage of complementarity. Seidman (chap. 12) proposes strategies that will lead to regional integration. In the case of mineral development, it is clear that regional integration among nations—linking countries with similar resources and potential for industrial growth can pay handsome dividends in the near future.

Linking LDNs is a problematic venture. A major difficulty with combination proposals is the inequality that seems to develop regionally. Thus, the East African community found it impossible to provide equity to Tanzania and Uganda vis-à-vis Kenya. All new proposals for "stratification" in Sahelian livestock management (e.g., reproduction in the Sahel, intensive feeding in the Sudanic zone, marketing on the Coast) only seem to enhance the peripheral and dependent role of the Sahelian nations.

Five years ago, when the present writers first identified the environmental marginality of LDNs, the latter were described as "least known" nations. They are still least known (except, of course, to their own inhabitants), for knowledge, like all investments, is related to rates of return. But enough is known from this and other studies to draw some central conclusions.

Nation-states, regionally peripheral in marginal environments, constitute a special case of development need. Irrespective of who will devise an ordering of socioeconomic well-being in the world community, these states will predominate in the lowest fifth of nations.

Given the fact that the least developed constitute a special case with special patterns, a development strategy addressed to their needs cannot simply reflect a modification of conventional policies, be it the conventions of industrialized capitalism or industrial socialism. To do so will surely not help; it might even hurt, thereby increasing regional dependency and subservience and threatening the life-support systems of the population in question.

The alternative approaches suggested in the preceding chapters are directions to be taken, not blueprints to be followed. Within the individual countries concerned, they call for redefinitions of what constitutes growth and progress, and for increased self-reliance. Between North and South they demand a new mini-economic order in terms of flows of commodities and donor relations. And among nations within the same regions they require greater solidarity and mutual support.

This constitutes a tall order, perhaps too much for a strife-torn world where the attention given to any single set of problems seems so limited. Five years ago we wrote: "Soon, hopefully, the rains will come again in the Sahel, and the herds and herders will turn northward. A government or two might have fallen, but the pressures of wealth—inflation pressure, resource scarcity, corruption in public life—will eclipse the news from far-off, distant places." In 1971 the flow of resources to all developing nations from the rich was less than one-half cent for every dollar earned, but the flow to the least developed was somewhat greater (five-sixths of one cent). The least developed represent neither powerful allies nor resources and markets. They do serve as a measure of the distributive justice of the world order. The latter has fared rather poorly despite the radiant visions of global village or spaceship earth. That measure of justice still remains to be fulfilled.

FOR FURTHER READING

Amin, Samir. 1974. *Accumulation on a World Scale*. New York: Monthly Review Press.

Baran, Paul. 1957. *The Political Economy of Growth*. New York: Monthly Review Press.

Campbell, D. and C. Katz. 1975. *Atlas of the Least Developed Nations: Groups and Characteristics*. Worcester, Mass.: Clark University.

Clark University Program in International Development and Social Change. 1974. *Delimitation of Groups of Least Developed Nations on the Basis of Socio-Economic, Political and Economic Data*. Worcester, Mass.: Clark University.

Frank, A. G. 1970. "The Development of Underdevelopment." *Imperialism and Underdevelopment*. Edited by Robert I. Rhodes. New York: Monthly Review Press, pp. 4–17.

George, Susan. 1977. *How the Other Half Dies*. Montclair, N.J.: Allanheld, Osmun.

Goulet, Denis. 1971. *The Cruel Choice*. New York: Atheneum.

Kjeshus, H. 1977. *Ecological Control and Economic Development*. London: Methuen.

Lappe, Francis and J. Collins. 1977. *Food First: Beyond the Myth of Security*. Boston: Houghton Mifflin.

O'Keefe, P. and B. Wisner. 1975. "The Process of Soil Erosion." *African Environment: Special Report I—Problems and Perspectives*. Edited by P. Richards. London: I.A.I., pp. 63–65.

Rostow, W. W. 1960. *The Stages of Economic Growth: A Non-Communist Manifesto*. New York: Cambridge University Press.

Seidman, A. 1974. *Planning for Development in Sub-Saharan Africa*. New York: Praeger.

———, ed. 1976. *Natural Resources and National Welare: The Case of Copper*. New York: Praeger.

Szentes, Tamas. 1971 and 1973. *The Political Economy of Underdevelopment.* Budapest: Akademiai Kiado.

Tanzania Delegation to Nonaligned Nations Summit Conference. 1971. "Cooperation Against Poverty." *The Political Economy of Development and Underdevelopment.* Edited by C. K. Wilber. New York: Random House, pp. 373–389.

BIBLIOGRAPHY

Adler, J. H., ed. 1967. *Capital Movements and Economic Development* New York: St. Martin's Press.

Ahn, P. M. 1970. *West African Soils.* New York: Oxford University Press.

Ajayi, J. F. A. and M. Crowder. 1976. *History of West Africa.* London: Longmans.

Allen, Philip M. 1970. "The Technical-Assistance Industry in Africa: A Case for Nationalization." *International Development Review*, no. 3: 8.

Amin, Samir. 1973. *Neo-Colonialism in West Africa.* Harmondsworth: Penguin.

———. 1974. *Accumulation on a World Scale.* New York: Monthly Review Press.

———. n.d. "Growth Is Not Development." *Development Forum.* [A selection of articles from previous issues] New York: United Nations Centre for Economic and Social Information, p. 7.

Amundsen, E. and K. W. Newell. 1975. "Health Service Development in the Third World." *WHO Chronicle* 29: 10–11.

Antoine, Pierre. 1959. "Qui est coupable?" *Revue de L'action Populaire*, no. 32 (November): 1055–1065.

Aron, R. 1962. *Dix-huit leçons sur la société industrielle.* Paris: Gallimard.

Asad, Talal. 1973. "The Bedouin as a Military Force: Notes on Some Aspects of Power Relations between Nomads and Sedentaries in Historical Perspective." *The Desert and the Sown: Nomads in the Wider Society.* Edited by Cynthia Nelson. Berkeley: University of California, Berkeley, Institute of International Studies, pp. 61–73.

Awad, Mohamed. 1959. "Settlement of Nomadic and Semi-Nomadic Tribal Groups in the Middle East." *International Labor Review* 79: 25–56.

Baier, S. B. 1974. "African Merchants in the Colonial Period: A History of Commerce in Damagaram (Central Niger), 1880–1960." Ph.D. dissertation, University of Wisconsin.

Bailey, Clinton. 1974. "Bedouin Star-lore in Sinai and the Negev." *Bulletin* [School of Oriental and African Studies, London University] 37: 580–596.

Baird, A. et al. 1975. "Towards an Explanation of Disaster Proneness." Disaster Research Unit. Occasional Paper, no. 10. Bradford, Eng.: University of Bradford.

Banarji, D. 1974. *Health Behaviour of Rural Populations.* New Delhi: Centre of Social Medicine and Community Health, Jawaharlal Nehru University.

Bank of Zambia. 1972. *Annual Report* [Year ending December 31, 1972].

Baral, Lok. Raj. 1976. "Party-like Institutions in 'Party-less' Politics: The GVNC [Go to the Village National Campaign] in Nepal." *Asian Survey:* 16, no. 7 (July): 672–681.

Baran, Paul. 1957. *The Political Economy of Growth.* New York: Monthly Review Press.

Bates, Daniel G. 1973. *Nomads and Farmers: A Study of the Yörük of Southeastern Turkey.* Anthropological Paper no. 52. Ann Arbor: University of Michigan, Museum of Anthropology.

Berger, Peter L. 1974. *Pyramids of Sacrifice.* New York: Basic Books.

Bergsten, C. Fred. 1973. "The Threat From the Third World." *Foreign Policy,* no. 11 (Summer): 102–124.

Berman, Mildred. 1971. "Social Change among the Beersheba Bedouin." *Human Organization* 26: 69–76.

Bernus, Edmond. 1966. "Les Touaregs du Sahel Nigérien." *Les Cahiers d'Outre-Mer* 19, no. 73: 5–34.

———. 1974a. "Géographie humaine de la zone sahélienne." *Le Sahel: bases écologiques de l'aménagement.* Paris: UNESCO, pp. 67–73.

———. 1974b. *Les Illabakan (Niger): Une tribu touarègue sahélienne et son aire de nomadisation.* Paris: ORSTOM.

———. 1975. "Les Composantes géographiques et souàles des types d'elevage en milieu Tanarey." *Pastoralism in Tropical Africa.* Edited by T. Monod. Oxford: Oxford University Press, pp. 239–244.

——— and Suzanne Bernus. 1972. *Du sel et des dattes: introduction à l'étude de la communauté d'In Gall et de Tegidda-n-tesemt.* Etudes nigériennes, no. 31. Niamey: Centre Nigérien de Recherches en Sciences Humaines.

Berry, E. 1976. "Facilitating Rural Change in Contemporary Africa." *Contemporary Africa: Geography and Change.* Edited by G. C. Knight and J. L. Newman. Englewood Cliffs, N.J.: Prentice-Hall, pp. 233–250.

Berry, Leonard. 1975. "Environmental Constraints and Development Policy." *Drought, Famine and Population Movements in Africa.* Edited by J. L. Newman. Syracuse University: Maxwell School of Citizenship and Public Affairs, pp. 32–55.

—— and J. Townshend. 1972. "Soil Conservation Policies in the Semiarid Regions of Tanzania: An Historical Perspective." *Geografiska Annaler* [series A] 53, nos. 3–4: 241–253.

—— and D. Ford. 1977. "Recommendations for a System to Monitor Critical Indicators in Areas Prone to Desertification." Mimeographed. Worcester, Mass.: Clark University.

Bisson, Jean. 1964. "Eleveurs caravaniers et vieux sedentaires de l'Air sudoriental." *Travaux de l'Institut de Recherches Sahariennes* 23: 95–110.

Björkman, Olle and Joseph Berry. 1973. "High-Efficiency Photosynthesis." *Scientific American*, 229, no. 4: 80–93.

Blaut, J. M.; N. R. P. Harman; M. Moerman. 1959. "A Study of Cultural Determinants of Soil Erosion and Conservation in the Blue Mountains of Jamaica." *Journal of Economic and Social Studies* 8: 403–420.

Bloomfield, Frena. 1976. "Birenda's King-sized Problem." *Far Eastern Economic Review*, November 19, pp. 32–33.

Blue, R. N. and J. H. Weaver. 1977. *A Critical Assessment of the Tanzania Model of Development*. Washington, D.C.: USAID Development Studies program. Paper no. 1.

Boahen, A. A. 1962. "The Caravan Trade in the Nineteenth Century." *Journal of African History* 3, no. 2: 349–359.

Boserup, E. 1965. *The Conditions of Agricultural Growth*. Chicago: Aldine.

Boudet, G. 1972. "Désertification de l'Afrique tropicale sèche." *Adansonia* [series 2] 12, no. 4: 505–524.

Box, Thadis, W. 1971. "Nomadism and Land Use in Somalia." *Economic Development and Cultural Change* 19: 222–228.

Brown, David G. 1976. "The Development of Vietnam's Petroleum Resources." *Asian Survey* 16, no. 6 (June): 553–570.

Bryant, John. 1969. *Health and the Developing World*. Ithaca: Cornell University Press.

Bryson, R. A. 1973. "Drought in Sahelia." *Ecologist* 3: 366–371.

Bugnicourt, J. 1974. *Un peuple privé de son environnement*. Programme formation pour l'environnement. Dakar: IDEP/UNEP/SIDA.

Bulliet, Richard E. 1975. *The Camel and the Wheel*. Cambridge: Harvard University Press.

Burton, I. 1977. "Safe Water for All." *Natural Resources Forum* 1:95–110.

——, R. W. Kates, G. F. White. 1978. *The Environment As Hazard.* New York: Oxford University Press.

Campbell, D. J. 1977a. "Strategies for Coping with Drought in the Sahel: A Study of Recent Population Movements in the Department of Maradi, Niger." Ph.D. dissertation, Clark University.

––––––. 1977b. "Land Competition at the Margins of the Rangelands: A Proposal for Research in Kajiado District." Working Paper No. 299. Nairobi: Institute for Development Studies, Univ. of Nairobi.

–––––– and C. Katz. 1975. *Atlas of the Least Developed Nations: Groups and Characteristics*. Mimeographed. Worcester, Mass.: Clark University.

Carter, L. J. 1977. "Soil Erosion: The Problem Persists Despite the Billions Spent on It." *Science*, April 22, pp. 409–411.

Chanda, Najan. 1976. "Vietnam's Joint Venture Plan." *Far Eastern Economic Review*, September 24, pp. 55–56.

Clark University Program in International Development and Social Change. 1974. "Delimitation of Groups of Least Developed Nations on the Basis of Socio-Economic, Political and Economic Data." Worcester, Mass.: Clark University.

Cochemé, J. and P. Franguin. 1967. *An Agroclimatology Survey of a Semiarid Area in Africa*, WMO Technical Note 86: Geneva: World Meteorological Organzation.

Collins, J. D. 1974. "Government and Groundnut Marketing in Rural Hausa Niger: The 1930's to the 1960's in Magasia. Ph.D. dissertation, Johns Hopkins University.

Conde, J. ed. 1971.*The Demographic Transition as Applied to Tropical Africa, with Particular Reference to Health, Education and Economic Factors*. Paris: OECD.

Conyers, D. 1973. "Agro-Economic Zones of Tanzania." *BRALUP Research Paper*, no. 25. University of Dar es Salaam.

Crowder, M. 1968. *West Africa under Colonial Rule*. Evanston, Ill.: Northwestern University Press.

Cummings, Ralph W. 1977. Minimum Information Systems for Agricultural Development in Low-income Countries." Seminar Report (September 14). New York: Agricultural Development Council.

Curtin, Philip et al. 1978. *African History*. Boston: Little, Brown.

CUSO. 1975. *The Third Imperative for Canadian Irrigation Policy: Interdependence with the Third World*. A submission to the Special Joint Committee of Parliament on Immigration Policy. June.

Dankoussou, I. et al. 1975. "Niger." *Population Growth and Socio-Economic Change in West Africa*. Edited by J. C. Caldwell et al. New York: Columbia University Press, pp. 679–693.

Dasmann, R. F.; J. P. Milton; P. H. Freeman. 1973. *Ecological Principles for Economic Development*. London: John Wiley.

Davidson, B. 1976. "Review of Abaar: The Somali Drought." *Review of African Political Economy,* May–August, pp. 110–112.

Davidson, S., and R. Passmore, 1969. *Human Nutrition and Dietetics*. Edinburgh and London: Livingstone.

Diakite, Y. 1971. "Migratory Movements in West Africa." *The Demographic Transition as Applied to Tropical Africa, with Particular Reference to Health, Education and Economic Factors*. Paris: OECD.

Downs, James F. 1964. *Animal Husbandry in Navajo Society and Culture*. Berkeley: University of California Press.

Dubourg, J. 1957. "La Vie des paysans Mossi: Le Village de Taghalla." *Les Cahiers d'Outre-Mer* 10, no. 40: 285–324.

Dupire, Marguerite. 1962. "Trade and Markets in the Economy of the Nomadic Fulani of Niger (Bororo)." *Markets in Africa*. Edited by Paul Bohannan and George Dalton. Evanston, Ill.: Northwestern University Press, pp. 68–93.

———. 1972. "Les Facteurs humaines de l'économie pastorale." *Etudes Nigériens*, 6. Niamey: CNRSH.

Dworkin, J. 1974. "Global Trends in Natural Disasters, 1947–73." Natural Hazard Research Working Paper, no. 26. University of Colorado.

Dyson-Hudson, Rada. 1972. "Pastoralism: Self-Image and Behavioral Reality." *Perspectives on Nomadism*. Edited by William Irons and Neville Dyson-Hudson. Leiden: E. J. Brill, pp. 30–47.

Eckholm, E. 1977. *Losing Ground: Environmental Stress and World Food Prospects*. New York: Norton.

The *Economist*. 1975. "Business Brief," August 16, pp. 60–61.

Edelman, John A., and Hollis B. Chenery. 1977. "Aid and Income Distribution." *The New International Economic Order: The North-South Debate*. Edited by Jagdish N. Bhaqwati. Cambridge, Mass.: MIT Press.

Elliot, David W. P. 1976. "Political Integration in North Vietnam: The Cooperativation Period." *Communism in Indochina: New Perspectives*. Edited by Joseph Zasloff and MacAlister Brown. Lexington, Mass.: Lexington Books, pp. 165–193.

Elliot, K. M., ed. 1974. *Human Rights in Health*. Ciba Foundation Symposium 23 [new series]. Amsterdam: Associated Scientific Publishers.

———, ed. 1975. *The Year of the Health Auxilliary? British Health Care Planning and Technology. The Year Book of the British Hospitals Export Council*.

de Fabrègues, B. E. Peyre. 1971. *Evolution des pâturages naturels sahéliens de Sud Tamesna (République de Niger)*. Etude agro-stologique, no. 32. Paris: Institut d'étude médecine vétérinaire des pays tropicale.

Falk, Richard A. 1975. *A Study of Future Worlds*. New York: Free Press.

Farvar, M. Taghi and J. P. Milton. 1972. *The Careless Technology: Ecology and International Development*. New York: Natural History Press.

Faulkingham, R. H. 1975. "Ecologic Constraints and Subsistence Strategies: The Impact of Drought in a Hausa Village—A Case Study from Niger." Mimeographed. Department of Anthropology, University of Massachusetts.

Feachem. R. et al., eds. 1977. *Water, Wastes, and Health in Hot Climates* New York: John Wiley.

Fendall, N. R. E. 1972a. "Auxilliaries and Primary Care." *Bulletin [of the]* New York Academy of Medicine 48: 1291–1300.

———. 1972b. "Primary Medical Care in Developing Countries." *International Journal of Health Services* 2: 297–315.

Forrester, Jay W. 1971. *World Dynamics*. Cambridge, Mass.: Wright-Allen Press.

Frank, Andre G. 1967a. "Sociology of Development and Underdevelopment of Sociology." *Catalyst*, No. 3. Buffalo, N.Y.: University of Buffalo.

———. 1967b. *Latin America: Underdevelopment or Revolution—Essays on the Development of Underdevelopment and the Immediate Enemy*. New York: Monthly Review Press.

———. 1970. "The Development of Underdevelopment." *Imperialism and Underdevelopment*. Edited by Robert I. Rhodes. New York: Monthly Review Press, pp. 4–17.

Fromm, Erich, ed. 1966. *Socialist Humanism*. New York: Doubleday, Anchor Books.

Gallais, Jean. 1972. Les sociétés pastorales ouest-africaines face au développement." *Cahiers de'etudes africaines* 12: 353–368.

Gange, Frederick H. 1976. *Regionalism and National Unity in Nepal*. Berkeley: University of California Press.

Ganon, M. F. 1975. "The Nomads of Niger." *Population Growth and Socio-Economic Change in West Africa*. Edited by J. C. Caldwell et al. New York: Columbia University Press, pp. 694–700.

Ghali, Mirrit Boutros. 1972. *Tradition for the Future*. Oxford: Alden Press.

Ginsburg, Norton. 1961. *An Atlas of Economic Development*. Chicago: University of Chicago Press.

Glassner, Martin I. 1974. "The Bedouin of Southern Sinai under Israeli Administration." *Geographical Review* 64: 31–60.

Goodman, S. 1971. "The Foreign Exchange Constraint." *Constraints on the Economy of Zambia*. Edited by C. Elliot. Nairobi: Oxford University Press.

Goulet, Denis. 1966. "Secular History and Teleology." *World Justice* 8, no. 1: 5–19.

———. 1971. *The Cruel Choice*. New York: Atheneum, pp. 255–263.

———. 1974a. "Development Administration and Structures of Vulnerability." *The Administration of Change in Africa*. Edited by E. Philip Morgan. New York: Dunellen, pp. 27–58.

———. 1974b.*The New Moral Order*. Maryknoll, New York: Orbis Books.

Green, R. H. and A. Seidman. 1968. *Unity or Poverty? The Economics of Pan Africanism*. Harmondsworth: Penguin African Library.

Greene, Mark. 1975. "Impact of the Sahelian Drought in Mauritania." *African Environment* 1, no. 2: 11–21.

Groth, E., III. 1975. "Increasing the Harvest—Meeting Social, Not Sales, Goals." *Environment* 17, no. 1 (January–February): 28–39.

Haraldson, S. R. S. 1970. "Appraisal of Health Problems and Definition of Priorities in Health Planning." *Ethiopian Medical Journal* 8: 37.

———. 1973a. "Health Problems of Nomads." *World Hospital* 9: 176–177.

———. 1973b. *Evaluation of Alaska Eskimo Health Services*. Geneva: WHO Report.

———. 1975. "Alternative Approaches to Health Services for the Least Developed Countries." Paper read at the Wingspread Conference on the Least Developed, October 19–22, 1975, at Racine, Wisconsin.

Hargreaves, John D. ed. 1969. *France and West Africa: An Anthology of Historical Documents*. London: Macmillan.

Harriman, James. 1976a. "Ne Win Faces Up to Failure." *Far Eastern Economic Review*, December 24, pp. 20–21.

Harriman, James. 1976b. "Burma's First Steps to Capitalism." *Far Eastern Economic Review*, December 24, pp. 100–101.

Harvey, C. R. M. 1971. "Financial Constraints on the Economic Development of Zambia." *Constraints on the Economic Development of Zambia*. Edited by C. Elliot. Nairobi: Oxford University Press, p. 245.

Heady, Harold F. 1972. "Ecological Consequences of Bedouin Settlement in Saudi Arabia." *The Careless Technology: Ecology and International Development*. Edited by M. Taghi Farvar and John P. Milton. New York: Natural History Press, pp. 683–693.

Heilbroner, Robert L. 1975. *An Inquiry Into the Human Prospect*. New York: Norton.

Helleiner, G. K. 1976. "Transnational Enterprise, Manufactured Exports and Employment in Less-Developed Countries." *Economic and Political Weekly* [annual number] 11, nos. 5–7 (February).

———. Forthcoming. "Aid and Dependence in Africa: Issues for Recipients." *Politics of Africa: Dependence and Development* Edited by T. M. Shaw and K. Heard.

Hernandez, M. et al. 1974. "Effect of Economic Growth on Nutrition in a Tropical Community." *Ecology of Food and Nutrition* 3: 283–293.

Hewapathirane, D. 1975. "Flood Hazard in Sri Lanka, Human Adjustments and Alternatives." Ph.D. diss., University of Colorado.

Hewitt, K. and L. Sheehan. 1969. "A Pilot Survey of Global Natural Disasters of the Past Twenty Years." Natural Hazard Research Working Paper, no. 11. University of Colorado.

Hirschman, A. O. 1968. "The Political Economy of Import Substituting Industrialization in Latin America." *Quarterly Journal of Economics* 82, no. 1: 1–32.

———. 1973. "The Changing Tolerance for Income Inequality in the Course of Economic Development." *Quarterly Journal of Economics* 81: 544–566.

Holling, C. S. 1973. "Resilience and Stability of Ecological Systems." *Annual Review of Ecology and Systematics* 4: 1–23.

Horowitz, Irving L. 1966. *Three Worlds of Development*. London: Oxford University Press.

Howe, James W. and John W. Sewell. 1975. "Let's Sink the Lifeboat Ethics." *Worldview* 18, no. 10 (October): 13–18.

Imboden. 1977. "Planning and Design of Rural Drinking Water Project: A Research Framework to Analyze Experience with Rural Drinking Water Schemes." Paper no. 2. Paris: OECD Development Center, CD–R [77] 22.

International Monetary Fund. 1970. *Surveys of African Economies*. 3 vols. Washington, D.C.: International Monetary Fund.

Islam, M. A. 1970. "Human Adjustment to Cyclone Hazards: A Case Study of Char Jabbar." Natural Hazards Research Working Paper, no. 18. University of Colorado.

Janzen, D. 1973. "Tropical Agroecosystems." *Science*, December 21, pp. 1212–1219.

Jayaramen, T. K. and O. L. Shrestha. 1976. "Some Trade Problems of Landlocked Nepal." *Asian Survey* 16, no. 12 (December): 1113–1123.

Johnson, Douglas L. 1969. *The Nature of Nomadism: A Comparative Study of Pastoral Migrations in Southwestern Asia and Northern Africa*.

Research Paper, no. 118. University of Chicago, Department of Geography.

———. 1973. "The Response of Pastoral Nomads to Drought in the Absence of Outside Intervention." United Nations Secretariat, Special Sahelian Office, ST/SSO/18.

———. 1974a. "Changing Patterns of Pastoral Nomadism in North Africa." *Spatial Aspects of Development*. Edited by B. S. Hoyle. London: John Wiley, pp. 147–66.

———. 1974b. "L'Etat du nomadisme pastoral dans la zone sahélienne." *Le Sahel: bases écologique de l'aménagement*. Paris: UNESCO, pp. 75–88.

———. 1975. "The Status of Pastoral Nomadism in the Sahelian Zone." *The Sahel: Ecological Approaches to Land Use*. MAB Technical Notes. Paris: UNESCO, pp. 75–88.

Johnson, K. 1977. "Do As the Land Bids." Ph.D. dissertation, Clark University.

al-Kasab, Nafi Nasser. 1966. *Die Nomadensiedlung in der Irakischen Jezira*. Geographische Studien, no. 20. Tübingen: Geographischen Instituts der Universität Tübingen.

Kates, R. W. et al. 1976. *Population, Society and Desertification*. Conference on Desertification. Nairobi: UNEP/UN.

Keatley, P. 1963. *The Politics of Partnership: The Federation of Rhodesia and Nyasaland*. Harmondsworth: Penguin African Library.

Keenan, Jeremy H. 1972. "Social Change among the Tuareg." *Arabs and Berbers: From Tribe to Nation in North Africa*. Edited by Ernest Gellner and Charles Micaud. Lexington, Mass.: Lexington Books/ Heath, pp. 345–360.

Keller, Gordon N. 1972. "Bicultural Social Work and Anthropology." *Social Casework* 53: 455–465.

Kelly, T. J. 1975. "Climate and the West African Drought." *Drought, Famine and Population Movements in Africa*. Edited by J. L. Newman. Syracuse Univeristy: Maxwell School of Citizenship and Public Affairs, pp. 14–31.

Kesic, G. C. and J. L. Newman. 1976. *Contemporary Africa: Geography and Change*. Englewood Cliffs, N.J.: Prentice-Hall.

Kimambo, Isaria N. and A. Temu. 1969. *A History of Tanzania*. Nairobi: East Africa Publishing House.

Knight, G. G., and J. L. Newman. 1976. *Contemporary Africa*. Englewood Cliffs, N.J.: Prentice-Hall.

Konczacki, Z. A. 1967. "Nomadism and Economic Development of Somalia" *Canadian Journal of African Studies*. 1: 163–175.

Kornfeld, L. et al. 1977. *AID Involvement in Traditional Agriculture*. American Technical Assistance Corp.

Kramer, Kim St. Clair. 1975. "Valleys without Rain: Teda Pastoralism in the Libyan Tibesti." Paper read at the Second Conference of the Faculty of Arts, March 1975, University of Benghazi ["The Geography of Libya"].

Labret, L. J. 1961. *Dynamique concrète de Développement*. Paris: Les Editions Ouvrières.

Lallemand, S. 1975. "La sécheresse dans un village Mossi de Haute Volta." *Sécheresses et famines du Sahel, II*. Edited by J. Copans. Paris: Maspero, pp. 44–61.

Lance, L. M. and E. E. McKenna. 1975. "Analysis of Cases Pertaining to the Impact of Western Technology on the Non-Western World." *Human Organization* 34, no. 1 (Spring): 87–94.

Lattimore, Owen, 1962. *Nomads and Commissars*. New York: Oxford University Press.

Laya, Diuldé. 1975. "Interviews with Farmers and Livestock-Owners in the Sahel." *African Environment* 1, no. 2: 49–93.

Lees, Susan H. and Daniel G. Bates. 1974. "The Origins of Specialized Nomadic Pastoralism: A Systemic Model." *American Antiquity* 39: 187–193.

Lewis, I. M., ed. 1975. *Abaar: The Somali Drought*. London: International African Institute.

Lewis, J. 1975. "Proposals for a Working Method of Indigenous Resource Coordination as Part of a Pre-Disaster Plan." Disaster Research Unit Occasional Paper, no. 3. Bradford, Eng.: University of Bradford.

Libyan Arab Republic, Council for Agricultural Development. 1974. "Short Account on Jabel El Akhdar Development Project." Mimeographed.

Lin, Paul T. K. 1975. "Development Guided by Values: Comments on China's Road and Its Implications." *International Development Review* 17, no. 1.

Little, Kenneth. 1965. *West African Urbanization*. Cambridge: Cambridge University Press.

Loche, Massimo. 1976. "Foundations for the Year 2000." *Far Eastern Economic Review*, December 24, pp. 23–24.

Lofchie, M. F. 1975. "Political and Economic Origins of African Hunger." *Journal of Modern African Studies* 13, no. 4: 551–567.

Lovejoy, P. E. and S. Baier. 1976. "The Desert-side Economy of the Central Sudan." *The Politics of National Disaster: The Case of the Sahel Drought*. Edited by M. H. Glants. New York: Praeger.

Low, Helen C. and James W. Howe. 1975. "Focus on the Fourth World."

The U.S. and World Development: Agenda for Action, 1975.
Washington, D.C.: Overseas Development Council, p. 36.

McHale, John and C. Magda. 1975. "Human Requirements, Supply Levels
and Outer Bounds: A Framework for Thinking About the Planetary
Bargain." Policy Paper. Aspen Institute for Humanistic Studies,
Program in International Affairs.

Marano, S. 1964. "Protectionism and Industrialization in Latin America."
Economic Bulletin for Latin America. March.

Maystre, Y. Idelovitch and I. E. Burton. 1973. *Technology Assessment and
Research Priorities for Water Supply and Sanitation in Developing
Countries (with Special Reference to Rural Populations and Small
Communities)*. Ottawa: International Development Research Centre.

Mazrui, Ali A. 1975. "The New Interdependence: From Hierarchy to
Symmetry." *The U.S. and World Development: Agenda for Action,
1975*. Washington, D.C. Overseas Development Council. New York:
Praeger.

Mbithi, P. and C. Barnes. 1975. *Spontaneous Settlement Problems in
Kenya*. Nairobi: East African Literature Bureau.

―――― and B. Wisner. 1972. "Drought and Famine in Kenya: Magnitude and
Attempted Solutions." Discussion Paper 174. Nairobi: Institute for
Development Studies, Univ. of Nairobi.

Meadows, D. H. et al. 1972. *The Limits to Growth*. A Report for the Club of
Rome's Project on the Predicament of Mankind. New York: Universe Books.

Mendlovitz, Saul H., ed. 1975. *On the Creation of a Just World Order*. New
York: Free Press.

Mezger, D. 1976. "The European Copper Industry and Its Implications for
the Copper-Exporting Underdeveloped Countries, with Special
Reference to CIPEC Countries." *Natural Resources and National
Welfare: The Case of Copper*. Edited by A. Seidman. New York:
Praeger, pp. 60–91.

Ministry of Water Development and Power. 1973. Taarifa ya Maendeleo ya
Utekelezayi wa Shughuliza Maji. Progress Report on Water Development Activities. Dar es Salaam.

Mujwahuzi, Mark R. 1976. "Self-help in the Development of Improved
Rural Water Supply: Tanzania Experience and Potential." Ph.D.
diss., Clark University.

Mumford, Lewis. 1934. *Technics and Civilization*. New York: Harcourt
Brace.

Myrdal, Gunnar. 1970. *The Challenge of World Poverty*. New York:
Pantheon.

————. 1974. "The Transfer of Technology to Underdeveloped Countries." *Scientific American* 231, no. 3, pp. 172–182.

Myrdal, J. 1963. *Report from a Chinese Village*. London: Heinemann.

Nash, Manning. 1965.*The Golden Road to Modernity*. Chicago: University of Chicago Press.

National Academy of Sciences, Ad Hoc Panel of the Advisory Committee on Technology Innovation. 1974. *More Water for Arid Lands: Promising Technologies and Research Opportunities*. Washington, D.C.: National Academy of Sciences.

National Academy of Sciences. 1977. *Resource Sensing from Space: Prospects for Developing Countries*. Washington, D.C.: N.A.S.

National Christian Council of Kenya. 1968. *Who Controls Industry in Kenya?* Nairobi: East African Publishing House.

Navarro, V. 1973. "The Underdevelopment of Health or the Health of Underdevelopment." Paper read at the Pan American Conference on Health Manpower Planning, Ottawa, September 10–14.

Newell, K. W., M. H. King. and Saroso J. Sulianti. 1975. "The Health Care Package." *WHO Chronicle* 29: 12–18.

Newlyn, W. T. and D. C. Rowan. 1954. *Money and Banking in British Colonial Africa*. Oxford: Oxford University Press.

Nicholaisser, Johannes. 1963. *Ecology and Culture of the Pastoral Tuareg: With Particular Reference to the Tuareg of Ahaggar and Ayr*. Copenhagen: National Museum.

Nicolas, G. 1960. "Un village Haoussa de la République du Niger: Tassao Haoussa." *Les Cahiers d'Outre-Mer* 13, no. 52: 421–454.

————. 1962. "Un village Bouzai du Niger: Edute d'un Terroir." *Les Cahiers d'Outre-Mer* 15, 58: 138–165.

————. 1963. "Notes ethnographiques sur le terroir, l'agriculture et l'elevage dans la vallée de Maradi." *Etudes Nigériens, 8*. Niamey: IFAN-CNRSH.

————. 1966. "Essai sur les structures fondamentales de L'Espace dans la cosmologie Hausa." *Journal de la Société des Africanistes* 36, no. 1: 65–108.

————, H. Magaji, and M. Mouche. 1968. *Problèmes posèes par l'introduction de techniques agricoles modernes au sein d'une société africaine—vallée de Maradi Niger.* Faculté des Lettres et Sciences Humaines. Université de Bordeaux.

Nyerere, Julius K. 1977. *The Arusha Declaration Ten Years After*. Dar es Salaam: Government Printer.

O'Keefe, Phil. 1975. "The Process of Soil Erosion." *African Environment:*

Special Report I—Problems and Perspectives Edited by Paul Richards. London: I.A.I., pp. 63–65.

——— and B. Wisner. 1975. "The Process of Soil Erosion." *African Environment: Special Report I—Problems and Perspectives.* Edited by P. Richards. London: I.A.I., pp. 63–65.

Omololu, A. 1971. "Changing Food Habits in Africa." *Ecology of Food and Nutrition* 165–168.

OECD. 1972. *Development Cooperation: Efforts and Policies of the Members of the Development Assistance Committee, 1972 Review.* Paris: OECD.

———. 1977. *Development Cooperation: Efforts and Policies of the Members of the Development Assistance Committee, 1977 Review.* Paris: OECD.

Pan-American Health Organization (PAHO) 1973. *Report of the Inter-American Investigation of Mortality in Childhood.* Scientific Publications, no. 262. Washington, D.C.: PAHO.

Pearson, Lester. 1969. *Partners in Development.* Report to the World Bank. New York: Praeger.

Peattie, Lisa R. 1969. *The Views from the Barrio.* Cambridge, Mass.: M.I.T. Press.

Peil, M. 1971. "The Expulsion of West African Aliens." *Journal of Modern African Studies* 9, no. 12: 205–209.

Pelissier, P. 1951. "Sur la désertification des territoires septentrionaux de l'A.O.F." *Les Cahiers d'Outre-Mer* 4, no. 13: 80–85.

Perroux, François. 1958. *La Coexistence pacifique.* Volume 3. Paris: Presses Universitaires de France.

Petrov, Victor P. 1970. *Mongolia: A Profile.* New York: Praeger.

Pineo, Charles S. and D. Donaldson. 1976. "Rural Water Supply Problems and Potential Solutions in Latin America." Unpublished manuscript prepared for the United Nations Water Conference, Mar del Plata, 1976.

Pouquet, J. 1956. "Aspects morphologiques du Fouta Dialor régions de Kindia et de Labé Guinée Française, A.O.F. Caractères alarmants de phénomènes d'erosion de sols déclenchés par les activités humaines." *Revue de géographie alpine* 44: 231–247.

van Raay, H. G. T. 1975. *Rural Planning in a Savanna Region.* Rotterdam: Rotterdam University Press.

Raulin, H. 1969. "Communautés d'entraide et développement agricole du Niger: l'exemple de la Majya." *Etudes Rurales* 33: 5–26.

Raynaut, C. 1971. *Soumarana—notes sur le terroir et l'économie.* Centre d'Etude et de Recherche Ethnologues. Université de Bordeaux.

———. 1975. *Le Cas de la région de Maradi (Niger): sécheresses et famines du Sahel, II.* Edited by J. Copans. Paris: Maspero, pp. 5–43.

République de Niger, 1961. *Etude démographique et économique en milieu nomade.* Niamey.

Richard-Mollard, J. 1944. "Essai sur la vie paysanne au Fouta-Dialon: le cadre physique, l'économie rurale, l'habitat." *Revue de géographie alpine*, 32, no. 1: 135–239.

Rigby, Peter. 1972. "The Relevance of the Traditional in Social Change." *African Review* 2: 309–321.

Rodd, F. 1929. "A Second Journey among the Southern Tuareg." *Geographical Journal* 62, no. 1: 1–19.

Rodney, Walter. 1974. *How Europe Underdeveloped Africa.* Washington, D.C.: Howard University Press.

Roscher, W. H. 1861. *Ansichten der Volkswirtschaft aus dem Geschichtlichen Standpunkte.* Stuttgart.

Rosenthal, Jerry E. 1973. "The Creeping Catastrophe." *Africa Report* 18, no. 4: 6–13.

Rostow, W. W. 1960. *The Stages of Economic Growth: A Non-Communist Manifesto.* New York: Cambridge University Press.

Rouch, J. 1956. "Migrations au Ghana." *Journal de la Société des Africanistes* 26, nos. 1–2: 31–196.

———. 1957. *Rapport sur les migrations nigériennes vers la basse: Côte d'Ivoire.* Niamey: ORSTROM-IFAN.

Salifou, A. 1975. "When History Repeats Itself: The Famine of 1931 in Niger." *African Environment* 1, no. 2: 22–48.

Salzman, Philip C. 1971. "Adaptation and Political Organization in Iranian Baluchistan." *Ethnology* 10: 433–445.

Sandberg, A. 1973. "Ujaama and Control of Environment." Paper No. 5. Annual Social Science Conference of the East African Universities: December 1973, at the University of Dar es Salaam. Bureau of Resource Assessment and Land Use Planning. Dar es Salaam.

———. 1974. "Saio Economic Survey of Lower Rufiji Flood Plain: Rufiji Delta Agricultural System." Research Paper No. 34. Bureau of Resource Assessment and Land Use Planning. University of Dar es Salaam.

Saul, J. 1973. "The Political Aspects of Economic Independence." *Economic Independence in Africa.* Edited by D. P. Ghai. Nairobi: East African Literature Bureau.

———. 1975. "Free Mozambique." *Monthly Review* 27, no. 7 (December): 8–22.

Saunders, Robert J. and Jeremy J. Warford. 1976. *Village Water Supply: Economics and Policy in the Developing World*. World Bank Publication. Baltimore: John Hopkins University Press.

Sawadogo, P. 1974. "Situation médico-nutritionelle des nomades refoulés par la sécheresse, Niger." Programme formation pour l'environnement. Dakar: IDEP/UNEP/SIDA.

Scudder, T. 1972. "Ecological Bottlenecks and the Development of the Kariba Lake Basin." *Careless Technology: Ecology and International Development*. Edited by M. Taghi Farvar and John P. Milton. New York: Natural History Press, pp. 206–235.

Seidman, A. 1962. "Development in Africa: Aims and Possibilities." *UNECA Economic Bulletin* 2, no. 2. (June): 26–36.

———. 1972. *Comparative Development Strategies in East Africa*. Nairobi: East African Publishing House.

———. 1973. "The Have–Have Not Gap, or What Happens to the Investable Surpluses in Zambia?" Mimeographed. Lusaka: University of Zambia.

———. 1974a. "The Distorted Growth of Import Substitution Industry: The Zambian Case." *Journal of Modern African Studies* 12, no. 4: 601–631.

———. 1974b. *Planning for Development in Sub-Saharan Africa*. New York: Praeger.

———. 1976. *Natural Resources and National Welfare: The Case of Copper*. New York: Praeger.

Semin-Panzer, Ursula. 1975. "Strategies against Neo-Colonialism: Angola, Mozambique, Guinea Bissau." Paper read at the Conference on Dependence, Crisis and Transformation in the World System, June 1975, London.

Sheets, Hal and Roger Morris. 1974. *Disaster in the Desert*. Washington, D.C.: Carnegie Endowment for International Peace.

Skinner, E. P. 1965. "Labor Migration among the Mossi of the Upper Volta." *Urbanization and Migration in West Africa*. Edited by H. Kuper. Berkeley: University of California Press.

Stebbing, E. B. 1935. "The Encroaching Sahara: The Threat to West African Colonies." *Geographical Journal* 86, no. 5: 506–524.

Sterling, Claire. 1976. "Nepal." *Atlantic,* October, pp. 14–25.

Stott, D. H. 1969. "Cultural and Natural Checks on Population." *Environment and Cultural Behavior*. Edited by Andrew P. Vayda. New York: Natural History Press.

Sukkar, M. Y. et al. 1971. "The Nutritional Status of Children in Rural Khartoum." *Sudan Medical Journal* 9: 23–38.

——— and O. M. Belsil. 1975a. "Current Directions in Medical Education in the Sudan." *Sudan Medical Journal*. 13.

————; J. Z. Boutros; and M. K. Yousif. 1975b. "The Composition of Sudanese Foods." *Sudan Medical Journal* 13: 54–61.

Swift, J. 1975. "Pastoral Nomadism as a Form of Land Use: The Tuareg of Adrar n Iforas." *Pastoralism in Tropical Africa.* Edited by T. Monod. Oxford: Oxford University Press, pp. 443–54.

Szentes, Tamas. 1967. "Introduction to the Economy of Tropical Africa." *Studies on Developing Countries* no. 12. Budapest: Institute for World Economics of the Hungarian Academy of Sciences.

————. 1971. *The Political Economy of Underdevelopment.* Budapest: Akademiai Kiado. Reprinted 1973.

————. 1972a. "Socio-Economic Effects of Two Patterns of Foreign Capital Investments." Paper presented at a seminar on the Use of Foreign Funds, April 1972, Dar es Salaam. IDEP. ET/CS/2367-8.

————. 1972b. "The Structural Background of the Problem of Land-locked Countries." Paper for seminar on land-locked countries of Africa, September 1972, Oslo.

————. 1973. "Some Peculiarities of the Socio-Economic Development of Tropical Africa, with Special Regard to the Policy to Be Adopted in Our Relations with Them." Paper presented at the Africanist Conference, Warsaw.

————. 1975. "International Trade and the New Economic Order." Paper presented at the Symposium on the New International Economic Order, May 1975, The Hague.

Talbot, Lee M. 1972. "Ecological Consequences of Rangeland Development in Masailand, East Africa." *The Careless Technology: Ecology and International Development.* Edited by M. Taghi Farvar and John P. Milton. New York: Natural History Press.

TANU Guidelines, 1971. [Cited in the *Nationalist,* February 1971, p. 3, and in *Mazungunzo* (Michigan), 1971, p. 59.]

Taylor, C. E. and M. F. Hall. 1967. "Health, Population and Economic Development." *Science,* August 11, 1967, pp. 651–657.

Temple, R. S. and M. E. R. Thomas. 1973. "The Sahelian Drought: A Disaster for Livestock Populations." *World Animal Review* 8: 1–7.

Tendler, Judith. 1975. *Inside Foreign Aid.* Baltimore: Johns Hopkins University Press.

Tenu, P. and A. Seidman. 1973. "Study of Comparative Costs of Living for Tazara Employees." Mimeographed report. Lusaka and Dar es Salaam.

Tinker, Hugh. 1976. "Burma: Separations as a Way of Life." *The Politics of Separation.* Edited by W. H. Morris-Jones. London: Institute of Commonwealth Studies, pp. 57–68.

Tricart, J. 1956. "Dégredation du milieu nativel et problèmes d'Amenagement au Fouta-Djallon (Guinée). *Revue de géographie alpine* 44: 7–37.

Tschannerl, G. 1976. "Periphery Capitalistic Development: A Case Study of the Tanzanian Economy." *Utaliti* 1: 5–46.

Turner, A. K. 1963. "The Control of Roadside Erosion." *Overseas Bulletin 17.* Crowthorne, U.K.: Road Research Laboratory.

UNCTAD. 1971. *Special Measures in Favour of the Least Developed among the Developing Countries.* Report of Ad Hoc Group of Experts. New York.

———. 1975a. "Review of Progress in the Implementation of Special Measures in Favour of the Least Developed among the Developing Countries, Statistical Annex." TD/B/AC.17/3/ Add 1. Mimeograph June 2. New York.

———. 1975b. "An Assessment of Constraints to Development and the Role of External Assistance in the Least Developed Countries." TD/B/AC.17/Misc. 1. Mimeographed. June 2. New York.

———. 1976a. *Least Developed among Developing Countries, Developing Island Countries, and Developing Land-locked Countries.* Item 13—Main Policy Issues. TD/191. Nairobi.

———. 1976b. *International Financial Cooperation for Development.* Item 11—Supporting Paper: Addendum. TD/188/Supp. 1. Add. 1. Nairobi.

———. 1976c. *Economic Cooperation among Developing Countries.* Item 14—Supporting Paper. TD/192/Supp. 1. Nairobi.

UNICEF/WHO. 1969. "Assessment of Environment Sanitation and Rural Water-Supply Programs Assisted by the United Nations Children's Fund and the World Health Organization (1959–1968)." Joint Committee on Health Policy. 16th Session. Geneva. March. Document JC.16/UNICEF-WHO/69.2

———. 1971. "Assessment of UNICEF/WHO–Assisted Education and Training Programs." Joint Committee on Health Policy, 18th Session. Document JC. 18/UNICEF/Wab/2.

United Nations Department of Economic and Social Affairs. 1971a. *A Concise Summary of the World Population Situation in 1970.* New York. [Reprinted in *Population Studies,* no. 48, pp. 24–25.]

———. 1971b. *World Economic Survey, 1969–70.* New York.

———. 1971c. *Report on the World Social Situation.* New York.

United Republic of Tanzania, 1969. *Second Five-Year Plan for Economic and Social Development, 1 July 1969–30 June 1974.* Vol. 1. Dar es Salaam.

Wallman, S. 1972. "Conceptual Barriers to Cross-Cultural Communication." *Cultural Adaptation within Modern Africa.* Edited by S. H. Irvine and J. T. Sanders. New York: CEA/Teachers College Press.

Ways, Max. 1959. *Beyond Survival.* New York: Harper & Row.

White, A. V. 1974. "Global Summary of Human Response to Natural Hazards: Tropical Cyclones." *Natural Hazards: Local, National, Global.* Edited by G. F. White. New York: Oxford University Press, pp. 255–264

———— and Chris Seviow. 1974. *Rural Water Supply and Sanitation in Less-Developed Countries—A Selected Annotated Bibliography.* Ottawa: International Development Research Centre.

White, G. F. 1974a. "Domestic Water: Good or Right?" *Human Rights in Health.* Edited by K. M. Elliot. Ciba Foundation Symposium, 23 [new series]. Amsterdam: Associated Scientific Publishers, pp. 36–54.

————, ed. 1974b. *Natural Hazards: Local, National, Global.* New York: Oxford University Press.

————; D. J. Bradley; and A. V. White. 1972. *Drawers of Water—Domestic Water Use in East Africa.* Chicago: University of Chicago Press.

———— and J. E. Haas. 1975. *Assessment of Research on Natural Hazards.* Cambridge, Mass.: MIT Press.

Whitworth, William. 1970. "A Reporter at Large: Some Questions about the War." *The New Yorker,* July 4, pp. 30–46.

WHO. 1971. *International Standards for Drinking Water.* Expert Committee on International Standards for Drinking Water. Geneva: WHO.

————. 1973a. "Organization Study on Methods of Promoting the Development of Basic Health Services." WHO Executive Board. *Official Records,* no. 206, pp. 103–115.

————. 1973b. "Report of a Meeting of Regional Advisers in Environmental Health." Unpublished document EH/73.12.

————. 1974a. "Malnutrition and Mental Development." *WHO Chronicle* 28.

————. 1974b. *Health Education Program Review.* Geneva: WHO.

————. 1974c. *Alternative Approaches to Meeting Basic Health Needs.* Document JC 20/UNICEF-WHO/75.2.

————. 1974d. "Fifth Report on the World Health Situation: Part II." Unpublished document A27/10.

————. 1975. "Meeting Basic Health Needs in Developing Countries: Alternative Approaches." *WHO Chronicle* 29: 168–187.

————. 1976. *Mid-Decade Progress Report* (1975). Geneva: WHO.

Whyte, A. V. 1976. "Towards a user-choice philosophy in rural water supply programmes." *Carnets de l'enfance,* no. 34. New York: UNICEF, pp. 35–54.

———. 1977. *Guidelines for Field Studies in Environmental Perception.* MAB Technical Notes 5. Paris: UNESCO.

Winstanley, Derek. 1973. "Rainfall Patterns and General Atmospheric Circulation." *Nature,* no. 245: 190–194.

Wisner, Benjamin G., Jr. 1977. "The Human Ecology of Drought in Eastern Kenya." Ph.D. diss., Clark University.

World Bank. 1975. *Annual Report.* Washington, D.C.

Zhdanko, T. 1966. "Sedentarization of the Nomads of Central Asia, including Kazakhstan, under the Soviet Regime." *International Labor Review* 93: 600–620.

LIST OF CONTRIBUTORS

LEONARD BERRY
Professor of Geography
Co-Director of the International
    Development Program
Clark University

IAN BURTON
Research Professor
Institute for Environmental Studies
University of Toronto

DAVID CAMPBELL
Research Associate
Institute for Development Studies
University of Nairobi

CYNTHIA H. ENLOE
Professor of Government
Clark University

RICHARD B. FORD
Associate Professor of History
Director of the International
    Development Program
Clark University

DENIS GOULET
Overseas Development Council
Washington, D.C.

SIXTEN HARALDSON
Director and Professor of
    Community Preventative Medicine
Scandinavian School of Public Health
Goteborg, Sweden

G. K. HELLEINER
Professor of Economics
University of Toronto

DOUGLAS L. JOHNSON
Associate Professor
Graduate School of Geography
Clark University

ROBERT W. KATES
University Professor and Professor
    of Geography
Graduate School of Geography
Clark University

CINDI KATZ
Research Fellow
Graduate School of Geography
Clark University

MARK MUJWAHUZI
Research Associate Professor
Bureau of Resource Assessment and
    Land Use Planning
University of Dar es Salaam

HILARY RENWICK
Research Fellow
Graduate School of Geography
Clark University

ANN SEIDMAN
Visiting Professor
Department of Sociology
Brown University

MOHAMMED Y. SUKKAR
Professor of Anatomy
Faculty of Medicine
University of Khartoum

TAMAS SZENTES
Professor of Economics
Institute for World Economics
   of the Hungarian Academy
   of Sciences
Budapest

FARRON VOGEL-ROBOFF
Research Fellow
Graduate School of Geography
Clark University

ANNE WHYTE
Research Professor
Institute of Environmental Studies
University of Toronto

INDEX

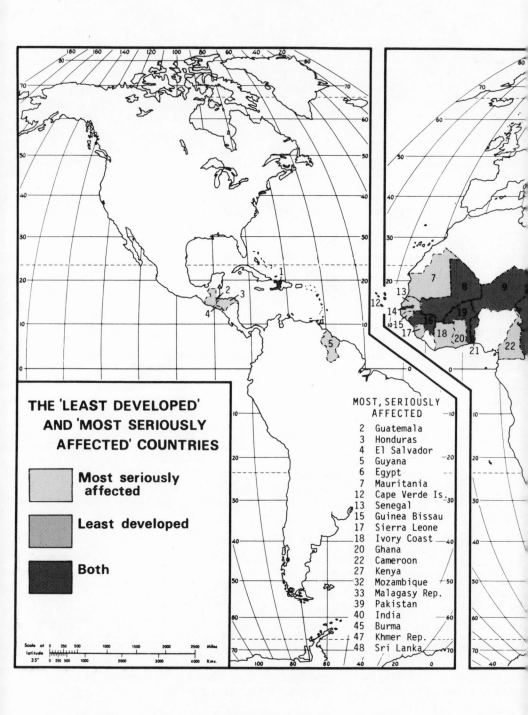

THE 'LEAST DEVELOPED'
AND 'MOST SERIOUSLY
AFFECTED' COUNTRIES

Most seriously
affected

Least developed

Both

Scale at   0 250 500   1000   1500   2000   2500   Miles
latitude ┣┳┳┳┳┳┫
35°   0 250 500   1000   2000   3000   4000   Kms.

MOST, SERIOUSLY
AFFECTED

2   Guatemala
3   Honduras
4   El Salvador
5   Guyana
6   Egypt
7   Mauritania
12 Cape Verde Is.
13 Senegal
15 Guinea Bissau
17 Sierra Leone
18 Ivory Coast
20 Ghana
22 Cameroon
27 Kenya
32 Mozambique
33 Malagasy Rep.
39 Pakistan
40 India
45 Burma
47 Khmer Rep.
48 Sri Lanka